Foreign-Language Learning with Digital Technology

Also available in the Education and Digital Technology Series

Music Education with Digital Technology – John Finney and Pamela Burnard
Drama Education with Digital Technology – Michael Anderson, John Carroll and
    David Cameron
Mathematics Education with Digital Technology – Adrian Oldknow and Carol
    Knights

Also available from Continuum

Learning Cultures in Online Education – Robin Goodfellow and
    Marie-Noëlle Lamy
Attitudes to Modern Foreign Language Learning – Brendan Bartram
Digital Games and Learning – Sara de Freitas and Paul Maharg

Foreign-Language Learning with Digital Technology

Edited by
Michael J. Evans
Education and Digital Technology Series

continuum

Continuum International Publishing Group

The Tower Building　　　　　80 Maiden Lane
11 York Road　　　　　　　 Suite 704
London SE1 7NX　　　　　　 New York, NY 10038

www.continuumbooks.com

© Michael J. Evans and Contributors 2009

First published 2009
This paperback edition published 2011

British Library Cataloguing-in-Publication Data
A catalogue record for this book is available from the British Library.

ISBN:　978-1-84706-041-9 (hardback)
　　　　978-1-4411-0441-0 (paperback)

Library of Congress Cataloguing-in-Publication Data
A catalog record of this book is available from the Library of Congress.

Typeset by Newgen Imaging Systems Pvt Ltd, Chennai, India

Contents

Notes on contributors

Carl Blyth is the Director of the Texas Language Technology Center (TLTC) and Associate Professor of French Linguistics in the Department of French and Italian at the University of Texas at Austin. Carl has written various journal articles, chapters and books. Most notably, he was author of *Untangling the Web: Nonce's Guide to Language and Culture on the Internet* (New York: Wiley/Nonce, 1999) and editor of *The Sociolinguistics of Foreign Language Classrooms* (Boston: Heinle, 2003). With his colleagues at the University of Texas, he has developed French online materials (*Tex's French Grammar* and *Français interactif*). More recently, he co-authored with Stacey Katz (University of Utah) *Teaching French Grammar in Context* (New Haven, CT: Yale University Press, 2007). Currently, he serves as the series editor of Issues in Language Program Direction, an annual volume devoted to foreign-language study in higher education. As his publications indicate, his main research interests lie at the intersection of discourse analysis, sociolinguistics and language learning.

Cal Durrant is Chair of Initial Teacher Education and lectures in English Curriculum and Media Education at Murdoch University. He was a member of the successful Deakin/Murdoch/Australian Association for the Teaching of English (AATE) team that delivered the $2.4 million Australian government's 'Summer School for Teachers of English' initiative in January 2008, and has been involved in a number of projects that have applied ICTs to various aspects of teaching and learning. Cal is currently on the Executive Council of the AATE and serves on the editorial board of 'English in Australia'. In 2001, he co-edited with Catherine Beavis *P(ICT)ures of English: Teachers, Learners and Technology* (Kent Town: Wakefield Press). His most recent project is an edited text on media education with Andrew Burn from the Institute of Education at the University of London entitled *Media Teaching: Language, Audience and Production* (Kent Town: Wakefield Press, 2008).

Michael Evans is Deputy Head of Faculty and Senior Lecturer in Education at the University of Cambridge. He has considerable experience in foreign-language teacher education and directs the MPhil in Research in Second Language Education. He is co-director (with Linda Fisher) of a study funded by the Department for Children, Schools and Families (DCSF), 'Language learning at KS3: the impact of the KS3 Modern Foreign Languages Framework and changes to the curriculum on provision and practice' (2006–8). He has published on a number of second-language education topics including the use of ICT by language learners and the impact of study abroad on language proficiency. He is co-author, with Norbert Pachler and Shirley Lawes, of *Modern Foreign Languages: Teaching School Subjects 11–19* (London: Routledge, 2007).

Linda Fisher is Lecturer in Education at the Faculty of Education, University of Cambridge. Before moving to Higher Education, she taught German and French in a number of secondary schools and was Head of Department. She coordinates the MFL PGCE programme and is involved in extensive work with secondary teachers of MFL. She jointly plans and delivers faculty-wide mentor training, and teaches and supervises on the MEd, MPhil and PhD programmes. She has experience of qualitative and quantitative research projects and is co-director of the DCSF-sponsored research project 'Language learning at Key Stage 3: the impact of the Key Stage 3 Modern Foreign Languages Framework and changes to the curriculum on provision and practice'. Publications include: (2007) 'Pedagogy and the curriculum 2000 reforms at post-16: the "learn it, forget it" culture?' *Curriculum Journal*, 18, (1), 103–114; (2005) 'Measuring gains in pupils' foreign language competence as a result of participation in a school exchange visit: the case of Y9 pupils at three comprehensive schools in the UK', *Language Teaching Research*, 9, (2), 173–92; and, with Michael Evans and Edith Esch, (2004) 'Computer-mediated communication: promoting learner autonomy and intercultural understanding at secondary level', *Language Learning Journal*, 30, (Winter), 50–8.

Miranda Hamilton has taught for several years at two leading TEFL colleges in the UK. She has had four articles published in *Modern English Teacher* about the integration of technology in the EFL classroom, as well as an article in the *Guardian Weekly* about the exploitation of the interactive whiteboard (IWB) in the EFL learning environment. She has also delivered papers at three international conferences about the integration of ICT in the EFL classroom. She is currently completing a PhD on the development of linguistic and learner autonomy within the context of a technological learning environment, focusing on the use of the medium by trainee teachers of English as a foreign language in a university in Mexico.

Rachel Hawkes has extensive experience as a classroom teacher of French, German and Spanish at secondary level. She has several senior management roles at Comberton Village College, Cambridgeshire, including Assistant Principal, Director of Language College, Head of Modern Languages, Advanced Skills Teacher, Specialist Schools Trust Lead Practitioner and Regional Subject Advisor for the roll out of the new secondary languages curriculum in England. For the past few years she has provided in-service training to languages teachers at national conferences (organized by the Centre for Information on Language Teaching (CILT) and the Specialist Schools and Academies Trust (SSAT)); at regional network training meetings (Association for Language Learning (ALL), Comenius East); and by inviting participants from all over the country to 'in-house' training sessions at Comberton Village College. She is currently pursuing a part-time PhD at Cambridge University on teacher and learner second language (L2) talk in the secondary languages classroom, with a particular focus on the role of dialogic teaching strategies in L2 development.

Iain Mitchell taught Modern Languages in comprehensive schools for 18 years, including nine as Head of Department, and was then Curriculum Support Teacher for Cambridgeshire LEA until 1993. Since then he has worked as an Independent Advisory Teacher for Modern Languages, providing advice and training to modern-language teachers in England, Wales and Northern Ireland. He provides in-service training for local education authorities, for national organizations such as ALL and CILT, contributes to the University of Cambridge MFL PGCE course, works with individual schools and teachers on curriculum and individual professional development, and runs his own courses for MFL teachers in venues all over England. He also runs masterclasses for gifted and talented students. He has contributed to a variety of textbooks including *Logo 4*, *Formule X 3* and, most recently, CILT Classic Pathfinder 5 *Learning by Ear and by Eye*. He has a long-standing relationship with the Mother Tongue Section of the London Borough of Tower Hamlets and has produced for them an Assessment Framework and a non-language-specific Scheme of Work for primary age learners.

Series editors' foreword

A critical and central issue for this series is to explore the ways in which digital technologies can be said to enhance teaching and learning. In this second book in the series, *Foreign-Language Learning with Digital Technology*, we investigate this question with a particular focus on the role of technologies in bringing about frameworks for innovation; and from a range of perspectives, which explore classroom approaches for a wide range of language learners.

This volume is organized around two major areas: the first looks at the fascinating question of the relationship between digital technologies and pedagogy. Do digital technologies enable a redefinition of approaches to language learning and therefore new classroom practices? Or do technologies simply enhance existing good practices? This is a conundrum which has taxed many educators: are good classroom strategists simply those who will use and develop exciting resources as a matter of course – and are digital technologies simply such a resource? Or are there deeper questions to be asked about how far such technologies actually transform teaching approaches? Do they make us, as practitioners, reconsider learning in all its complexity and thus bring about a re-evaluation of what it means to learn a language? And critically, how is evidence pertaining to this question used in policy making? Evans's own first chapter, an analysis of comparative policy approaches in the USA, Australia and the UK, is an excellent account of how such evidence is generated, its strengths and limitations, and the implications for practitioners. Fisher continues this type of analysis with a report on a qualitative research project into pre-service teachers' attitudes towards and use of digital technologies, based on students taking the course she coordinates at the University of Cambridge, UK.

The second equally interesting and valuable area is that of effective language learning in classrooms. Here Evans has skilfully brought together an excellent selection of chapters on international practitioner classroom-focused research, which demonstrate not only effective practice, but the effective thinking which sits beneath such practices. Too often in teaching we are offered piecemeal (and occasionally patronizing) examples of 'new approaches' without any connecting threads of intellectual engagement being evident. Evans's approach here is quite different: he is concerned to ensure that the practices we are exploring in the use of digital technologies in MFL are clearly rooted in practitioner understanding of the issues which frame the practices. The resulting coherence of these chapters is refreshing, but also importantly reminds us of the centrality of the role of practitioners in both defining and creating teacher knowledge. Thus Mitchell, Hawkes, Durrant, Hamilton, Blyth and Evans offer persuasive and lively accounts of the impact of digital technologies on classroom practices across a range of countries, and of the decision-making processes which accompany such developments, with a clear expectation that readers will want to explore and critique the writers' approaches and ideas.

It is thus our great pleasure to invite you to explore, engage with and debate the issues on foreign-language learning with digital technology represented within this volume; our thanks go to all contributors to this book and particularly to Michael Evans, whose thoughtful and careful editing has crafted a volume we are delighted to be able to include in this series.

Sue Brindley and Tony Adams
Series editors

Introduction

Michael Evans

As always with language, the choice of label to express a key notion that is the focus of a book like this is not only problematic in itself but also a sign of the diversity and complexity of the reality to which it purports to refer. 'Digital technology' or 'Information and communication technology'? The former term is more familiar to readers in the USA and the latter to readers in the UK. In the latter case, the term ICT is accepted and used as an abbreviation by everyone in education (policy-makers, teachers, pupils, etc.) and yet it is very likely that there are some individuals, at least, in each of these categories who are not entirely clear what the *I* and *C* stand for, either linguistically or conceptually. Nevertheless, the acronym serves as a serviceable term with a more-or-less-common frame of reference for all users. Comparing the two labels, it is of passing interest to note that while ICT makes some attempt to allude to areas of use by the technology (namely, information and communication), the label used in the USA (and other countries such as Canada) focuses exclusively on the technical medium itself (digital). The point I am making here is that the label is arbitrary, for even 'information' and 'communication' are selective referents and do not represent the full range of areas in which technology is used in teaching and learning. In this book we use both terms interchangeably to refer to the use of digital technology as a vehicle for language teaching and learning.

In the case of foreign-language learning, the labelling issue is further complicated by the fact that our discipline very quickly generated its own subject-specific term (computer-assisted language learning or CALL) which, as is discussed in Chapter 1, began by referring to a specific kind of computer use by language learners (characterized mainly by drill and practice format) but soon presented educators with the dilemma of whether or not it should encompass broader uses of technology in language learning. For instance, in 2000 Chapelle asked the question: 'Is network-based learning CALL?' Chapelle has also drawn our attention to the different focal concerns of different formulations of this hyphenated label, and how they have depicted different roles for computer technology in the language-learning process: 'computer-assisted language learning', 'computer-based language learning', 'computer-enhanced language learning' (2001: 1–26).

While relevant, these definitional issues and developments do not constitute the focus of this book. They are inevitably in the background and inform the perspectives adopted by the authors of the different chapters as well as influencing the pedagogical settings and viewpoints expressed by the teachers and learners described in them. Ultimately, though, the labels and their corresponding definitions remain arbitrary, contingent, transient and partial. More than most other forms of teaching and learning, those that depend on digital technology are particularly prone to the effects of change, innovation and transience, making it difficult for teachers to time their assimilation of the technology effectively into their students' learning programmes before the march of innovation has moved on and new digital challenges and opportunities present themselves to language teachers and learners.

The focus of the chapters in this book is precisely on accounts, examples and descriptions of effective ways in which the technology can enhance language teaching and learning aims. As Stockwell has pointed out, the relationship between technology and language pedagogy 'may be seen as "the chicken or the egg?"' conundrum whereby at times the technology has generated ' "new possibilities in pedagogy" ' and at others the reverse is true, pedagogical innovation has triggered technological innovation: 'many pedagogies exist as a result of technology and many technologies exist as a result of pedagogies' (2007: 118). Can the same be said of the relationship between technology and learning? Is there also here a mutually redefining relationship? Does technology produce new language learning processes or only facilitate and support processes that already exist in conventional learning contexts? The chapters in this book do not claim to provide an answer to these questions but, beyond their immediate specific aims, they are all concerned with qualitative accounts of how the digital environment affects language learners and language learning. This, then, forms one basis for the collection of chapters in this book. A second rationale underlying the collection is that of bringing together insights that relate to a diversity of language learners. It is clear that if talking about language teachers as a homogeneous entity is problematic and reductive, this is all the more so with reference to language learners. This book juxtaposes insights and perspectives on a wide range of categories of language learners: secondary school learners of foreign languages; university students of foreign languages; EFL students; language students enrolled on distance-learning courses; and student teachers of foreign languages. Readers are encouraged to make their own inferences about the similarities and differences between these perspectives. However, a comprehensive understanding of the project of language teaching and learning (and the role of digital technology within that project) is only possible if we look at all the parts that make up the whole. A third rationale for the book is that the authors all frame their discussions within the context of language learning in Anglo-Saxon countries: Australia, England and the USA. One of the interesting aspects of international comparisons of this topic is that while pedagogical approaches draw on universal ideas and perspectives from the literature that transcend national boundaries, the educational cultures of these countries shape the experiences of language teachers and learners in different, locally determined ways. Finally, and perhaps most importantly, a common thread that runs through all the chapters and stories in this book is that the authors seek to identify, in different ways and in the different domains which they deal with, how the technology can be embedded in the broader context of foreign-language teaching and learning. The theme of integration runs through the book, sometimes implicitly, sometimes explicitly, as different kinds of boundaries are explored in the search for a clearer understanding of the educational use of the medium.

In Chapter 1, 'Digital technology and language learning: a review of policy and research evidence', I review governmental policy-making on the role of ICT in foreign-language education, particularly in relation to schooling in Australia, England and the USA. I also consider research evidence on the impact of the policies on language learning in these countries. Evidence from these educational studies tends to be quantitative and dominated by a positivist epistemology. Impact evidence is most commonly based on effects in terms of provision and usage of technology, on pupil motivation and (in rare cases) on learning outcomes, usually measured by examination results. In the second half of the chapter I review some of the key findings reported in the CALL literature, and follow Warschauer and other writers' categorization of trends in CALL pedagogy and research that have developed over time: namely, 'structural CALL', 'communicative CALL' and 'integrative CALL'. My argument is that while educational research has the weakness of over-hasty generalization and a reductive conception of impact evidence, its strengths are that broader socio-educational variables are factored into the equation. Conversely, the weakness of CALL approaches and studies is that they are usually small scale, tend to be clinical in approach and do not take account of the naturalistic classroom and educational setting, and are more often focused on more advanced language learners. Their strengths are that they examine in greater depth the language teaching and learning issues and are usually explicitly related to theories and thematic concerns developed with the subject domain of second-language education.

In Chapter 2, 'The potential of the internet as a language-learning tool', Mitchell presents us with a series of creative and innovative ways of exploiting the internet productively for teaching and learning languages at secondary school level. The many examples are directed at French and German as target languages, and the key theme of integration which runs throughout this book is tackled from the point of view of integrating tasks that exploit different types of textual and sound data from the internet within the boundaries of classroom learning. For Mitchell the internet provides valuable authentic cultural material that can be assimilated within the parameters of language learning at this level.

In Chapter 3, 'Trainee teachers' perceptions of the use of digital technology in the languages classroom', Fisher analyses the way personal, pedagogical and social factors influence the rate at which teachers of foreign languages completing a pre-service training course assimilate and acculturate the aims and practice of e-learning in their classrooms. Fisher examines the tensions brought about by prior experiences of technology and existing beliefs about priorities and approaches to language teaching, and shows how the trainees' programmed exposure to and use of computers in their professional placement work during the training year transforms their pedagogic perspectives. Fisher's account of the process in which technology use becomes an accepted integral part of the trainees' pedagogical mindset is based on qualitative interviews and observation of case studies of four trainees recently completing Fisher's own training course at Cambridge University.

In Chapter 4, 'Digital technology as a tool for active learning in MFL: engaging language learners in and beyond the secondary classroom', Hawkes vividly depicts the story of her own experiences as a highly innovative teacher of foreign languages at a secondary school in England, and reveals how the use and perception of technology as an educational tool has evolved in her department over time under her leadership. The core concept in her conceptual framework is that of 'active learning', which serves as the vehicle for the widespread use of digital technology for teaching and learning in her department. The theme of integration in this narrative account takes the form of the development of a departmental culture of language teaching in which the potential of technology is extended to all corners of the language-learning experience, such as target language use, grammar teaching, assessment, oral production, pupil production of video recordings, blogging and parental involvement in the learning process through email communication.

In Chapter 5, 'Engaging pupils in bilingual, cross-cultural online discourse', I report on a project I directed over four years that involved asynchronous Computer-Mediated Communication (CMC) between 14–16-year-old pupils in England learning French and pupils of similar age in francophone countries such as France, Canada and Senegal learning English. As well as discussing principles of task design and general planning and procedural issues, I present an analysis of the interactions produced and show how the pupils developed relationships and understandings through interaction over time. Integration in this context took on a mental and attitudinal dimension, in that the pupils developed cross-cultural collaboration and feelings through discussion of topics of mutual interest, in which the pupils confronted instances of agreement and disagreement in views on topics such as the war in Iraq or the existence of the devil. The chapter also provides examples of how the pupils scaffolded each other's language learning. Data from pupil interviews provides insights into the pupils' perceptions of the value of using CMC as part of their language-learning experience.

In Chapter 6, 'SIDE by side: pioneers, inventors and the tyranny of educational distance', Durrant reports on a project that supports the teaching of languages to secondary school pupils living in rural and remote regions of Western Australia. The author explores how digital technology (including the use of telephones, email, interactive multimedia and satellite technology) is being used to reduce the isolation aspect of distance education so that language students are able to learn in a teaching environment similar to that of a conventional school classroom.

In Chapter 7, 'Teacher and student perceptions of e-learning in EFL', Hamilton analyses the responses of teachers and young adult students to the experience of engaging with a Virtual Learning Environment (VLE) as a platform for learning English as a foreign language. The activities on the VLE included synchronous and asynchronous interaction between students within the class as well as a jigsaw reading activity. Hamilton's detailed analysis reveals the different ways in which the two teachers in the study adapted to the pedagogical directions elicited by the digital medium, and how these confirmed or clashed with the teachers' pre-existing pedagogical beliefs and preferences. The issue of integration here is seen from the perspective of teachers', and learners', personal conceptualizations of the e-learning, how they 'make sense of and cognitively map' the challenge of this new experience.

Finally, in Chapter 8, 'From textbook to online materials: the changing ecology of foreign-language publishing in the era of ICT', Blyth presents 'a case study of the development and impact' of two websites (*Tex's French Grammar* and *Français interactif*) which he has developed and produced at the University of Texas at Austin, and which together form part of an online course for undergraduate students of French. Blyth uses the 'metaphor of ecology of language use' to depict a process whereby digital technology is seen as being an integral part of a language curriculum rather than standing out as a supplementary resource. Blyth provides a powerful depiction of the developmental process that took place over a period of eight years, in which online courses produced by his department have refined a learning environment and curriculum which focus on the learner and which challenge some of the pedagogical norms present in commercial textbooks. Key features of Blyth's approach which stand out as innovative and effective are: the switch from native speakers to multilingual speakers as role models in pedagogical materials; incorporating a focus on informal oral grammar; the use of unplanned discourse, including mother tongue or first language/second language (L1/L2) codeswitching (or using more than one language in conversation); and greater attention to naturally occurring language play in everyday discourse.

References

Chapelle, C. (2000), 'Is network-based learning CALL?', in M. Warschauer and R. Kern (eds) *Network-Based Language Teaching: Concepts and Practice*. Cambridge: Cambridge University Press, pp. 204–28.

Chapelle, C. (2001), *Computer Applications in Second Language Acquisition*. Cambridge: Cambridge University Press.

Stockwell, G. (2007), 'A review of technology choice for teaching language skills and areas in the CALL literature'. *ReCALL*, 19, (2), 105–20.

Chapter 1

Digital technology and language learning: a review of policy and research evidence

Michael Evans

International policy-making on technology and language learning

Because the concepts of language and language learning are universal and boundless, it is easy to make the error of assuming that educational priorities, perspectives and policies that are developed to support them are also universal and interchangeable. Aspects of them, of course, are but there are important differences of emphasis and of focus of which one may not always be conscious. Does it matter? Do language teachers, and the language-education community generally, in any given country need to know what the macro context of their educational setting is and how it differs from those in other countries? To some extent the answer must be 'yes', because awareness of divergence in international priorities can remind us that the national decisions and priorities made on our behalf are 'situated', contingent and therefore not necessarily fixed forever. Take, for instance, the recent National Security Language Initiative (NSLI) launched by George Bush whereby foreign-language education in 'critical' languages such as Arabic, Chinese, Russian, Hindi and Farsi is justified on the basis of the fight against terrorism:

> An essential component of US national security in the post-9/11 world is the ability to engage foreign governments and peoples, especially in critical regions, to encourage reform, promote understanding, convey respect for other cultures and provide an opportunity to learn more about our country and its citizens. To do this we must be able to communicate in other languages, a challenge for which we are unprepared. (www.clta.net/policy/natlinterest.html)

Justifying foreign-language learning on the basis of international security considerations is not, as yet at least, a policy adopted by European countries, for instance, where top-down pressure has, on the contrary, been to promote integration of multilingual communities within host states by focusing on the learning of the national language. In the UK, for instance, English has been described as 'the language of integration' (O'Leary 2008). This suggests that while, for the time being at least, European language-education policies have been concerned to strengthen the role of national and European languages and identity through assimilation, the NSLI initiative in the USA is promoting a different perspective: let's learn *their* languages so we can protect ourselves better. Perhaps the ultimate objective is the same but the message of the policy and the means for achieving it are different, and the latter are what contribute to the educational framework within which language teachers are required to operate.[1] So let us look at some of the key documents that have defined the parameters of language education in the UK and elsewhere, with particular reference to the role played by ICT. After that, we can look at what researchers have found on the impact of ICT policy on language teaching and learning.

In the USA, national guidelines for language learning at K-12[2] were produced by a consortium of professional associations led by the American Council on the Teaching of Foreign Languages, funded by the federal government, and these have set the framework for classroom language-learning objectives and, increasingly, served as sets of objectives for language teaching: these guidelines were, namely, the *National Standards for Foreign Language Education* (1996), revised in 2006. This task force identified five goal areas that together are seen to encompass the diversity of language-learning needs and objectives; these areas are mnemonically summarized as the 'five Cs of foreign language education':

Communication: communicate in languages other than English

- *Standard 1.1*: students engage in conversations, provide and obtain information, express feelings and emotions and exchange opinions.
- *Standard 1.2:* students understand and interpret written and spoken language on a variety of topics.
- *Standard 1.3:* students present information, concepts and ideas to an audience of listeners or readers on a variety of topics.

Cultures: gain knowledge and understanding of other cultures

- *Standard 2.1:* students demonstrate an understanding of the relationship between the practices and perspectives of the culture studied.
- *Standard 2.2:* students demonstrate an understanding of the relationship between the products and perspectives of the culture studied.

Connections: connect with other disciplines and acquire information

- *Standard 3.1:* students reinforce and further their knowledge of other disciplines through the foreign language.
- *Standard 3.2:* students acquire information and recognize the distinctive viewpoints that are only available through the foreign language and its cultures.

Comparisons: develop insight into the nature of language and culture

- *Standard 4.1:* students demonstrate understanding of the nature of language through comparisons of the language studied and their own.
- *Standard 4.2:* students demonstrate understanding of the concept of culture through comparisons of the cultures studied and their own.

Communities: participate in multilingual communities at home and around the world

- *Standard 5.1:* students use the language both within and beyond the school setting.
- *Standard 5.2:* students show evidence of becoming lifelong learners by using the language for personal enjoyment and enrichment (p. 4).

Commenting on the implementation of these standards in classrooms in the USA in the decade or so since their inception, Magnan points out that the Communication standard has been frequently given pre-eminence over the other objectives by teachers and language educators, but that technology has been primarily used to address the Communities standard:

Most often, however, the profession turns to [. . .] technology to address the Communities standard through virtual communities [. . .] Darhower (2006) stressed how internet access to other cultures fits the 'social turn'

(Block 2002: 31) in second language theory because it creates a new realism for the Communities standard by engaging learners in 'multilingual communities at home and around the world in a variety of contexts and in culturally appropriate ways'. Technology is already fulfilling its promise to take language learning out of the classroom. (2008: 360)

In England the National Curriculum for Modern Foreign Languages, aimed at Key Stages 3 and 4 (11–16-year-olds), includes a programme of study that categorizes learning objectives under the following headings:

1. acquiring knowledge and understanding of the target language
2. developing language skills
3. developing language learning skills
4. developing cultural awareness

(DfEE 1999: 16–17)

The role of technology in this schema is mainly linked to the skills and cultural awareness sets of objectives, and the nature of the suggested use of the resource is primarily that of strengthening literacy-related skills by accessing ICT-based written text:

- *2h* techniques for skimming and scanning written texts for information, including those from ICT-based sources
- *2j* how to redraft their writing to improve its accuracy and presentation, including the use of ICT
- *4a* working with authentic materials in the target language, including some ICT-based sources

(DfEE 1999: 16–17)

The more recently produced *Key Stage 2 Framework for Languages*, which targets the teaching of languages at primary school to pupils aged 7–11 years, structures the learning objectives according to three core strands: oracy, literacy and intercultural understanding; and two cross-cutting strands: knowledge about language and language learning strategies. Perhaps benefiting from technology and pedagogy-related innovations in the intervening period between the publication of the two documents, one can see that the KS2 Framework presents a more integrated and multi-modal approach to the use of technology including more learner-focused productive uses such as multimedia presentations in support of the oracy strand, PowerPoint support for literacy activities and multimedia communications with native speakers in order to develop intercultural understanding.

Evidence of the impact of educational technology on language learning in schools

England

In a review of six large-scale studies of the impact of ICT on pupil attainment, motivation and learning in schools in England, Pittard et al. (2003: 3) draw the following conclusions:

- Generally, something positive happens to the attainment of pupils who make (relatively) high use of ICT in their subject learning.
- School standards are positively associated with the quality of school ICT resources and quality of their use in teaching and learning, regardless of socio-economic characteristics.
- Use of ICT in class generally motivates pupils to learn.
- Achieving positive impact of ICT on attainment, motivation and learning depends critically on the decisions of schools, teachers and pupils on how it is deployed and used.

One of the studies whose evidence is central to Pittard et al.'s review is a national study entitled *ImpaCT2* which was funded by the DfES (now the DCSF) and whose broad aim was to evaluate the government's ICT in Schools programme. Harrison et al. (2002) carried out the research in 60 schools in England, selected on the basis of high inspection ratings for quality of ICT learning opportunities in Ofsted school inspections. Analysis of the research – in which 2,100 pupils participated – focused on the impact on attainment and motivation. Findings related to the impact on attainment are particularly interesting from a foreign-language teaching and learning perspective since the study showed that attainment gains in GCSE exam results in languages were strongly related to the level of subject ICT use in the schools. Compared with correlations between ICT use and GCSE exam scores in other subjects, performance in foreign languages revealed the strongest impact: 'The greatest differences in mean performance between high-ICT-using pupils and low-ICT-using pupils is found in MFL, despite the fact that overall levels of use were low' (2002: 40–1).

More specifically, the researchers found that the difference between high and low use of ICT amounted to the equivalent of 0.8 of a grade at GCSE, while similar calculations with respect to other subjects yielded much lower gains: English 0.13, maths 0.02, science 0.56, geography 0.37, history 0.03, and design and technology 0.41. The authors surmise that in part this difference between effects in English, maths and history, on the one hand, and science, design and technology, and modern foreign languages, on the other, may be due to the fact that with the latter group ICT use in lessons was integral to subject learning whereas with the former group of subjects ICT was 'skill-oriented' and 'did not further pupils' subject knowledge and understanding' (2002: 32).

Evidence of the impact of computer use in lessons on language-learner motivation has been intuitively accepted for a long time, and collectively there is a good deal of evidence that pupils on the whole enjoy this. For instance, in a recent small-scale study of six secondary schools in London, in which 300 Y9 pupils completed a survey on their views about language learning, ICT was one of the most commonly cited enjoyable aspects of the experience:

> The four features receiving most positive mentions were visits abroad (64 per cent), teachers making lessons lively/fun/interesting (63 per cent), learning new words (59 per cent) and using ICT (52 per cent). (QCA 2006: 15)

In a large-scale survey carried out in 2002, 48 per cent of KS3 pupils across different subjects said that using computers motivated them in their schoolwork. Passey et al. (2004) report that ICT impacts positively on both boys' and girls' motivation for learning, but in particular found that its use could move the pattern of boys' work from 'burst' approaches (short intensive periods of working) to 'persistent' approaches (more time investment in tasks).

In its 2004 report on the impact of ICT on modern languages in schools in England, Ofsted concluded that 'in one in three departments in the sample' of schools visited between April 2002 and December 2003, 'the impact that using ICT had on teaching and pupils' achievement was at least good; in one in twelve it was very good'. This represented a 'slowly improving picture' on the situation outlined in Ofsted's report two years earlier (Ofsted 2002: 4). The effects on pupil learning that Ofsted identified were, from a current perspective, fairly modest from a pedagogical and learning point of view. The two main areas of positive impact were consolidation and practice through teacher use of interactive whiteboards (IWBs) in whole-class presentation of language, and through developing pupils' independent language learning through activities such as word-processor-based redrafting exercises completed individually by pupils or in collaboration through email. On the negative side, Ofsted pointed to a detrimental effect on the amount of target-language communication taking place in the languages lesson as a result of inclusion of computer-based activities:

> Worryingly, the use of ICT is still frequently at the expense of teachers' and pupils' use of the modern foreign language in lessons. On the whole, teachers do not plan lessons to ensure that pupils speak in the language in lessons where they use ICT, and they often miss exploiting unplanned opportunities which present themselves. Even the notion of a plenary in the respective language to demonstrate what pupils have learned is not regularly built into such ICT lessons. (2004: 9)

In its most recent report, Ofsted has commented on the lack of wide-spread substantial use of ICT by pupils in lessons:

> In just under a quarter of the schools surveyed in 2006/07, independent learning was enhanced by ICT and the use of revision websites for examination purposes had increased. However, regular access for lessons was still a problem and some teachers still lacked confidence to include ICT in their teaching. Using it for drafting and redrafting text to improve accuracy and style and for different purposes was limited. (2008: 20)

However, there is evidence that in recent years the situation regarding neglect of speaking in ICT-based lessons may be altering, driven in part by the inexorable development and accessibility of technology. If we look at examples of innovative school language teaching currently taking place in England, we find that there is a growing focus on use of the technology as a vehicle for pupils' creative oral and audio-visual production of the target language. Examples of innovative practice in this area can be found in the account of 25 action research projects involving innovative ICT-related work by modern languages teachers funded by CILT and ALL between 2004 and 2007 (www.languages-ict.org.uk/action/index.htm). It is interesting that the focus of almost all the projects is on pupil use of the technology in pursuit of the development of productive use of the target language. Ten of the projects aim to develop speaking skills (including pronunciation), eight focus on the development of writing skills (including creative writing and narrative skills), a further eight consisted of presentational tasks involving internet research and multimedia outputs. The speaking-oriented projects involve the use of more recent technological resources (including the use of sound recording and editing software such as Garageband and Audacity, as well as iPods and MP3 players). One feature of this type of work is that it can confer a sense of star status to the learners as performers on the electronic stage. This feature of innovative practice is also exemplified in some of the work described in this book. For instance, Hawkes (Chapter 4 in this volume) points to the notion of audience as a motivating factor in her Y9 pupils' video recordings in the target language. Conversely, from the audience point of view, young learners tend to be more motivated to listen to each other than to native speakers. Similarly, in his analysis of the impact of *Français interactif,* an online course for undergraduate students of French as a foreign language, Blyth (Chapter 8 in this volume) reports that the videos used on the course, which were produced by students during their year abroad in France, had the effect of granting star status to the students who appeared on the video in the eyes of the next cohort of students, who completed the online course in preparation for their own year abroad. Blyth also found that users of *Français interactif* paid more attention to non-native speakers than to native speakers in the videos. Participants also commented that watching non-native speakers in the videos gave them 'a more realistic picture of [. . .] their own language development' (p. 283).

USA

The structure and politics of the educational system in the USA is characterized by different levels of independence in decision-making and funding: national, state, district and regional. In the case of technology-related policy-making, the focus at the national level has been in recent years on increasing hardware provision in schools and in the development of virtual schools, which in turn meets the growing enrolment of students in distance-education courses. In 2005–6 there were 22 states with virtual schools (www.ed.gov/technology) and in 2001–2 9 per cent of all schools had students enrolled on distance-education courses (about half of these were in rural areas or high-poverty districts).

One of the first comprehensive overview studies of the general impact of educational technology on educational achievement (Schacter 1999) in schools in the USA was based on an analysis of findings from seven major studies, including one which consisted of a meta-analysis of 500 separate empirical studies that had been published on this topic. Schacter's conclusion was that different forms of computer use in education (namely, computer-assisted learning, integrated learning systems technology, simulations, collaborative networked technologies, design and programming technologies) showed 'positive gains in achievement on researcher construct tests, standardized tests and national tests' (1999: 10). However, there was also evidence that 'learning technology is less effective or ineffective when the learning objectives are unclear and the focus of the technology use is diffuse' (1999: 11). Similar conclusions were drawn by a US Department of Education review of empirical studies of the impact of technology on learning in schools. Positive impacts were identified on achievement and student attitudes (www.nsba.org/sbot/toolkit/tiol.html).

Research evidence of the impact of technology on foreign-language learning in schools in the USA on a national scale can be found in the US Department of Education-funded 'Foreign Language Instruction in the United States: A National Survey of Elementary and Secondary Schools', conducted by the Center for Applied Linguistics during 1997 and 1998 (Rhodes and Branaman 1999). This survey was based on questionnaires completed by principals and foreign-language teachers at 1,534 elementary schools and 1,650 secondary schools throughout the 50 states and the District of Columbia. The report indicates that while technology was still not among the most common media used as teaching materials in foreign language instruction, there was a significantly greater percentage of schools using the medium in 1997 than in the earlier survey carried out in 1987. In elementary schools the increase was from 14 per cent in 1987 to 41 per cent in 1997; and in secondary schools the increase was from 20 per cent to 52 per cent. At the present time of writing the Center is compiling a similar report based on an updated national survey completed in 2007.

In 2007 The American Council of Teachers of Foreign Languages (ACTFL) reported on a survey, completed by 2,236 teachers of foreign languages, on the use of technology in their lessons and found that the uses were as follows:

- grades/attendance 82 per cent
- language instruction 66 per cent
- proficiency assessment 38 per cent
- classroom management 22 per cent

(ACTFL 2008: 18)

This would indicate that, while instructional use continues to increase, it does not do so to a dramatic extent. It also suggests that computers are mostly being used for administrative purposes.

Australia

Similarly to the USA, educational and technology-oriented policy-making in Australia is dependent on national and state or territorial initiatives and therefore less centralized than is the case in the UK (though as of January 2009 responsibility for the curriculum in English, maths, the sciences and history will be overseen by the national government). On a national level, technology is seen as a key vehicle for meeting social and educational objectives. In a statement on education and training in the information economy, the Australian government defined the role of ICT in education and training in relation to the following aims:

- creating an innovative society
- ensuring that all learners achieve their potential
- improving quality and raising standards
- achieving efficiencies through sharing
- capitalizing on the internationalization of education

(MCEETYA 2005: 1)

In 2008, the Australian government introduced the Digital Education Revolution policy, 'committing $1.2 billion over five four years to provide computer technologies for secondary school students in the school years 9 to 12' (www.digitaleducationrevolution.gov.au/faqs/default.htm). The policy also commits the Australian government to provide broadband connections to schools, with fibre to the premises. The aim of the Digital Education Revolution is 'to contribute sustainable and meaningful change to teaching and learning in Australian schools that will prepare students for further education, training, jobs of the future and to live and work in a digital world' (www.digitaleducationrevolution.gov.au/about.htm).

The main languages taught in schools in Australia are Japanese (23.4 per cent of total number of students studying languages other than English), Italian (20.4 per cent), Indonesian (18.1 per cent) and French (13.2 per cent). The role of technology within this provision has been primarily in the context of provision of distance education and in the production of language-learning resources made available on the Web. In a major study of the state of language education in schools in Australia, funded by the government, Liddicoat et al. (2007) identify a number of key drivers and constraints. Factors promoting language education include the following: national collaboration between schools and in national projects; diversity of languages; schools that allocate sufficient time for languages; and schools where there is local community support for language teaching in the school. Factors that inhibit language education in Australia include: states where languages are not mandatory; where insufficient time is available for language learning on the timetable; diversity of provision; lack of qualified teachers; low attitudes to languages; and dissipation of limited resources.

In a comparative study of the impact of ICT on schools in Australia, England, USA and Hong Kong, Eadie concluded that ICT usage and integration were most advanced in countries where there was 'the most need to connect to information and institutions' (2001: 40). Schools in countries where 'there are geographic barriers to overcome', like Australia and New Zealand, provided instances of 'best practice ICT use' among those examined in Eadie's research.

However, need alone is not a sufficient driver for widespread national provision and use of technology in educational systems, as Owhotu has established, who identifies five implications of the development of open distance learning in developing countries:

1. Universities in these countries must approach their new roles cautiously and from a step-wise development strategy, covering issues and factors in policy, planning, transformations in traditions, processes and means or methodologies, funding space and time management, mass learner centredness, quality control, certification skill-employment and self-employment for the work world.
2. Teachers' roles need to undergo fundamental change as the learner becomes more empowered through self-learning and unlimited access to the world of information and knowledge that the ablest teacher may no longer control or possess.
3. Universities and tertiary sister institutions will have to play the top-to-bottom catalytic role in order to move innovations forward and especially influence relevant policy and applications of ICTs in school systems . . . and the great masses of learners of all ages and backgrounds.
4. New forms of interaction and expression are leading to the emergence of what has been referred to as the culture of interactivity. This fact challenges the typical communication processes of the traditional classroom, calling for more innovative learning materials that combine pedagogical effectiveness with easy-to-use mechanisms supporting interaction between learners, tutors and other peer groups.
5. Inclusive education is shown to involve the nomadic learners and other special groups.

(2006: 55)

Evidence from research in applied linguistics on the impact of e-learning on language learners

While generic educational research, particularly in the form of quantitative impact studies of centralized policy, has the merit of attempting to capture the reality of the integration of technology in learning within the contextual settings of national institutional systems, it has the drawback of eliciting excessively hasty generalizations and conclusions about causality between this medium and outcomes of learning. A different source of useful insights for foreign-language teachers and educators is the burgeoning research on the effects and use of technology in foreign-language teaching and learning within the field of applied linguistics. This body of research can also be seen to be marked by salient common features. Many of the influential studies are small scale, experimental and set in the context of adult and higher education. Most of the earlier studies (though this is changing) focus on learners of English as a foreign language who have a working proficiency in the language. Consequently transference of themes and findings to the experience of language learning in other sectors is often problematic. However, the value of this research (compared to or as a complement to the generic educational research described in the previous section) is that it provides qualitative and often detailed accounts of the processes by which technology can support language learning.

As with research on the impact of technology within educational research, so too in the applied linguistics field, there have, in recent years, been a growing number of meta-analyses and critical overviews that have sought to summarize and synthesize findings from studies on this topic within applied linguistics (for instance, Felix 2008, Lamy and Hampel 2007, Stockwell 2007). However, one should avoid reaching overhasty conclusions based on an aggregate of findings drawn from existing studies. The value of these studies is precisely in their individuality and in the themes that emerge through the analyses. Though different frameworks of CALL-related paradigms have been proposed by researchers, a useful distinction of theoretical perspectives, made by Warschauer (1996), Gruba (2004) and others is between 'structural CALL', 'communicative CALL' and 'integrative CALL'. Although some of the theoretical frameworks in the literature outline approaches which delineate research perspectives rather than pedagogical ones, for our purposes in this volume it will be important to maintain a dual focus based on the premise of a link between pedagogical and research objectives in computer-assisted language learning. A further point to note in relation to the following typology as formulated within the TEFL perspective is that the different types of CALL are defined in relation to syllabus design. Applying the typology to the broader educational context, including the different sectors of education, one cannot view technology as a defining factor in alternative syllabus modes. Instead, technology needs to be recognized as one of a range of different pedagogical and learning experiences within the broader constituent elements of classroom practice.

Structural CALL

Gruba describes the era of structural CALL as one where there was a 'strong emphasis on grammar' with the aim of helping 'students gain accuracy in their language usage' (2004: 628). Warschauer describes this phase of CALL, which dominated practice in the early days of technology use in the languages classroom, as 'behaviouristic CALL' since it 'entailed repetitive language drills' based on the notion of 'computer as tutor':

> In other words the computer serves as a vehicle for delivering instructional materials to the student. The rationale behind drill and practice was not totally spurious, which explains in part the fact that CALL drills are still used today. Briefly put, that rationale is as follows:
>
> - Repeated exposure to the same material is beneficial or even essential to learning.
> - A computer is ideal for carrying out repeated drills, since the machine does not get bored with presenting the same material and since it can provide immediate non-judgemental feedback.
> - A computer can present such material on an individual basis, allowing students to proceed at their own pace and freeing up class time for other activities.
>
> (1996: 4)

A recent example of structural CALL, and less narrowly based on drill-oriented tasks but nevertheless grounded in the notion of computer as tutor, are the distance language-learning courses that are currently flourishing in some countries, and in the USA in particular. An interesting account of analysis of the effects of this form of CALL is provided by Blake and Delforge's study of student use of *Spanish Without Walls*, an online course for undergraduates at the University of California, Davis (Blake and Delforge 2006). The authors' aim was to look for evidence of improved language-learning outcomes through the use of the online medium. In order to measure the existence or otherwise of such gains in learning, the authors adopted a comparative methodology, contrasting results from the students who completed one year's study using *Spanish Without Walls* with those of other students at the university enrolled on the conventional, textbook-based first-year Spanish course. The online course design consisted of multimedia language materials using *Tesoros* (a CD-ROM detective story), content-based website readings, Flash activities and collaborative asynchronous CMC. Students also chatted live with their instructor in groups of three or less at least once a week. The same grammatical tests were administered to both the *Spanish Without Walls* (SWW) group and the conventional group (classroom group). The authors report that 'on all of the discrete point grammar tests, the SWW students scored significantly higher' than the classroom group (2006: 138–9). By way of explanation, Blake and Delforge suggest that '[p]erhaps the more textual emphasis required by an online course affords the SWW students greater textual concentration and, therefore, greater awareness of grammatical details' (2006: 139). The authors also found that most of the interactions between instructor and students on the chat forum revolved around 'issues of formal accuracy and correct pronunciation' (2006: 142).

An earlier and narrower comparison of the relative effectiveness of online and textbook delivery of discrete skill language learning was carried out by Allum (2002). In this experimental study, 28 first-year university non-specialist students of English as a foreign language in Japan completed an eleven-week course involving completion of language exercises using the *Hot Potatoes 5.2* software accessed via the internet. The same pencil-and-paper pre- and post-tests were used with both groups, focusing on vocabulary learning, spelling, grammar, listening comprehension and written dialogue. Allum reported his findings as follows:

> The results overall confirm that the medium, if the two 'media' are teacher and CALL, is not especially important, at least for the measures taken and with students at this level. They also confirm that this is true across a range of exercises with different aims – teaching functional phrases, vocabulary, grammar, listening, and even spelling. Further, this is true even when simple CALL exercises are used, and the full power of CALL to provide more sophisticated feedback, branching, or higher quality visual information is not utilised. (2002: 157)

Allum concluded by supporting the claim that 'methodology is critical and media not' (2002: 161). The control over listening input available to the CALL group in his study did not improve their listening skills; and the repeated typing in of words did not lead to significant improvement in spelling as measured by his tests.

Chenoweth and Murday (2003) have conducted a comparative study of their students' engagement with the Language Online project at Carnegie Mellon University. Comparing the learning outcomes of students completing the online and offline versions of the course, the researchers aimed to see if there were differences in student gains in language skills between the two instructional formats (specifically, differences in listening comprehension, reading comprehension, grammar knowledge, oral production and written production):

> The participants in this study for the Spring 2000 semester were the students enrolled in the conventional Elementary French I (101) and in Elementary French I Online (103). Twelve students completed 101, and eight completed 103. The majority of the participants were undergraduate students, with three graduate students in 101 and one graduate student and one staff member in 103. Although different instructors taught the two courses and different instructional materials were used, the same syllabus was followed in both courses, and common sections of the final exam were administered in both. (2003: 292)

The results indicated that the online students did indeed appear to make sufficient and comparable progress as reflected by their performance on the measures used for this study. In fact, in written production, the online students scored higher than the offline students.

Communicative CALL

Gruba describes the aims of 'practices in communicative CALL' as 'help[ing] students develop their own mental models through the use of the target language' through 'exercises that guide meaningful peer interactions and promote fluency' (2004: 628–9). The use of CMC in language learning has resulted in a large number of studies that have analysed different aspects of the effect of this medium on the development of learners' communicative competence. Some studies have focused on the impact on linguistic features of the learners' interactions, usually elicited through pedagogically controlled tasks and often also analytically presented in comparison with classroom-based language production. González-Bueno (1998), for instance, highlighted the discourse features of interactions between first- and second-semester students of Spanish and their tutor at the University of Southwestern Louisiana. The author found that L2 CMC interactions mirrored several characteristics which have been observed in L1 CMC interactions (such as the use of markers like *OK, well, bien, pues* to manage the discourse). The discourse was also found to be characterized by expressive language either through the use of typographical features (e.g. *¡¡¡Muy fácil!!!*) or reuse of coined expressions learnt in the regular lessons (e.g. *tengo dieciocho [años] ¡Por fin!*). Sotillo (2000) compared synchronic with asynchronic modes of CMC interaction between two instructors and their respective advanced ESL classes at Montclair State University to see which resulted in 'more syntactically complex' student output (2000: 82). First, she found that synchronous discussions (instantaneous interaction taking place in real time) resembled face-to-face interactions more than asynchronous discussions did. The written output in asynchronous CMC, on the other hand, was syntactically more complex; longer texts were produced and, therefore, indicated greater self-monitoring and reflection. However, the discourse patterns were more limited and resembled the traditional pattern of classroom discourse: teacher request – student response – teacher evaluation:

> Synchronous communication seems to encourage communicative fluency, which is generally understood as a quality of oral communication that expresses itself in coherence, fluidity, and appropriate lexical choice. . . .
>
> In the asynchronous discussions (the threaded ESL discussion forum), students participated in information exchanges, challenged each other's views, questioned new concepts, but primarily responded to teacher and student questions. Thus the quantity and quality of interaction was largely constrained in this mode of CMC. Some topics generated more student interaction than others. (2000: 101 and 104)

Other researchers have focused on the process of interaction itself as part of the broader structure of communication. Abrams (2001) adopted a more sociocultural perspective by defining the 'participant roles' adopted by students using the CMC medium. Blake (2000) and Toyoda and Harrison (2002) have applied the Interaction Hypothesis to study how L2 learners 'negotiate meaning' through CMC interaction. The same construct is used by Pellettieri (2000) to refer to explicit and implicit corrective feedback between participants in a task-based synchronous forum discussing lexical, syntactic or semantic aspects of their discourse. Lee (2001) has examined the negotiation strategies used by university students of Spanish in synchronous online communication, and found that clarification checks, requests and self-corrections were the most frequently used strategies. Belz and Kinginger (2002) have explored the development of L2 pragmatic competence through use of a 'telecollaborative learning environment' (2002: 189). The case studies they reported on involved two first-year university students, one studying French and the other German at the same university. Both participated in a telecollaborative project with students of English in France and Germany, respectively. The researchers analysed the development of the students' competence in the use of the *tu/vous, du/Sie* distinction, drawing on a corpus of emails, synchronous chat transcripts, and a range of qualitative and quantitative data. The authors emphasize that their study does not allow them to make claims about the extent of the students' knowledge of the rules of pronoun use in the address form in German or French; however, they do report on increased proficiency in their use of the address form, which the authors link to the collaborative support provided by their interlocutors in the online environment:

> In the course of negotiation of social meaning in these interactions, however, the learners' attention was directed to these forms by native speaking partners, and participation in these events did lead to changes in the learners' language use. In each of the cases examined, the learners displayed dynamism over time in their use of the pronouns of address as well as evolution toward greater awareness of the use of the T forms of solidarity. (2002: 209)

Other studies in this area have targeted the cultural learning outcome of CMC as the object of research. Müller-Hartmann (2000) studied how the negotiation of meaning promoted intercultural learning in students participating in asynchronous cross-national CMC networks. Furstenberg et al. (2001) have analysed the development of 'cultural literacy' among students in France and the USA engaged in a programme of jointly completed cross-cultural tasks. Liaw and Johnson (2001) have described patterns of cross-cultural learning among US and Taiwanese participants engaged in a looser framework of CMC interaction. The authors found that 'cultural differences sometimes hindered effective communication' and sometimes participants strove to bridge 'cultural gaps' through different discourse strategies (2001: 246). What links this group of authors is their emphasis on the content of the discourse.

A different focus of researchers on the use of CMC by language learners is the effect on learners' anxieties related to communication in the target language. Arnold (2007) has looked at the relationship between CMC use and 'communication apprehension' in the case of 56 university students of German in the USA. Analysis was based on a comparison of responses from students engaged in face-to-face, synchronous or asynchronous communication. Arnold points out that prior research has suggested that there is a fall in levels of anxiety felt by language learners during participation in synchronous or asynchronous CMC. Proposed explanations of this finding are that the environment is more anonymous than classroom settings, that the absence of paralinguistic signs (such as raised eyebrows) can ease anxiety and that, for asynchronous users, time to participate at their own pace can have a similar reassuring effect (2007: 472). Arnold's study looked at the more permanent 'carry-over effect on learners' FL communication apprehension levels' (ibid.). Arnold found that the main factor influencing the growth in the participants' confidence in engaging in L2 interaction was the student-centred nature of the practice:

> Using regular student-centered discussion, be they in an electronic form or the traditional oral setting, can have multiple benefits. First, they can promote a new communicative awareness with less focus on form. Second, such discussions provide the opportunity for students to apply and practice the FL while experimenting with it and even making adjustments. The findings of this research also indicate that asynchronous CMC might not be a suitable environment for interactive, conversation-like exchanges. Instead, it seems to lend itself more to writing tasks. (2007: 483)

Integrative CALL

This category has been interpreted in different ways by authors, depending on the constituent features of the integration process. Some commentators focus on the combination of multiple language skills (speaking, reading, writing and listening) or of types of resources (visual, textual, aural), while for others the defining feature of the integration is the blending of computer use with the lessons and learning more broadly. It is Gruba, again, who provides us with a definition that is most appropriate from our point of view in this book. The key ingredients in Gruba's definition (drawing on Debski (2000) and Warschauer and Kern (2000) and others) are twofold. Integrative CALL 'make[s] full use of networked computers as a means to engage learners in meaningful, large-scale collaborative activities' (2004: 629). The second feature of this practice is that this form of computer-assisted collaborative activity involves learners in using the technology to produce tangible language/digital outcomes: 'Students are taught techniques in online publishing, and are urged to produce their own texts. Fostering learner agency [. . .] is a primary goal of integrative CALL' (ibid.). I would want to add a third, complementary dimension to this definition of integrative CALL. Through collaboration and productive, project-based work in (and around) the lesson and classroom environment, CALL is integrated more intricately with the teaching and learning process. The boundaries between CALL and 'conventional' activities in a lesson become blurred.

One way of illustrating the definition of the digital medium as an integrative tool within the broader context of language learning is by looking at the potential of particular multimedia digital tools which display a high degree of flexibility and portability. O'Bryan and Hegelheimer (2007: 166) have conceptualized the use of podcasts and podcasting within the framework of integrative CALL:

> The content of any out-of-class material – in addition to needing to be of reasonable quality and relevance – can serve various functions, ranging from reviewing lecture content to exemplifying difficult concepts through elaboration to preparing for the next class.

Podcasts can be used by teachers to provide extracts of authentic audio-visual material. They can also be downloaded from the internet by learners, including for use outside of lessons. Podcasts can also be easily produced by teachers, providing learners with supplementary pedagogical material that supports independent learning, revision, extension or 'catch-up' material. The production of podcasts by learners has also be found to be a motivating and creative medium in the languages classroom, as experienced for instance by Stanley in the context of the study of English as a foreign language:

> My own experience of producing a podcast with university students of tourism using http://themetourism.blogspot.com has also shown that publishing is a way of encouraging the learners to take greater care over the work that they do. The attention to detail and interest is superior to when learners are producing work which is only being seen by an audience of one (the teacher). Questionnaires given to the students after the course also showed they appreciated the value of the publishing project. One thing which is crucial is being able to demonstrate that the learners have an audience. For this project, promoting the address of the podcast

via various podcast directories and educational podcasting groups made it relatively easy to find an audience for the learners' work. Another thing that helped was displaying graphically the number of visitors to the site. (2006: 6)

Similarly, Fox (2008: 4–5) describes the following list of strategies for using a 'talk-radio-type podcast' entitled *Absolutely Intercultural* in English classes in Denmark and Germany:

1. Listening for pleasure and/or homework. This will indeed be mainly for the advanced and motivated learners. Follow-up discussion may help motivation.
2. Listening with a pre-prepared teacher glossary would help to make the show accessible to lower levels.
3. Listening to a short chunk. Most of our podcasts are divided into more-or-less independent sections which can be listened to on their own. This makes the task more manageable for lower levels.
4. Listening with a transcript (prepared by the teacher). This is a controversial issue. Many teachers see a transcript as an obstacle to learning and preparing transcripts is a time-consuming job which most podcasters do not do (but why not have the students make one, each a part of it?). The show notes provide a good summary of the content and in some cases are partial transcripts.
5. Using a chunk as dictation practice. This is a very useful exercise which many teachers reject as old-fashioned but which can highlight and train grammatical accuracy. A potentially more rewarding reason is that it could be used to heighten awareness of authentic speech and how it differs from formal written language. Such chunks could be placed in text-manipulation programs for further practice. For that matter, cumulative transcripts and show notes could comprise or contribute to a corpus for not only text manipulation but concordance/collocations exercises and analysis.
6. As part of a distance-learning course where there is a danger of too much reliance on written texts.
7. Listening to a slowed down version: Windows Media Player 10 (Microsoft Corp., 2007) now includes functionality to slow down the recording and some students may find this helpful. Audacity also does this, and with that program you can introduce silences to allow increased processing time (at natural speech speed, but the assumption is that the lack of pauses between utterances prevents time for reflection).

8. The *Absolutely Intercultural* podcast includes many non-native speakers of English and therefore provides ample opportunity for learners to deal with the accented English which they are most likely to meet.

Fox includes an extract of an interview with Steve Evans, a teacher from the British Council in Madrid who has created 'Madrid young learners podcast' (http://mylcpodcasts.blogspot.com). Evans describes how he used the *Absolutely Intercultural* site with students of English in Spain, aged 14–16 years, and based a lesson around the podcast during which the students listened to dialogues 'about what other people thought about what they thought was the truth about the Spanish diet, tapas and siestas' (Fox 2008: 6). The students subsequently posted their reactions to these beliefs on the blog which in turn triggered responses from other people who were interested in their views. This had a strong motivating effect on the students who then decided to produce a podcast of their own on aspects of Spanish lifestyle.

Conclusion

The dual focus of the review in this chapter, which has surveyed studies in the parallel fields of educational research and CALL that have focused on the use of technology in language teaching and learning, has indicated that there has been a growing rapprochement between the two perspectives in recent years. At first, the two perspectives reflected a clash of paradigms in terms of both pedagogical and research focus. Initially studies conducted within the educational research context were intent on measuring impact on learning, and were concerned with measuring patterns of generic use of the technology in the classroom. Early CALL studies and pedagogical uses of technology in TEFL were characterized by a narrowly focused, clinical examination of the impact of CALL activities and resources on improvement of language proficiency. In recent years teachers and researchers have shown a greater desire to explore a more holistic or synthetic perspective, such as discussed above in relation to 'integrative CALL'.

What might be happening here is a recognition of the interdependence between subject discipline needs and objectives and the more generic social context of classroom teaching and learning. Of course there is no guarantee that this perspective will provide a satisfactory account of the potential of digital language learning in instructional contexts. What is clear is that access and computer literacy alone is not a sufficient factor to promote consistent use of computers in teaching that would lead to transformative practice. As Larry Cuban has reported in his comparison of the classroom use of computers by Silicon Valley teachers in the 1990s with that of previous generations of less technologically literate members of the profession, there are 'unanticipated similarities' in the low level of usage by both groups:

> There is credible evidence, limited to be sure, that teachers' use of computers in Silicon Valley, an area marked by strong support for innovation and technological progress, is similar to earlier generations of teachers facing new machines that also promised much improvement in teaching and learning. (2001: 150–1)

Skill and access alone, therefore, would seem to be insufficient drivers for radical and pervasive use of the medium. The pursuit of a pedagogically transformative role for computers in language teaching and learning may turn out in the end to be a misguided and temporary educational blind alley. It is not always made clear on what grounds language pedagogy is in need of transformation. For the time being, however, it would seem fairly incontrovertible and uncontroversial to argue that language teaching and learning, at all levels, can benefit from the mediation of technology. It would seem equally clear that for radically effective mediation to take place, both technology and language pedagogy need to adapt and change in the interests of language learning and use. The chapters that follow in the rest of this book, therefore, are as much about language pedagogy and learning as they are about the use of digital technology by language teachers and learners.

Notes

1 For a lively and varied set of responses, both supportive and critical, to the NSLI initiative see the 'Perspectives' section of a recent issue of the *Modern Language Journal* (Blake and Kramsch, 2007: 247–283).
2 K-12 refers to the full span of years in schooling in the USA: from kindergarten to twelfth grade.

References

Abrams, Z. (2001), 'Computer-mediated communication and group journals: expanding the repertoire of participant roles'. *System*, 29, (4), 489–503.

ACTFL (2008), *Student Survey Report*. www.actfl.org/files/public/ACTFL_Final_2008_completeLOW.pdf.

Allum, P. (2002), 'CALL and the classroom: the case for comparative research'. *ReCALL*, 14, (1), 146–66.

Arnold, N. (2007), 'Reducing foreign language communication apprehension with computer-mediated communication: a preliminary study'. *System*, 35, 469–86.

Belz, J. and Kinginger, C. (2002), 'The cross-linguistic development of address form use in telecollaborative language learning: two case studies'. *Canadian Modern Language Review*, 59, (2), 189–214.

Blake, R. (2000), 'Computer mediated communication: a window on L2 Spanish interlanguage'. *Language Learning & Technology*, 4, (1), 120–36.

Blake, R. and Delforge, A.-M. (2006), 'Online language learning: the case of Spanish Without Walls' in R. Salaberry and B. Lafford (eds) *The Art of Teaching Spanish*. Washington, DC: Georgetown University Press, pp. 127–47.

Blake, R. and Kramsch, C. (eds) (2007), 'The Issue: National Language Educational Policy'. *The Modern Language Journal*, 91, (ii), 247–83.

Block, D. (2002), *The Social Turn in Second Language Acquisition*. Washington, DC: Georgetown University Press.

Chenoweth, N. and Murday, K. (2003), 'Measuring student learning in an online French course'. *CALICO Journal*, 20, (2), 285–314.

Cuban, L. (2001), *Overused and Underused: Computers in the Classroom*. Cambridge, MA: Harvard University Press.

Darhower, M. (2006), 'Where's the community? Bilingual internet chat and the 'fifth C' of the National Standards'. *Hispania*, 89, (1), 84–98.

Debski, R. (ed.) (2000), 'Project-oriented CALL: implementation and evaluation'. *Computer Assisted Language Learning*, 13, 4–5.

DfEE (Department for Education and Employment) (1999), *Modern Foreign Languages: The National Curriculum for England*. London: DfEE and QCA.

DfES (Department for Education and Skills) (2005), *The Key Stage 2 Framework for Languages*. London: DfES.

Eadie, G. (2001), *The Impact of ICT on Schools: Classroom Design and Curriculum Delivery: a Study of Schools in Australia, USA, England and Hong Kong*. Wellington: Winston Churchill Memorial Trust.

Felix, U. (2008), 'The unreasonable effectiveness of CALL: what have we learned in two decades of research?'. *ReCALL*, 20, (2), 141–61.

Fox, A. (2008), 'Using podcasts in the EFL classroom'. *TESL-EJ*, 11, (4), 1–11.

Furstenberg, G., Levet, S., English, K. and Maillet, K. (2001), 'Giving a virtual voice to the silent language of culture: the Cultura project'. *Language Learning & Technology*, 5, (1), 55–102.

González-Bueno, M. (1998), 'The effects of electronic mail on Spanish L2 discourse'. *Language Learning & Technology*, 1, (2), 55–70.

Gruba, P. (2004), 'Computer assisted language learning (CALL)', in A. Davies and C. Elder (eds) *The Handbook of Applied Linguistics*. Oxford: Blackwell Publishing, pp. 623–48.

Harrison, C., Comber, C., Fisher, T., Haw, K., Lewin, C., Lunzer, E., McFarlane, A., Mavers, D., Scrimshaw, P., Somekh, B. and Watling, R. (2002), *The Impact of Information and Communication Technologies on Pupil Learning and Attainment*. DfES: London.

Lamy, M.-N. and Hampel, R. (2007), *Online Communication in Language Learning and Teaching*. Palgrave Macmillan: Basingstoke.

Lee, L. (2001), 'Online interaction: negotiation of meaning and strategies used among learners of Spanish'. *ReCALL*, 13, (2), 232–44.

Liaw, M.-L. and Johnson, R. (2001), 'E-mail writing as a cross-cultural learning experience'. *System*, 29, 235–51.

Liddicoat, A., Scarino, A., Curnow, T., Kohler, M., Scrimgeour, A. and Morgan, A.-M. (2007), *An Investigation of the State and Nature of Languages in Australian Schools: Department of Education, Employment and Workplace Relations: Canberra*. www.dest.gov.au/sectors/school_education/publications_resources/profiles/investigation_languages_in_schools.htm.

Magnan, S. (2008), 'Re-examining the priorities of the National Standards for Foreign Language Education'. *Language Teaching*, 41, (3), 349–66.

MCEETYA (Ministerial Council on Education, Employment, Training and Youth Affairs) (2005), *Joint Statement on Education and Training in the Information Economy*. www.curriculum.edu.au/verve/_resources/infoeconomy2005_file.pdf.

Müller-Hartmann, A. (2000), 'The role of tasks in promoting intercultural learning in electronic learning networks'. *Language Learning & Technology*, 4, (2), 129–47.

National Standards in Foreign Language Education Project (1996), *The Standards for Foreign Language Learning: Preparing for the 21st Century (SFFLL)*. Lawrence, KS: Allen Press.

National Standards in Foreign Language Education Project (1999, 2006), *The Standards for Foreign Language Learning in the 21st Century (SFFLL*, 2nd & 3rd edns.). Lawrence, KS: Allen Press.

O'Bryan, A. and Hegelheimer, V. (2007), 'The role of podcasting in an ESL listening strategies course'. *ReCALL*, 19, (2), 162–80.

Ofsted (Office for Standards in Education) (2002), *ICT in Schools: Effect of Government Initiatives: Secondary Modern Foreign Languages*. London: HMSO.

—(2004), *2004 Report: ICT in Schools: the Impact of Government Initiatives: Secondary Modern Foreign Languages*. Available at www.ofsted.gov.uk/assets/3644.pdf (accessed 4 January 2008).

—(2008) *The Changing Landscape of Languages: an Evaluation of Language Learning 2004/07*. Available at www.ofsted.gov.uk/assets/Internet_Content/Shared_Content/Files/2008/july/The_changing_landscape_of_languages.pdf (accessed 2 July 2008).

O'Leary, D. (2008), 'Language of Integration'. *Guardian*, Tuesday April 29.

Owhotu, V. (2006), 'Higher education, open distance learning and virtual universities', in Owhotu, V. (ed.), *An Introduction to Information Technologies in Education*. Lagos: Sibon Books Ltd, pp. 34–66.

Passey, D., Rogers, C., Machell, J. and McHugh, G. (2004), *The Motivational Effects of ICT on Pupils*. DfES: London.

Pellettieri, J. (2000), 'Negotiation in cyberspace', in M. Warschauer and J. Kern (eds) *Network-Based Language Teaching: Concepts and Practice*. Cambridge: Cambridge University Press, pp. 59–86.

Pittard, V., Bannister, P. and Dunn, J. (2003), *The Big PICTure: The Impact of ICT on Attainment, Motivation and Learning*. DfES: London.

QCA (Qualifications and Curriculum Authority) (2006), *Pupils' Views on Language Learning*. www.qca.org.uk/qca_6973.aspx.

Rhodes, N. and Branaman, L. (1999), *Foreign Language Instruction in the United States: a National Survey of Elementary and Secondary Schools*. Washington, DC: Delta Systems Co. Center for Applied Linguistics and NSLI.

Schacter, J. (1999), *The Impact of Educational Technology on Student Achievement: What Most Current Research Has to Say*. Santa Monica, CA: Milken Exchange on Educational Technology.

Sotillo, S. (2000), 'Discourse functions and syntactic complexity in synchronous and asynchronous communication', *Language Learning & Technology*, 4, (1), 82–119. *Standards for Foreign Language Learning in the 21st Century* (2006), Lawrence, KS: Allen Press (www.actfl.org/files/public/execsumm.pdf).

Stanley, G. (2006), 'Podcasting: audio on the internet comes of age' *TESL-EJ*, 9, (4), 1–11.

Stockwell, G. (2007), 'A review of technology choice for teaching language skills and areas in the CALL literature'. *ReCALL*, 19, (2), 105–20.

Toyoda, E. and Harrison, R. (2002), 'Categorization of text chat communication between learners and native speakers of Japanese'. *Language Learning & Technology*, 6, (1), 82–99.

US Department of Education, *Technology's Impact on Learning*. www.nsba.org/sbot/toolkit/tiol.html.

US Department of Commerce and US Department of Education, *Visions 2020: 2 Student Views on Transforming Education and Training Through Advanced Technologies*. www.ed.gov/about/offices/list/os/technology/plan/2004/site/documents/visions_20202.pdf.

Warschauer, M. (1996), 'Computer assisted language learning: an introduction', in S. Fotos (ed.) *Multimedia Language Teaching*. Tokyo: Logos International, pp. 3–20.

Warschauer, M. and Kern, R. (eds) (2000), *Network-Based Language Teaching: Concepts and Practice*. Cambridge: Cambridge University Press.

Chapter 2

The potential of the internet as a language-learning tool

Iain Mitchell

Modern-language teaching in schools in England has until recently been mainly concentrated on the secondary level (ages 11–18) with the main languages being: French, German and Spanish, in that order. Recent changes, however, have included: the development of language teaching in the KS2 sector of primary education (ages 7–11); a general broadening of the languages being offered, with increasing popularity for Spanish, Japanese and Chinese; and significantly, initiatives aiming at providing consistency across the curriculum including, of particular importance for language learning, the National Literacy Strategy. This strategy, as it applies to second-language learning (The National Languages Strategy), places particular emphasis on the need to develop an awareness of how language works at different levels: word, sentence, text. Traditionally, language teachers may focus on word (vocabulary) and sentence (syntax and grammar) work and view text work as an outcome of the first two. The National Languages Strategy aims to put text-level work on an equal footing with word and sentence work. Equally, an extra strand of the Strategy highlights the importance of the development of cultural awareness, an awareness and understanding of the settings, the societies where the language is used. In this chapter, the author will suggest how the use of authentic, up-to-date texts, such as exist on the Web, can be said to achieve all of these aims.

Authentic texts and tapes

The use of *authentic* texts and tapes in the MFL classroom has often been viewed as problematic. The lack of easy and up-to-date access to such material has, in the past, limited their use and effectiveness. The development of the internet, however, has led to a previously unimaginable, immediate resource for language learners. The vast availability of original, authentic texts, and also, more recently, audio and DVD files, can provide instant contact and stimulus for the language learner. Nonetheless, such material, produced for native speakers of the language, can, for many language learners (and their teachers), be viewed as 'difficult'; the lexis and structures may be far beyond what has been encountered so far, and the subject matter may relate to a culture of which the learner has little or no experience.

Added to which, particularly in the English educational system, pressures of time can lead languages teachers to focus mainly on the development of reading and listening skills as they relate to assessment criteria of the exam system: 'prove to me that you know what (all) these words mean.' While there undoubtedly is a place for measurement of comprehension in language learning, it is also crucial to develop learners' confidence in facing the unpredictable challenges of authenticity and their awareness of the cultures where this language is the main means of communication and expression. Authentic texts available on the internet illustrate how technology can be used to *assist* in language learning.

This chapter is based on work that I have undertaken over many years as a modern-languages teacher in the English state system. For the last fifteen years, I have worked as a trainer, an independent Advisory Teacher for Modern Languages, with serving teachers, trainee students and pupils of all abilities in all parts of the country. The examples discussed are generic and can be replicated in any language. They are appropriate for whole class or individualized learning, for traditional low-tech presentation or for use in electronic form. The *same* original texts can be exploited with learners of different ages and levels of ability. Also, crucially, the time taken in their preparation need not be disproportionate to their use and effectiveness.

Summary

1. exploiting news websites
2. exploiting commercial websites
3. websites specifically for young people
4. culturally authentic sites
5. strategies for reading authentic texts: becoming an intelligent reader

Where to start? Exploiting news websites

Text-based pages

Thanks to the internet, news from the target-language country is no more than a click away. Any major portal can lead to news from the major press or media organizations. Typically, the first page of a news website offers a menu of different categories: Actualités: = Monde; France; Sport; People and so on. Choosing, for example, *France* will then reveal a variety of further subcategories and, most usefully, the most prominent headlines of the day. Although, with some more advanced, autonomous learners this initial direction could be all that is required ('choose, report, summarize, research further, comment on') most learners will benefit from some minimal intervention and preparation of the material by the teacher. The following steps suggest how this can be done practically.

Teacher preparation

Choice of appropriate headlines

To provide a good variety requires about 12–15 recent headlines. They should be chosen irrespective of their linguistic difficulty and, to an extent, of their content. However, it is unrealistic to focus on some themes such as Spanish domestic politics or the latest French financial scandal. The aim should be a good variety of types of news stories and there can be overlap of types, or even of the same story. (Some discretion should perhaps be exercised in ensuring that a few recurring themes do not over-predominate, such as disasters, murders, or industrial strikes!) To achieve this variety might involve some trawling through headlines from previous days, but keeping in mind that up-to-date authenticity is one of the main attractions of such material.

Editing of material

It is important to resist the temptation to edit the language of the headlines. The main editing should only be to copy and paste the material into a manageable, useable format such as Word, to number the headlines and to present them either in printed hard copy or electronically.

Example: www.yahoo.fr/actualités/France (21.10.07)

Les actualités

1. Nicolas Sarkozy propose une refonte du système social français
2. le cancer première cause de mortalité des Français
3. obésité: l'UFC veut interdire certaines pubs télé pour enfants
4. le juge Van Ruymbeke sera jugé devant le CSM le 25 octobre
5. les Etats-Unis voient une solution diplomatique à la crise en Iran
6. la durée de la crise radicalise les Flamands en Belgique
7. l'UE veut aider les pays pauvres sur le réchauffement climatique
8. mondial: Vincent Clerc a des fourmis dans les jambes
9. eBay retire une annonce qui mettait la Belgique en vente
10. incendie dans une centrale nucleaire japonaise
11. l'accès à Ground Zero refusé au président iranien
12. pesticide aux Antilles: une situation 'très grave', selon Barnier
13. besoin d'un alibi? Des sites internet prêts à vous les concocter
14. la doyenne des Français décède à l'âge de 113 ans
15. le rappeur américain 50 Cent annule sa tournée européenne, sans motif

Exploitation

The main temptation for the teacher may be initially simply to ask the learners what the headlines mean in English. This can then throw up the problem of the perceived difficulty of the language and even the 'so what?' issue of 'who cares about *le juge* Van Ruymbeke anyhow?'. A more useful approach can be to turn such perceptions on their head and encourage the learners to view the difficulties of authenticity as a challenge to which they can rise. It is important for all learners that they are not limited by their own (or our own) feelings of what is difficult, of what they know about what is happening in the world at large, or in one particular country. The claim that many learners have limited awareness of what is happening in their own country should not discourage us from opening their eyes to the issues that are deemed to be important in other cultures.

Familiarization with the text: starter activities

It is useful initially to treat the group of headlines as one text despite the layout and numbering. This can link with aspects of text-level work as highlighted in the cross-curricular National Literacy Strategy and the MFL KS3 Strategy. To avoid intimidation by the difficulty of the text, the learners can initially be asked simply to find certain categories of language. An accessible starter activity can be: 'how many names of people can you find in 45 seconds?' and then 'how many names of places?'. This can then be followed by a simple sound-spelling task: 'which number headline am I reading out?'/'c'est quel numéro?' These basic scanning activities perform a crucial role of creating a 'can-do' atmosphere, and equally allow the learner to revisit the whole text, but each time from a slightly different angle. As yet, there is no stress on 'what does it all mean?', although strikingly if the brain is not required to do something particular, it will often do it, in its own way. At this point learners may offer, of their own volition, comments such as: 'is that one about that fire in Japan?' Unexpected bonuses perhaps, but ones that will become more frequent, over time, as learners develop their confidence. Also, should the task be deemed too unchallenging by some learners, the tables can be turned and the task can be to identify a certain category of language and corresponding examples: one group suggested titles for people (*président, rappeur, doyenne, juge*) or acronyms.

Levels of meaning: word level

To ease the learners into the meaning of the text the teacher can identify some relatively unusual vocabulary, such as: *mortalité; en vente; une refonte; annule; incendie; crise; décède; sans motif; réchauffement climatique.*

Possible tasks can, cumulatively, include:

- find and highlight these words in the text
- work out what you think they mean from the whole sentence

or

- match them up from the English: *fire; an overhaul; crisis; passes away; global warming; without reason; up for sale; cancels; forbid*

Or simply, for the more able:

- identify the English concepts in the French text

The choice of such vocabulary may seem somewhat arbitrary and peripheral, especially for less able learners. But there is certainly a case to be made, even with less able learners, of occasionally introducing them to language which does not appear in the more predictable lexis of well-worn topics. It can also be an enjoyable challenge for the teacher and a method of developing their own subject knowledge of current language usage! The word-level language is, however, only part of the process, and a stepping stone to the next level.

Levels of meaning: sentence level

This level of meaning – 'what do the sentences actually mean?' – is probably traditionally where most teachers and learners would presume to start (and finish). It is, however, important to stress the danger of omitting the previous tasks. The learner crucially needs *time* to absorb the nature of the whole text, to consider it in a variety of different ways and to develop confidence along the way.

While more able learners may now be able to identify what many of the sentences mean (also with the help of the word-level vocabulary tasks above), there are a variety of useful ways to develop an understanding of meaning at sentence level. Paraphrasing of the basic meanings in English by the teacher can aid gist understanding as in the following type of task:

Match up the following English newspaper headlines with their French equivalents:

A: ban on 'fat' advertisements
B: President's proposals
C: Belgium in crisis
D: number 1 cause of death
E: rugby player has pins and needles
F: Iran's president refused access
G: aid to combat global warming
H: oldest woman in France dies
I: alibis for every occasion
J: nuclear accident in Japan

Such a task can allow for a variety of learning situations:

- If the pupils are working individually at computer terminals, they can cut and paste the English to the French.
- A whole-class activity with an IWB can similarly allow pupils physically to drag and match the English to the French.

- A4 printouts for each individual headline can be displayed round the classroom walls. To complete the task the learner must leave their seat and find and note the matching texts. To increase the challenge a time limit can be set.
- Use of the PowerPoint feature of a timed slide show can allow each English headline to be shown in sequence for a certain length of time. The sole requirement is to match the number of the French headline with the letter of the English. The whole sequence can be run at least twice (and more often if required) to reduce stress at missing one the first time through. This provides an interesting example of dynamic reading that our learners are becoming more used to in their everyday lives, such as ticker-tape messages that often appear in the media. It also moves reading away from the static text that may not appeal to our learners.

With this, and indeed with all of the activities described so far, it can be beneficial for learners to work in pairs helping and monitoring each other.

This may be all that the teacher wants to do with this text. Even such exploitation might spread over two lessons (although its immediacy is a core issue).

Other ways to develop the text include

- Grammar: expand selected headlines into grammatically complete sentences (headlines often lack articles and finite past tense verbs).
- Reading: reduce the headlines to their core meaning: 'can you select for your billboard the three most crucial words that convey the meaning of this headline?'
- Speaking: select, order and record in pairs your main headlines for a radio newsflash ('Voici les infos avec . . .; . . . Le prochain bulletin sera à . . . heures') with the challenge of an exact time limit.
- Writing: 'In a personal journal/diary select and copy (and comment on) four important news items for that day.' If this was done even only five times over a year, it would still constitute a valuable personal record of what the pupils had discovered of what had been going on in France. An approach to cultural awareness that even the best textbook cannot provide.
- Cultural awareness: 'Copy onto sticky labels any headline with a geographical place in the country mentioned. On a wall-display map, find the place and attach to the map.'
- With the help of Google Images find the people mentioned in the news items and create a display (electronic or hard copy).

Is it all worth the effort?

To justify its topical but short shelf life, such an activity needs to earn its keep. It must be capable, in a teacher's busy day, of being used and adapted, while retaining the core principles of progression, for pupils of significantly different abilities and ages from even a Y8 (second year of language learning) group right up to Y12/Y13 learners. A scheme of work that could include such work at least once a half-term would considerably improve learners' reading skills, their general confidence and perception of the status of the subject ('challenging but rewarding').

Audio: use of sound files

In the last few years, the scope of internet-based material has developed to include sound and DVD files as well as text. This again opens up a whole range of possibilities for the languages classroom and can hugely enhance the role of listening in language acquisition. Perhaps even more so than with reading, listening in the languages classroom, usually to material provided with a commercial course, can be seen by our learners primarily as a form of assessment. 'Is this a test?' is a query that many teachers will have had to deal with on appearance of the tape recorder in the classroom. While course-book material is produced to a high standard and benefits from clarity and manageable pace of delivery, like reading (as discussed above), listening tasks can often lack immediacy and relevance to the country, and do not necessarily prepare the learners for the alarming moment when faced with native speakers, responding at seemingly breakneck speed to apparently straightforward questions. The design of listening tasks, perhaps even more than that of reading tasks, needs considerable focus if we are to give our learners the confidence to deal with the onslaught of the real language out there, in the real world.

Listening in the languages classroom,
but (perhaps) not as we know it (so far)

The numerous and varied news media sites available on the internet give access not only to texts but to audio sound files. These can be found intermittently on newspaper media sites but more consistently on radio sites such as:

- France Inter: www.radiofrance.fr/franceinter
- Norddeutscher Rundfunk: www1.ndr/radio

This is a whole new landscape, given that only recently, and only with considerable commitment and good geographical positioning on the part of teachers, was it possible to record from even a few stations in neighbouring countries. It is now possible to listen regularly to all types of speech programmes with good sound quality. Sound clips can also now be successfully downloaded into WAV or MP3 files using, for instance, basic audio-editing software such as Audacity (http://audacity.sourceforge.net/).

This does still beg the question of practicality of use in the classroom. It is probably unrealistic to consider regular transcriptions of even short audio extracts for equivalent news headlines (such as have been described above for text reading). The apparent speed of delivery can certainly make pure, unsupported listening to a France Inter news bulletin, for example, demanding for even the most able linguists. But therein lies a useful challenge.

Listening is arguably the most fundamental of the four language skills. It is what we have done for the longest length of time in our mother tongue. For years before we start to speak, to use language in an identifiably communicative form, we have been listening not just for meaning but to sounds, rhythm and intonation of language. Without that crucial phase of listening we would be unable ever to speak in our first language. Yet this step is often missing for second-language learners who are expected, from the first lesson onwards, to speak, communicate and use new sounds and new intonation patterns from a standing start. English mother-tongue speakers have a particular problem. Due to the ubiquity of English as a global means of communication, they may, in an anglophone country, never hear the sounds of the language they are learning outside the walls of the classroom. Compare this to the average second-language learner of English in almost any country in the world. As well as their own native language, they are hearing English, from an early age, through the media, through films, through music, but in an unstressed way. They are not being forced to understand it, but it exists all around them; they are immersed in English almost without realizing it. In some ways it could even be argued that there now exists a type of de facto bilingualism in many countries, certainly among the younger generations. The average teenager, in the Netherlands or Scandinavia, for instance, comes to the languages classroom to learn English swimming in the sounds of language, ready and able to deal with the more formal requirements of second-language learning. The challenge for languages teachers in an anglophone country is somehow to provide some of this background language, this chatter, albeit if only within the classroom. Some of the following activities can, thanks to the internet, provide such a linguistic background.

Extensive listening: listening to the day's news quickly

A downloaded recording of a 2–3-minute on-the-hour news bulletin from a news website may not be exploited as thoroughly as the text-based news described above, but it can still provide an invaluable focus, particularly at the start of the lesson. The following tasks exploit news broadcasts in ways that are accessible to most young learners:

- Listen (twice) to this news bulletin and count the number of different items you hear. Do you hear anything at all that might give you a clue as to what any one of the items might be about?

This is not meant as a test, but rather as a confidence booster: 'even if you understood very little, it is still worthwhile building up your confidence, accepting that 95 per cent of what you hear may not be understood.' Such a task is ideal as a group or class activity where different learners may pick out different parts of the spoken input. Other supportive tasks that can train the ear to listen, without the undue stress of trying to comprehend what is heard, include:

- Here are the news items from the bulletin – what order do they come in?
- Here are a variety of news items – which ones appear in the bulletin? (This could work well in conjunction with the reading tasks described above: 'which of the 15 news items we have read about are actually mentioned in this radio broadcast?')

Even something as basic as the following is not a dumbed-down language task:

- Listen to this news broadcast and tell me how many different voices you hear.

The learners are being asked to listen, in a focused manner, in a 'surface' task where they know there is a reasonable probability that they will be successful. But at a deeper level they are absorbing, and almost without realizing it, the sounds and patterns of words, sentences, monologues or dialogues.

Such tasks lend themselves to whole class activities, but with the interesting proviso that the teacher does not pause the recording and will play it several times, or as often as is requested by the learners. An intriguing aspect of this approach is that it forces the teacher to stop talking, to stop being centre stage, to enact a significant part of the learning process, that of 'teacher fading', for at least a few minutes! Conversely, if the sound file is provided individually for the learner on a computer screen, or downloaded to an MP3 file for homework, the learner can take control, pause and replay as they often as they need, but still with a clear, manageable task in mind.

Intensive listening

For some more able learners it may be appropriate to develop part of such a sound file for more intensive listening. Activities that can be quickly put together by the teacher can include:

- Listen now to this one news item – which of the following phrases did you actually hear? What order did you hear them in?
- Look at the transcript of this item. Is the text exactly the same as what you hear? Are there any differences between the written and the heard?

Modern audio software (such as Audacity) can allow the teacher (or the learner) to slow down the speed of the language without noticeable distortion. While this might appear to go against the philosophy of helping the learner to cope with undiluted speed, it can, if used judiciously, help to develop the learner's comprehension skills, and begin to focus on specific meaning. But even an overtly non-linguistic editing task such as:

- Listen and follow the sound-file graph of this news item. It lasts 19 seconds. The programme producer needs it edited down to 15 seconds.

can probably be done purely by the removal of several short silences or of one short sentence (or even speeding it up slightly!). Such a task is a type of problem-solving that may engage students who may not view themselves as traditional, successful language learners. They may not be working at a high level of comprehension but they are still being exposed to the language, and at a subliminal level, their awareness of the language and its sounds is being developed.

Focused listening

Occasionally it may be worthwhile for the teacher to spend more time on preparation, especially if the recording is characterized by a specific type of language. The sound file concerning the fate of the French aircraft carrier Clémenceau is a short extract from an online news bulletin. The language is fast and as a listening task would tax most learners. It is, however, particularly characterized by the use of numbers. The task devised consequently is a traditional gap-fill, but focusing on numbers. The sentences appear in the order that they are heard and able students could conceivably complete it without any extra support.

Le porte-avions 'Clémenceau'

Sa coque a le numéro _____	10
Il a fait un voyage de _____ kilomètres	2
Le voyage a duré _____ mois	4
Il est arrivé ce matin à _____ heures au	12
quai numéro _____	Q790
Il date de _____	266
Il mesure _____ mètres de long et _____	5
mètres de large	18000
Son arrivée à Brest va durer _____ jours!	51
Tout ça coûte cher– _____ millions d'euros	1961

FIGURE 1 Le porte-avions 'Clémenceau'

Many learners would nonetheless benefit from support even for this task.

- *Before* listening to the tape it would be beneficial for the learners to focus on the specific language of the numbers (for instance, they could practise recognizing them or practise saying them) so that they are sensitized to the language that they are going to hear.
- Also, and this is a crucial learning strategy, they could predict what they think are the most plausible numbers for each sentence. This is not part of a test, and it will not matter if the learners make false predictions. What is important is that they have time to reflect on the meaning of what they are going to hear and that they have their own particular reasons for wanting to listen to the tape.

This in no way devalues the task as a listening exercise. The learners are being exposed to challenging language (designed for a native-speaker audience); they can accept they will not understand all the language heard, but they will have done useful work on numbers and context. Although this could be argued to be 'hot news' that will date quickly, it can equally well be viewed as an interesting archive of recent French history and could be used for some considerable time after the actual event.

Blurring the skills: mixing listening with reading

The above example suggests how the standard assessment task of gap-filling can be used to help the learners improve, rather than just to measure their performance. All assessment task types can benefit from such a focus.

The task of synonym matching can cause particular problems for many learners; for example, the question includes the word *fumer* but the learners will hear the word *cigarette*. The following example exploits the richness and variety of language that native speakers use instinctively when speaking and at the same time usefully deconstructs the synonym assessment task. As the focus is not overtly on listening comprehension the skills of reading and listening can be blurred together.

Mangez les fruits et les légumes – mais qui dit quoi?
les consommatrices? le présentateur? l'expert?

- Je mange beaucoup, beaucoup, beaucoup de fruits!

- C'est bon pour la santé.

- En 1976 on mangeait plus de légumes et de fruits.

- Mange ce que tu aimes mais avec les fruits ou les légumes.

- Mange ton dessert avec du fruit.

Il faut consommer les légumes non pas à la place de leur plat favori mais avec.

Ça a beaucoup de vitamines! ça empêche de manger d'autres choses plus calorifiques, ça garde en bonne santé.

J'achète des kilos, des kilos de fruits.

Depuis trente ans la consommation de fruits et légumes a chuté de 20 pour cent.

Tu prends la glace, d'accord, mais la glace à la vanille tu vas la prendre avec une petite salade de fraises ou avec une demi-pêche.

Je mange les fruits et les légumes tous les jours.

FIGURE 2 Mangez les fruits et les légumes

The sound file is taken from an internet-based news website (www. radiofrance.fr/franceinter 20.05.06) consisting of sound bites from a variety of shoppers in a French market. The transcripts written by the teacher for all of these short sound bites are presented in random order at the bottom of the page/screen. The extra preparation for the teacher involves devising synonym sentences for each of the sound bites and arranging them on the right, but *in the order* that the sound bites will be heard on the pro-gramme. The task for the learners, before they listen to the sound file, is to match up and place the sound bites in order beside the synonyms. If the matching is correct it will 'read' as a transcript of the whole sound file. Thus the transcript becomes the 'answer' to the reading task. This can work most effectively where the dragging of the sentences can be seen to be done on an IWB or computer screen. What might otherwise have been material which was too challenging for a standard listening activity is thus transformed:

- The learners are given *time* to reflect on the nature of synonyms through the reading.
- They can be made aware of new language, of different ways of express-ing the same idea.
- The 'answer' to the task does not appear to come from the teacher, but from the sound file itself. As has already been mentioned, any instance of 'teacher fading', of appearing sometimes not to be the centre of attention and font of all knowledge, can have a positive effect on the learners.

This example gains from its immediacy and authenticity, from the fact that these are real people and from using language in a naturalistic manner. At the same time, useful work has been done through the deconstruction of a potentially difficult assessment task-type. Such an activity probably has a longer shelf life than some of the news activities described above. The time taken in preparation can be offset by the fact that it can become part of a 'healthy-eating' module than can remain valid, at least for several years, as and when it appears in a syllabus.

Internet-based, authentic material: variety of types of texts; variety of approaches

So far the focus has been on news-based generic sites. There are other types of sites worth considering as a source of authentic material.

Exploiting commercial websites

Many of the major company names we encounter in our daily lives are now global concerns and will almost certainly have websites in the language being studied. While in the classroom we will hardly be using such websites (like French eBay or German Ikea) for the purpose for which they are originally intended (to make purchases), their immediacy and credibility with our learners can be significant. Different methods of exploitation in the foreign languages classroom are possible.

Preparatory editing by the teacher for whole class work

www.ebay.fr (22.04.07)

The following is a section of selective editing of an eBay webpage on 'vêtements de sport':

Baskets Neuves Junior Décathlon Point. 35/36	**5,00 EUR**	–	8h 44m
Body vert pour le sport en salle Taille 40	**1,00 EUR**	1	9h 13m
Ensemble brassière + short gris taille L	**1,00 EUR**	1	9h 18m
Caleçon sport pour danse ou gym gris Taille 4	**1,00 EUR**	–	9h 21m
Superbe veste de survêtement LACOSTE bordeaux	**20,00 EUR**	6	10h 14m
LOT DE 2 BAS DE SURVÊTEMENTS LACOSTE	**11,50 EUR**	7	10h 33m
Kimono Judo enfant T-150	**1,00 EUR**	2	11h 3m
Combinaison Ski neuve T-M	**15,50 EUR**	6	11h 22m
FIGO MAILLOT FOOTBALL REAL MADRID	**19,99 EUR**	–	14h 4m
NISTELROOY MAILLOT FOOTBALL MAN UTD	**19,99 EUR**	–	14h 4m

This material lends itself to a variety of quick starter activities at the beginning of a lesson:

- for number practice (prices, times, quantities) both for listening and speaking tasks
- vocabulary classification of different types (sports, clothes)

and also for more extended work such as:

- j'achèterais/je n'achèterais pas . . . parce que . . .
- an auction sketch
- create a short TV advertisement for ebay.fr using this material

Online/on-screen work

www.ikea.com/de (accessed 10.12.06)
There may be quite specific reasons within a school environment for pupils not being able to work directly online. If need be, an 'online environment' can be simulated by downloading in advance the required webpages.

This example allowed Y9 students to plan and budget for their teacher's Christmas shopping:

'Ich kaufe jetzt meine Weihnachtsgeschenke aber ich habe nur €500. Ikea ist mein Lieblingsgeschäft aber ich habe keine Zeit zum Einkaufen. Kannst du mir helfen?'

- meine Schwester mag kochen. Ich suche etwas für ihre Küche
- mein Bruder hört gern Musik, aber er hat zuviele CDs!
- meine Freundin liebt Pflanzen
- mein Kollege studiert an der Uni. Er braucht etwas für sein Büro
- und für mich selbst bitte: zwei Überraschungsgeschenke!
- und, wenn dir was übrig bleibt, kauf dir selbst was Schönes!

This is a problem-solving task where learners, working to a budget, can, with a considerable level of choice, buy a range of presents for a busy teacher.

Websites for young people

No matter what language is being studied, it will be possible to find websites specifically aimed at young native speakers of the language. While perhaps not all the material can be exploited in the classroom, some lateral thinking on the part of the MFL teacher can pay significant dividends. One of the most successful websites for young French people is www.momes.net. Its target range is from about 8–14 so at least some of the pages have content appropriate to our own learners. The challenge, as ever, is matching appropriate content to accessible language.
www.momes.net (accessed 16.06.07)
Some of the most useful pages on any such site can be the topic discussion pages (*le forum*). These are more structured than normal 'chat' pages, and would appear to be effectively supervised. Topics, which vary hugely, are proposed for discussion by participants. Responses can equally vary hugely and sometimes unpredictably. Although aimed primarily at native speakers from all parts of the global francophone community, contributions are also welcome from second-language learners. Even a small

selection from the index to the forum can in itself be a useful initial stimulus for learners:

Débats: des sujets qui passionnent

- l'argent de poche après les bonnes notes?
- service militaire: filles et garçons ou garçons seulement?
- pour ou contre la viande de cheval?
- quel métier aimeriez-vous faire plus tard?
- pour ou contre les zoos?
- avez-vous des craintes de prendre maintenant l'avion?
- êtes-vous pour ou contre l'arrêt de l'école à 16 ans?
- pour ou contre le paintball?
- boycottez-vous les vêtements Tommy?
- dans quel pays aimeriez-vous vivre?
- êtes-vous pour ou contre la légalisation du cannabis?
- la discrimination des blonds
- l'argent de poche (pour ou contre)
- changer de prénom
- vous aimez l'école?
- croyez-vous aux extra-terrestres?

Tasks based around these (and possibly other) subjects could include:

- choose five that might interest you
- are there any that strike you as unusual?
- using mostly language from the subjects, can you invent a few more?

While this is an obvious area where the learners could have some free access to at least some of the pages, the teacher could also develop some of the pages in a manner appropriate to the needs of their learners. It will occasionally involve some choice and editing and even, if felt necessary, corrections to the contributors' accurate use of French!

http://forum.momes.net/: example A

Pensez-vous que le cheval est un animal que l'on peut manger comme le boeuf ou les poules . . .?

This example selects a very small, manageable selection from the comments available, and the teacher has added a basic task which would be appropriate for a whole-class activity:

- *tatiana76* On ne mange ni les chiens ni les chats ni les rats ni les tigres ni les zèbres ni les lions ni les girafes ni les singes. Alors pourquoi mangerait-on du cheval?
- *Miki* On mange du boeuf, du porc, du poulet, du veau, alors pourquoi ne mangerait-on pas de cheval?
- *kelly* Alors mangeons-les tous!! même les singes . . . Bon appétit!
- *ataboy* vous me donnez faim! LoL

Here are some possible tasks:

- soulignez tous les animaux
- remplacez tous ces animaux par d'autres exemples!

Once this has been exploited as a whole-class modelling activity, learners could then be directed to further pages of comments, allowing the learners to choose to continue with the task as above, and finally, if appropriate to their ability, to write their own comments using a variety of language they have encountered.

http://forum.momes.net/: example B

LA LANGUE FRANÇAISE VA-T-ELLE DISPARAÎTRE?
L'anglais est de plus en plus présent dans notre vie quotidienne. Est-ce un risque pour le français? Qu'en pensez-vous?

- Beaucoup de langues ont déjà disparu, chaque semaine une langue disparaît. Mais une langue qui disparaît c'est également une culture qui s'éteint à tout jamais de la surface de la Planète. *Bernard*
- Ici aux États-Unis nous nous demandons si l'espagnol remplacera l'anglais d'ici quelques années! *Jenny, 15 ans*
- Le risque pour moi, c'est que bientôt on ne pourra plus travailler en français. Vive la langue maternelle et dégagez-moi ces anglophiles de nos lieux de travail. *Orlando, Belgique*
- Je suis prof de français dans un collège italien. Mes élèves aiment bien la langue française, sa culture mais ce sont leurs parents qui voient dans l'anglais le futur de leurs fils. Je suis un peu fatiguée de combattre cette guerre, je suis toute seule!!! SOS pour la langue française! *Teresa, Italie*
- Bien sûr, le français est en train de disparaître maintenant même. L'anglais envahit tout et cette langue est omniprésente. Nous sommes

la dernière génération de francophones au Québec et en Amérique du Nord. *Jean, Québec*

- Je pense que le français ne disparaîtra pas tant qu'il y aura la volonté politique des pays francophones de le promouvoir. *Sven, Suisse*
- Cela dépend de nous, il ne faut pas se contenter de dire aux gens de ne pas parler anglais, il faut surtout donner des synonymes en français des mots que nous disons en anglais. *Muriel, Belgique, 13 ans*
- Chez nous la langue française est encore apprise, même si la langue anglaise gagne de plus en plus une place importante dans notre société. *Blaise, Italie*

Translation:
Is the French language about to disappear?
English is more and more present in our daily life. Is French at risk? What do you think?

- Many languages have already disappeared, each week a language disappears. But when a language disappears, that amounts to a culture disappearing for ever from the surface of the planet. *Bernard*
- Here in the USA we are wondering if Spanish will replace English in a few years! *Jenny, 15*
- The risk for me is that soon we will no longer be able to work in French. Long live the mother tongue and take away those Anglophiles from our workplaces! *Orlando, Belgium*
- I am a teacher of French in an Italian school. My pupils like the French language a lot, its culture but it's their parents who see English as part of their children's future. I am a little tired of fighting this war, I am all alone!!! SOS for the French language! *Teresa, Italy*
- Of course French is in the process of disappearing even now. English invades everything and this language is everywhere. We are the last generation of francophones in Quebec and in North America. *Jean, Quebec*
- I think that French will not disappear so long as there is the political will in francophone countries to promote it. *Sven, Switzerland*
- It's up to us, we mustn't be content with telling people not to speak English. We must above all use the French synonyms of words we say in English. *Muriel, Belgium, 13 years old*
- With us French is still studied, even though the English language has a bigger and bigger place in our society. *Blaise, Italy*

This is an almost random selection of the many comments that this topic stimulated. The language is more complex than in Example A and it would be unrealistic to expect all pupils to understand every word. However two basic types of activities could benefit all learners:

- scanning and gist understanding
- the language of opinions

Possible activities might include:
Complète la grille

nom	*jeune personne*	*adulte?*	*langue maternelle?*	*langue étrangère?*	*pays?*
Orlando	• (?)		•		Belgique

Extra!

- qui a des attitudes plutôt optimistes? Plutôt pessimistes? Rangez les opinions en ordre d'importance!
- faites un poster en français pour promouvoir le français!

This type of grid-filling activity can, however, sometimes create its own problems. If a grid has six columns and ten rows, is the expectation that 60 boxes must be filled to successfully complete the task? (In fact there are only 40, as two are alternatives, but it may not seem so to a learner, who might find the whole concept dauntingly vast.) Given the different speeds that learners work at, there will inevitably be those who take longer than others, and particularly in a whole-class setting, who do not get enough time to complete everything to their own satisfaction.

A more profitable approach could be to encourage the individual learner to *choose* two columns on which they will initially concentrate, and then to work vertically on each column (for instance, insert all the names, then all the countries). This can create some sense of ownership and more of a feeling of a series of small tasks being completed. It might also guide the learners to cast their eyes over the whole text several times, gradually assimilating information and avoiding getting blocked at the top, never getting to the bottom or the perceived end of the task.

An instruction from the teacher could be: 'I want everybody to complete at least two vertical columns, but to think carefully about which two you choose. I will be very pleased if people manage to do more than this, and I expect quite a few of you to finish at least three if not all the columns!'

This is effectively a type of differentiation by outcome. The *Extra!* tasks of course do run the risk of being perceived as 'more work for those who work hard' but they are a different type of task, and the optimist/pessimist activity does allow more able learners to look at the text again to gauge the attitudes of the contributors. It is fairly open-ended and not all who start it would necessarily finish it completely. The poster activity is an example of the reuse of language encountered. It is probably better done at another point and would make a good homework/consolidation activity.

A further language development activity identifies the core language of the opinions and, as above, there would not necessarily be an expectation that every learner matches everyone of them. 'Everybody should aim to match at least ten of the phrases but I will be very impressed by anybody who manages to get more than that':

français	*anglais*
je ne crois pas	but
je ne le trouve pas bien	fight this war
sera parlé	first language
au contraire!	French speakers
c'est l'anglais qui gagne	French-speaking countries
ce n'est pas la peine	have already disappeared
Cela dépend de nous	I don't think so
ces anglophiles	I don't think that's good
combattre cette guerre	I think that
des pays francophones	in the process of disappearing
des synonymes en français	is disappearing
disparaît.	is going to stay
disparaîtra	is not going to disappear
elle ne disparaîtra jamais	it will not disappear
en train de disparaître	it's English that's winning
francophones	it's not worth the effort
Il est idiot d'avoir peur	it's stupid to be frightened
je crois que	let die
la langue maternelle	lovers of English
laisser mourir	quite the opposite
mais	similar words in French
ne va pas disparaître	that depends on us
ont déjà disparu	will be spoken
remplacera	will disappear
va rester	will replace

All of these activities can work well in a whole-class environment but also lend themselves to an electronic form, for individualized learning or for whole class activities with an IWB.

http://forum.momes.net/: example C

Horror book reviews: first uncorrected, written drafts by Y9 students (in 3rd year of language learning):
Frissons, chair de poule

La Cadillac de Dolan *de Stephen King*

J'ai lu un livre de Stephen King qui m'a fait très peur; il s'appelle *La Cadillac de Dolan*. Ça ne m'a pas fait peur, j'ai même trouvé ça amusant! Certains de ses livres font peur alors que d'autres non. On dirait même des livres comiques. La dernière fois à la télé j'ai vu le film *Shining*, ça ne m'a pas marqué du tout, je n'ai même pas eu peur. Moi ce que je recherche ce sont des livres qui foutent vraiment la trouille. Pouvez-vous m'aider à en trouver? Merci d'avance.

Le Tueur à la rose

Mon coup de coeur est: *Le Tueur à la rose* de la collection Frissons. Je n'ai jamais lu un livre aussi bon. Un mélange de suspens, d'amour . . . C'est l'histoire de Babette qui vit dans une ville où en deux mois, trois filles assez jolies pour être mannequins se font tuer. Le tueur dépose toujours une rose sur son corps. Personne n'ose plus sortir. Je vous laisse découvrir la suite . . . *Julie, 12 ans*

L'Accident *coll. Frissons*

Une jeune fille nommée Marianne rencontre un fantôme dans son miroir. Celui-ci lui demande de faire un échange assez spécial. L'échange de sa vie avec la sienne durant une semaine complète. Mais malheureusement, le fantôme décide de garder la vie de Marianne pour toujours . . . Marianne réussira-t-elle à reprendre sa vie? Ce petit article s'adresse à tous les passionnés de lecture qui ne savent pas quoi lire. Je conseille en particulier les livres Frissons. *Jennyfer*

L'Auberge de l'horreur *coll. Evado*

Ça se passe dans une auberge de la Nouvelle Arcadie, loin de tout mais surtout là où des choses bizarres se passent. Il y a quatre livres pour l'instant: 1: *L'Auberge de l'horreur*, 2: *Chambre n° 13*; 3: *La Piscine*; 4: *Le Grenier. Nadia, 14 ans*

D'autres titres

Le Camp de la terreur; *Le Dernier Refuge*; *La Foire aux horreurs*; *L'Inconnu du cimetière*; *La Maison tête de pioche* . . .

At first glance this may seem somewhat esoteric. Book reviews of horror fiction in a second language could appear a challenging concept for many learners. However, rather than focus on detailed comprehension of each contribution, the core task for learners may be nothing more than to react to the titles of these horror stories by saying which ones might appeal to them. A basic substitution task could be to develop their own 'catalogue' of horror titles by minimal substitution of the above titles:

- *Le Collège de la terreur*
- *La Piscine aux horreurs*
- *Le Prof du cimetière*

An extension task could be to use the language of horror storybook reviewing to invent their own publicity blurb for the hit horror story that they are 'about to write'. While not linguistically perfect, these reviews have been written with enthusiasm by students who would not normally have been engaged by traditional writing activities. They are *first* drafts that with consultation with the teacher can be improved on.

All three of these examples of stimuli from the forum.momes.net website benefit from being written (authentically) by young people, on topics that could be of interest to young learners and on subjects that might not appear in more traditional forms of text. For all of them there is the implicit invitation that 'if you were interested by that there is a lot more that you can access on the Web on these and on other topics'.

Très excitant!!!!!

Le fantôme de la maison c'est très effrayant et c'est
même trouvé ça amusant!!!!
Alors, les escaliers se secouent, les planchers craquent.
les fenêtres claquent, les tuyaux crèvent..
Tu veux avoire peur??????

Bonne lecture!!!!

Je lui accorde 10/10!!!!

 Le Fantôme des bijoux

Le Fantôme des bijoux

Collection chair de poule.

Un livre de R.L.Stine. Mustapha
et Gary prennent les vacances a
Paris. Ils vont au Museé de
Bijoux. Ils regardant un
fantôme! Le fantôme tue
Mustapha! Quel fantôme? Est-
ce que Gary est mort aussi?
Pour en savoir plus, lisez ce
livre...
Un roman plein de suspense!

« C'est super! » Le Guardian

« C'est fantastique! » Le Temps

FIGURE 3 La maison de l'horreur and R. L. Stine

Culturally authentic sites: intellectually challenging and stimulating?

The internet allows immediate access to a vast range of factual information about the country being studied. It is ideal for cross-referencing of information encountered during classroom work. The BBC TV series for Y9 learners of French is based in the small Provençal town of Collobrières. An obvious extension task can be to discover more about the town and the area through the internet. However, with the best will in the world, there can be a certain 'sameness' to such sites and the implicit question of 'what do we actually do with this information once we have found it?'. Comprehension tasks on a text about a French locality abound, in course books and in exam questions, and more able learners can probably accurately predict what information they will be required to discover ('What can you do in this town?', 'What is the most famous monument?', 'What happened in 1587?', etc.). The main webpage for Collobrières (www.collobrières.fr) corresponds to such a text.

Collobrières

Collobrières est un village de 1600 âmes niché dans un creux de verdure entre les collines cristallines du massif des Maures.

Son charme, vous l'apprécierez en parcourant ses forêts de châtaigniers, de chênes lièges, d'arbousiers . . ., mais aussi en flânant dans ses rues caladées qui grimpent jusqu'à l'ancienne église Saint Pons ou le long de son cours d'eau, le Réal Collobrier.

Les premières traces de vie à Collobrières datent de l'époque pré-romaine. Immergé dans la forêt des Maures, le village a toujours vécu des resources de celle-ci: pâturage, élevage, exploitation du bois. C'est un enfant du pays, Aumeran qui alla chercher en Espagne le secret de la transformation du liège en bouchon.

En 1850, Collobrières comptait 17 bouchonneries, 3 scieries, et plusieurs mines de plomb, cuivre, fer.

Les maisons de maître qui longent la rue principale racontent l'histoire de ces industries jadis florissantes et contrastent étonnamment avec les maisons médiévales du vieux village.

Aujourd'hui, la forêt reste un élément important dans la vie et dans le Coeur des Collobriérois.

Office de tourisme de Collobrières

Indeed, a more challenging task for more able learners could be to take on the role of exam setter, to produce a grid or multiple-choice items for others to use. A more interesting starting point may be to challenge the learners about the nature of the text, with questions such as:

- who devised this text? An employee of the local tourist board
- what is their purpose? To encourage visitors

And without looking at the text,

- how could this affect the way it is written?

This last question offers learners the chance to reflect, in general, on how language is used in certain contexts: for instance, in tourist material: 'lots of: imperatives, adjectives and superlatives'; 'lists – you can . . . and . . .'; 'exaggerations . . . un-truths' were some of the responses from an able group of learners.

The challenge for the learners can then be to discover examples of such use of language in the Collobrières text. Working in groups on different parts of the text (and with dictionaries), the language one class discovered included:

- ces industries jadis florissantes
- datent de l'époque pré-romaine
- en flânant dans ses rues
- immergé dans la forêt
- l'ancienne église
- la forêt reste un élément important
- les maisons médiévales du vieux village
- niché dans un creux de verdure
- son charme
- un village de 1600 âmes
- vous l'apprécierez

Once the language had been identified, it could then be used in a new context such as to describe their own home area, using as many of the above phrases as possible, with minimal substitutions. There are various possible outcomes; not necessarily just a standard tourist brochure but, for example, a page for their own locality's website, in French for French visitors, or a 30-second radio advert for French tourists.

Strategies for reading authentic texts:
becoming an intelligent reader

There are many different ways in which native speakers will approach and engage with a text. They may be looking for very specific information:

- From a Eurostar timetable: what time does the first train to Paris leave on a Sunday morning?
- From a menu: are any of the dishes here suitable for a vegetarian?
- From a review of a film: they may want their own opinion confirmed – does the reviewer of this film feel the same way as I did about it?
- When reading a thriller: 'I think X did it!', 'I am sure that . . . will happen now', 'I reckon I will be proved right'.

Our learners can also adopt similar strategies, but there is another, much more fundamental and more conscious level at which young language learners can operate.

www.olympiade.de (accessed 20.08.04)

Deutschlands Handballer haben die olympische Goldmedaille knapp verpasst. Der Europameister verlor im Finale von Athen gegen Weltmeister Kroatien 24:26 (12:11) und verspielte damit den ersten Olympiasieg einer deutschen Auswahl nach dem Erfolg der DDR-Mannschaft 1980 in Moskau. Bereits 1984 in Los Angeles hatte die Auswahl des Deutschen Handball-Bundes erst im Finale verloren und Silber geholt.

Auch Ronald Rauhe und Tim Wieskötter wurden im Zweier-Kajak ihrer Favoritenstellung gerecht. Das Duo aus Potsdam zog vom Start weg davon und brachte die Führung auch ins Ziel. Silber ging an die Australier Clint Robinson/Nathan Baggaley, Bronze sicherten sich Raman Piatrutschenka/Wadsim Machneuw aus Weißrussland.

There are key questions that the learners can engage with *before* they start reading in any great detail. With only the briefest glance at the title (e.g. 10 seconds), they could respond to the following:

- What sort of a text is this?
    - Possibly a sports report from the Olympics, i.e. not a tourist brochure; not a recipe; not a report of a car crash.

- What language do I already know connected with sports?
  - o Brainstorm of vocabulary: Fussball; Skilaufen; Volleyball spielen; Tor schiessen.
- What sort of language (that I may not know) might I encounter on an Olympics webpage such as this one?
  - o The language of results; teams; medals; countries.
- What sort of phrases and sentences might I expect in such a sports report?
  - o 'came third', 'the gold was won by'.
- What general knowledge do I have about this that might be useful?
  - o 'I know that Germany does well in', ' it is unlikely to be about'.

Following class or group brainstorming along these lines, the learners might *only now* be asked to look at the text in detail and apply these strategies to it (i.e. look at it several times, from different angles), and try to work out in reasonable detail what it is all about. It is not a test, and the strategies used may not always yield as much information as they might want. However, it crucially gives the readers a positive focus for this activity of reading, allows them to understand that reading can be more than just answering ten comprehension questions, and also indicates how they can apply and use similar techniques with quite different texts in the future.

Conclusion

The authentic material available on the internet is thus infinitely varied; but material itself is not a magic bullet, and will not in itself transform a foreign-languages classroom. Just as much as the appropriate choice of material, it is *how* the material is exploited that is crucial. The examples discussed above can only be effective if they are integrated into an overall philosophy of second-language pedagogy and acquisition. Although the internet is an ideal way to foster positive cultural awareness of the country in question, almost more emphasis needs to be put on the generic issues such as: how do we become successful readers and listeners *no matter what the source material might be?* How do we scan a text? How do we extract specific information? How do we react to an initially alarming wall of sound? How can we develop our own language from authentic source material, rather than from the teacher? Addressing all of these questions is vital, and even more importantly is: how do we develop our own confidence when faced with such challenges? A sense of 'can-do', no matter whether we are beginners or experienced linguists, regardless of our apparent level of ability, is something all can benefit from.

Chapter 3

Trainee teachers' perceptions of the use of digital technology in the languages classroom

Linda Fisher

Trainee teachers are in a unique situation when it comes to learning about ICT and its uses in the MFL classroom. All teachers work with learners and are themselves learners, but it might be argued that trainee teachers, insofar as they have less well-established identities as practitioners, come fresh to consider the benefits of ICT as a tool for learning that they can assimilate into their practice.

On beginning their courses, trainees' beliefs about the potential of digital technology for enhancing teaching and learning in the languages classroom will have been informed by a number of factors. They will have had experiences involving ICT that will have given them a view as to the extent of potential efficacy in the classroom: were they themselves taught languages using ICT, and did they consider this useful? What have they read or heard about digital technology's role in the classroom? What is their level of competence and confidence with ICT? All prior experiences will have contributed to the formation of beliefs about the value of ICT as a possible teaching tool for MFL, and these in turn influence the willingness to incorporate ICT into classroom practice, the speed of this incorporation and the variety of teaching approaches to digital technology adopted.

During their training, beginner teachers' views about ICT are likely to change. A number of factors are implicated in this, such as:

- increased exposure to ICT in practice (for example the modelling of teaching using ICT that trainees observe)
- course requirements
- their own developing competence and the acquisition of new skills
- the facilities encountered in schools
- their learning through reading and discussion
- peer influences

This chapter considers the perceptions of a small number of trainee teachers over the nine months of their postgraduate training course in England, regarding ways in which their beliefs and practice changed and the stimuli for this change.

Education policy and digital technology

All teachers, whether trainees or not, are expected to incorporate ICT into the teaching and learning of their classrooms. The National Curriculum (NC) of 1999 states that languages teachers are expected to promote the six Key Skills in their teaching, one of which is the development of IT, which should be achieved: 'through using audio, video, satellite television and the internet to access and communicate information, and through selecting and using a range of ICT resources to create presentations for different audiences and purposes' (1999: 8). The use of ICT is also stipulated in the Programme of Study. The new NC (2007) requires under 'Curriculum Opportunities' that pupils should have the opportunity to: 'use a range of resources, including ICT, for accessing and communicating information in the target language' (2007: 169). Neither qualified teachers nor trainees, therefore, have free rein to decide whether ICT is a suitable fit for their pedagogy, as they are required to incorporate it.

In addition, trainee teachers must demonstrate knowledge and competence in ICT in order to gain Qualified Teacher Status (QTS). First, this means providing evidence that they have met the QTS standards. For the cohort of trainees under the spotlight here, this meant demonstrating for example that 'they know how to use ICT effectively, both to teach their subject and to support their wider professional (TTA, 2003; 9) and that they 'use ICT effectively in their teaching' (TTA, 2003; 13). Second, trainees must also sit and pass an ICT test, centrally administered by the Training and Development Agency for schools (TDA), requiring competence at a certain level on leaving the course. These measures can be seen as government trying to ensure that new teachers leave training courses digitally proficient by requiring that all trainee teachers engage with it. Making trainees gain certain technical understandings and competences (the skills test), and guaranteeing they have experience of using it in their work in the classroom (the QTS standards), is a way of spreading more use of ICT into schools, with trainees potentially functioning as agents of change within subject departments.

Background: developing pedagogic practice

Despite the fact that it is a requirement to incorporate ICT into secondary classrooms, changing established teachers' pedagogic practice is not easy. It has been well documented that change is non-linear (for example, simply providing access to technology does not ensure its use), is complex and needs to be rooted in support structures that are embedded within teachers' social and working contexts (see Eraut 1994; Hoban 2002). As for other teachers, modern languages teachers of many years' standing have established aspects of their identity as successful practitioners that involve certain pedagogic approaches. While there is evidence to suggest that teachers may now be digitally proficient (see Ofsted 2005), experienced teachers may still show reluctance about abandoning their existing pedagogy (Hennessy et al. 2005). In addition, it is true that 'school subject cultures are built on deep traditions' (John 2005: 408), making it more difficult for teachers within certain subject-department contexts to change their approaches. All in all, therefore, it would be an easy assumption to make that trainees, since they have yet to establish their identities as successful practitioners, and have yet to become acculturated into an existing subject culture, would come very open-minded to the use of digital technology as a pedagogical tool.

As ever in the context of human learning, the situation is more complicated. Experienced subject teachers in MFL are likely to have a variety of responses to the incorporation of digital technology into their teaching, with some more open to change than others. It is clear that there are a number of teachers who have incorporated ICT very effectively. For example, whilst the evidence is based only on small-scale studies, Condie and Munro (2007) report that a number of MFL teachers particularly seem to be profiting from the use of new technology, especially from the use of online resources and digital video, and incorporating it into their work. In the same way as experienced teachers vary in their responses, so trainee teachers come to their training courses with a variety of beliefs about the use of ICT for personal and professional purposes, beliefs which vary from person to person and change in differing ways as their education in teaching progresses.

Worth bearing in mind when considering how trainees are likely to respond to the opportunities of using digital technology is the often-quoted idea that teachers revert to the style of teaching that they themselves experienced in school (Lortie 1975). What does this mean for trainees? Despite the internet's appearance only in the mid-1990s, and relatively few resources in schools until the massive government investment in the late 1990s and early 2000s, the general demographic of trainees (mode age 25 for the cohort under discussion) means that they are likely to have encountered some teaching with ICT during their own languages education. The expansion in use of digital technology for languages teaching means that soon the trainees arriving to learn to teach will almost certainly have had exposure to teaching using ICT, which may in turn mean that they are more likely to use it in their own classrooms.

Profile of the trainee teachers

During 2006–7 the trainee teachers referred to in this chapter completed a 36-week secondary PGCE course in a UK university, preparing modern foreign-language teachers in French, German, Spanish and Italian for the 11–18 age range. Of the 36 weeks, a total of 12 were university-based and 24 school-based. In the university, explicit input on digital technology for languages teaching and learning happened through a variety of workshops on word processing (WP), PowerPoint, use of the internet and working with IWBs. Implicit learning/input included witnessing staff use of the technology in their own teaching, peer resource-sharing and engagement in a bulletin board where trainees could discuss and share resources. In school, learning was planned explicitly through weekly sessions with the mentor (the teacher responsible for their ongoing progress in teaching while on school placement) and group workshops with PGCE trainees from other subject areas. There was also observation of the teaching given by modern-languages staff using ICT and peer learning from other trainees in their placement school (usually in subjects other than MFL). Trainees were required to incorporate ICT into their languages teaching for an early written assignment.

The learning journeys outlined below were based on interviews with five trainees towards the end of their PGCE course. As their course tutor, I asked the 19-strong PGCE group for volunteers to discuss ICT and language learning. The five chosen (four females and one male French native speaker, all in their twenties) were loosely representative of the group in that they represented male/female native speaker/non-native speaker ratios. The pre-course ICT skills audit showed that all had some basic understanding of WP and two were experienced in PowerPoint. Semi-structured interviews were conducted lasting around 40 minutes each, with questions on the following areas: how trainees felt about ICT and its affordances on beginning the course; how this developed over the year; how they had used digital technology for languages teaching and learning; any cautions about its use; projections for future use.

The summary below is structured around the trainees' initial thoughts about ICT and its potential for languages teaching, the influence of 'the subject culture' in moving their thinking and practice on ICT, the trainees' developing understanding of the 'fit' of ICT with MFL pedagogy, their uses of ICT for personal learning, cautions about the use of ICT and their thinking on its future use. Names have been altered to preserve anonymity.

Beliefs about ICT and its potential

When reflecting on how they viewed ICT's potential contribution to their teaching at the beginning of the course, all five interviewees noted that they had felt varying degrees of wariness and scepticism. They commonly mentioned 'fear'. Hannah, for example, said: 'I was a bit scared of it. I was not happy about trusting it. I didn't trust it at all. I felt nervous.'

Hannah was first of all afraid of things going wrong, of not being able to control the children when things, inevitably as she saw it, would break down. She could not really see any pedagogical benefits, only possible opportunities for disruption and problems.

For Michaela, the initial belief that she would not use a lot of digital technology in her own classroom was nothing to do with lack of confidence (she had just completed an internship in market research so was very proficient and confident), but she thought it was a gimmick introduced to try to distract unmotivated pupils:

I didn't really see the relevance of it to modern languages, other than looking things up on the internet. And I think it was more my own lack of knowledge about what it really was, how it worked . . . that made me think that'll disappear in five years. And I take that back, I was very wrong. And I'm glad that I was proved wrong.

Louis had taught before in the USA, and had probably the most prior experience with ICT. He had few concerns about his own competence and could see some of the benefits, but was still not convinced that it had a lot to offer in terms of teaching and learning in his classroom.

Claire described coming from a learning background where there was no ICT in the classroom at all, and could never imagine herself using it in her own teaching, which links back to Lortie's ideas of teachers teaching how they were taught:

> I think it's part of this watching-TV culture, and they know a lot more tech-nology than I know I do. And they've been brought up on it. We didn't have computers at primary school and early secondary school when I was there. And so that's partly why I think I wasn't confident. I wasn't brought up on it the same way. But they are and I think they expect it now.

Claire's confidence stood in stark contrast with that of the pupils when she said: 'I've never been confident with it, I think that's the main thing.'

Gemma's first reaction to thinking about using ICT in her classroom was: 'oh my God . . . this is going to be a nightmare.' Despite having passed an IT Basic Skills qualification whilst at university, Gemma professed not to enjoy using ICT, and had doubts about her ability to use it: 'when I started the course I wouldn't say I was competent, really.' Not only did she question her competence, but she also had doubts about the value of ICT in the classroom. She was mainly influenced by her aunt, a science teacher who was sceptical about ICT, and who had an IWB in her classroom, but was unable to use it. Gemma's beliefs about the dubious value of digital technology in the classroom were further reinforced during the very first week of the course, which was spent observing in a primary school. Here she saw 'the teacher get into a mess with it' and nothing would work. The teacher had a CD with which to teach music, but could not get it to work on the IWB:

> The tracks wouldn't play like they said. And I thought this is a waste of time. You know these poor kids sitting there behaving themselves when they could be . . . I think it was something to do with: if you blow across different tubes you get different sounds. It was like they could be here with the milk bottles having fun.

Gemma thought the use, or attempted use, of ICT was removing the possibility of children's active involvement in lessons; this use of technol-ogy required them to sit passively instead of engaging with learning activ-ities. She described this as the teacher 'fluffing around' and comments: 'I just thought this is technology for technology's sake. And it is not worth it.' Although this was a primary music lesson, Gemma had reinforced her belief that ICT served little educative purpose, and had made it more likely that she would need persuasion as to the benefits for her own teaching.

A general picture emerges from the trainees' interviews of at best nervousness and needing to be convinced, to at worst downright scepticism that ICT had any genuine benefits for pupil learning. The following section examines how this changed over the course of the year.

Moving forward: the influence of the subject culture

The influence of the subject culture in which teachers find themselves has been found to be of importance in their approach to integration of ICT into their work. John and La Velle (2004) note that different subject communities approach the adoption of the tool of ICT in differing ways and that, as might be expected, science and mathematics teachers, for example, are more open to exploring its affordances than the usually more sceptical humanities teachers. Selwyn (1999) argues that the computer is more congruent with the antecedent subculture of some subjects and therefore there is a better 'fit'. This brings a sense of ownership for some subjects, but not for others where it is met more with suspicion.

Trainee teachers are socialized and acculturated into the MFL subject setting as they complete the course. How this happens can influence the ways in which they view what it means to be a teacher of modern languages, and what it means in terms of pedagogy and the methodological tools to do the job. How then did the cultures of the MFL subject departments in which trainees spent most of their professional learning, as well as the culture of the faculty of education at university, influence their beliefs and practice about using digital technology?

Certainly, the influence of the culture of those around them was an important factor in the trainees' adoption of ICT in their teaching. Hannah described the environment of her first secondary placement, where she was advised not to bother with it by practising teachers:

> There were no interactive whiteboards. And the data projector I used twice. And I remember specifically . . . er . . . the second time when I was hunting for it, to try and book it. I remember a teacher saying to me 'I never bother with that because it takes so long to make the resource and then also to set it up and to tidy it away after'. So it wasn't really used that much and there weren't really any facilities.

The lack of facilities, combined with the fact that the teachers around her did not value or use the ICT that was available, meant that Hannah felt able to avoid using ICT. She was quite happy with this situation, as it was comfortable for her not to have to confront her own fears about using digital resources: 'I was quite happy that in my first placement there wasn't opportunity to because I was scared of it.'

This changed in the second placement because the departmental culture was different: 'The facilities were just better and everyone seemed to use ICT without thinking.' Hannah's comment reveals how embedded the use of digital technology was in this department, so much so that it had become second nature to use it as an integral part of the subject teaching, and this in turn influenced her own work.

Gemma, who as we saw had been highly sceptical, gradually began to change her views as a result of her experiences in her first secondary-school placement, where she saw a teacher who was able to use an IWB effectively. Several weeks into the course, when she had begun to engage with MFL teaching methodology, she could see how there may be aspects of the use of digital technology that might be more motivating and effective than other methods.

The influence of the culture around them was also reported as important by the other trainees, who commented on being gently pushed to develop their work with ICT and overcome their nervousness. Claire described receiving a lot of help on her first placement where the school was well resourced and the teachers in the department fully committed to using IWBs regularly in their teaching:

> They had it in every single room and they were very strong on it. We had several sessions on it, my mentor showing me how to use it. And that started me off on it really, that strength on the first placement.

Several mentioned how their departments had ICT fully embedded into the Schemes of Work, which included teaching ideas and centralized resources. This helped them to understand when and where ICT might be used and to experiment with using the technology in way that had already been identified as useful by experienced teachers. Helen felt that the fact that it was written into Schemes of Work in both placements pushed her, as she felt that she *should* use it:

> I mean it was there to use. I mean it was obvious; I thought 'Well, that's what they're recommending. That's what they say for that lesson; I feel I should be using it 'cos that then covers what they require.'

Louis made the point, though, that the inclusion of ICT in Schemes of Work was not always adequately thought through; for instance, a website reference might be included without detailed consideration as to how it might be used and the learning outcomes likely to arise.

In both of Michaela's placements she was encouraged by her mentor and other teachers in the department to use IWB and PowerPoint. In fact, she felt that she ought to use IWBs all the time in the first placement as the normal whiteboards were so small that it was too difficult for pupils to see them properly. Hannah, too, said that the fact that the technology was there was a factor in pushing her to use it: 'And to be honest it would have felt a bit daft to come in with flashcards and start dancing round when you could just flick it on and there you go.'

The school culture, where established teachers were using ICT in ways that trainees could model themselves on, was an important factor in moving them on. Gemma commented that, as she saw the ways teachers used the technology, she gradually understood that her judgment of herself as not very proficient was inaccurate, and this in turn increased her confidence: 'I think once I got into schools and I saw the different ways in which teachers used them, I realized that I was a bit more competent that I thought originally.'

Gemma described humorously as 'life changing' one of the Faculty sessions on how to make PowerPoint presentations, as from that time on she launched herself into creating resources and using them with her groups. The peer culture that arose amongst the MFL trainee group themselves was another strong influence. Louis commented on the subject culture that arose amongst the MFL trainees, saying that everyone seemed to be using ICT and that because everyone was using it, you would feel out of place if you didn't, echoing Hannah's comments earlier:

> But I do feel pressurized in some way where I'm showing what I do with other, you know, colleagues at PGC training . . . Everybody's showing PowerPoint, we're not really showing worksheets anymore. Basically, where is your PowerPoint? And so in that sense, yeah, you feel obliged to produce a few things like this, and to work on it with ICT.

Just as in the earlier section, where trainees were influenced by negative portrayals or incompetent use of ICT, so their acculturation into environments where ICT was being used effectively and often, had a great influence on their openness to explore the uses of digital technology for their own teaching. The subject culture was therefore an important factor in trainee learning.

Digital technology and the fit with
MFL subject pedagogy

John (2005) conducted an interesting study into how the subject teacher and the subject subculture (whether mathematics, science, MFL and so on) negotiate the relationship between ICT and learning. His interviews with 37 teachers across six subject areas found that there needed to be a blend of ICT with the subject pedagogy, but 'for the pedagogy to blend and for the ICT to have any learning effect, then the subject content had to have resonance with the technology, while the pedagogy used must be seen to fit with the learning outcomes (both tacit and explicit) designated by the teacher' (2005: 477).

These trainees found that in at least one subject department encountered during the training year, ICT was embedded and fully integrated into the teaching of the department. When discussing how they used ICT, it was clear that the trainees had drawn on their observations and on departmental suggestions for use and had developed their own practice, finding a blend between the subject pedagogy and the use of ICT. The following are some of the key aspects of digital technology's fit with MFL subject teaching that the trainees articulated in the interviews:

- *The teaching of vocabulary* was highlighted by all. Hannah explained how using ICT, particularly PowerPoint and the IWB, allowed for greater flexibility in vocabulary repetition techniques:

[There's] . . . better access to better resources by using the computer in your lessons. I think if you are teaching vocabulary and all you have is a picture, a cartoon picture of a car – something that you've drawn and printed out. You know if you use the computer you can have sounds, you can have real life pictures, cartoon pictures. You can . . . When the picture comes up, you can do a catch phrase . . . to try and recall the vocab. You've just got . . . Rather than just flashing and taking away, like 'What was it?', you've just got so much more scope for little games. To just try and test the vocab.

She describes the way that the technology enabled her to have a more multi-sensory approach to the presentation of new vocabulary, as well as a range of options for keeping the presentation varied and professional-looking. Claire also commented on the ways in which she was able to scaffold presentation of vocabulary, 'jumping back and forth' and varying activities so as to reinforce new language but keep it fresh. Consistency in using the same images in later lessons (and the ease with which these can be accessed) was highlighted as good for revision and revisiting language.

- *The link of words to voice via sound files.* As well as this flexibility in manipulating images for the introduction and repetition of vocabulary, the linking of sound to images was felt by several trainees to be an important use of the technology, especially for presenting new language. Drawing on internet resources for authentic native speaker voices was felt to be helpful in placing emphasis on pronunciation.
- *Presenting different grammatical forms.* The use of colour and the appealingly kinaesthetic nature of the IWB were noted by Louis, who found this especially helpful when working with 'lower-ability classes':

They really loved it. Really, really loved it. And that made sense, I had like a couple of sentences. Green words would be the verbs. Blue words the subject. Yellow would be, for example, the object. And the fact they had to drag and kind of inductively get to see that there was a column. . . . This was a Year 9 really really low-ability group.

Gemma also mentioned that ICT served grammar teaching well because of the immediate response possible from activities such as cloze exercises (an exercise in which the learner has to supply the missing words that have been removed from the text). She believed that showing mistakes and offering chances to redo immediately was helpful to learners, particularly mentioning success with this at A Level.

- *Making mistakes.* Daniella and others felt that using ICT diminishes students' fear of making mistakes. For example, they are willing to come up to the board and try something out. For language learning, where willingness to communicate, anxiety and fear of errors are issues for many language learners, this is an area where Michaela felt ICT offered potential. The same applied to working on word processors and working on websites, where she noted the pupils were not as afraid to try something out as they would have been to put pen to paper.
- *Recording and assessing the outcomes of projects.* Allowing pupils to record group oral activities by video, watching performances afterwards as a group and using them for peer assessment was seen as another benefit. Using Audacity software to record pupils and let them listen back was

also mentioned as very effective, as was running videotapes of pupils' performances through a moviemaker programme:

. . . and in the classroom you get pupils to record a little role play or something and then they can listen back to it, and then you can do some peer assessment. You can review what marks you should give them. I just think if you just had little tools like that and just little ideas up your sleeve, that you can work with on ICT, I just think that it . . . it just improves your teaching. It improves the subject for the pupils. *Hannah*

- *The improved quality of sound recordings.* On a practical level, Michaela noted access to a range of authentic native speakers via the internet and the improved sound quality of the listening passages on MP3 sound files:

They're normally much clearer than the cassettes. So the learners aren't put off by 'Oh I missed that. It's funny. It's fuzzy'. And it just makes it generally much less stressful for me as a teacher. Much less stressful for them as students.

- *Better pupil motivation through improved pace and quick changes of activity.* The trainees reported better motivation arising as a corollary of using the digital technology. This was true of their own practice and in observation of other teachers' lessons. Hannah said that she saw an MFL teacher 'throwing in a quick grammar exercise on the IWB' to pick up pupils' interest that was flagging during activities carried out using more traditional methods. While it is impossible to say whether it is the nature of the activity or the novelty of the IWB that needs crediting for the improvement in pupil engagement, all trainees judged motivation to be higher using ICT, though they noted some cautions. As we shall see later, trainees were able to distinguish between technology as simply a novelty engaging the pupils on a superficial level, and the real learning benefits that might arise from its use
- *Games.* All trainees noted how useful games were for practising language, and how particularly motivating they had found using technology for games: 'Really any kind of game that I've ever done with ICT has never really gone badly' (*Hannah*).
- *Developing independence, particularly in reading.* Michaela mentioned the motivational effects of working on websites, especially for developing independence in A-Level learners, who, watching the news and reading online current affairs, feel stimulated by seeing 'genuine things'. Louis

noted, though, that target language sites on the internet often need mediating in some way, so as not to be too complicated and therefore off-putting for the student even at A Level. In Key Stage 4, some of the boys in Michaela's classes seemed to particularly enjoy reading activities carried out using ICT; she described putting email reading texts on PowerPoint and how this seemed to grab their attention and make them want to answer, when previously they were disengaged and unmotivated by reading.

- *The teaching of culture.* Access to authentic sites on the internet was noted as an important gateway to the culture of the target language. Hannah described an example where she used her own photos of Normandy on PowerPoint, worked on key vocabulary arising and then had the pupils work on internet sites detailing tourist attractions. Gemma felt that the teaching of culture 'was transformed' through the use of ICT. She described what she saw as a very effective lesson, where she devised a series of activities leading pupils through a scenario in Paris, where they had to find their way to a restaurant (using the metro map) and then order particular things from the menu within a certain budget. Gemma felt the authenticity of the menu and maps, combined with the opportunity to see a real-life application of the French they had been learning in class, to be very successful and motivating: 'I think that's where it's most useful to us because we are not in France, we are not in Germany. But with the internet you kind of go there, so that's very helpful.'

Trainees were using a variety of technologies and finding a blend between the technology and the language learning outcomes they had identified. Their enthusiasm as to the potential of ICT was, however, tempered by some concerns as their training progressed.

Cautions: overexposure and privileging learning aims

Trainees expressed a number of cautions about ICT use, which serve to demonstrate the growing sophistication of their thinking about pedagogy as their training progressed. Mainly this happened during the second placement in school, about two-thirds of the way through the course when they had taken on full responsibility for the planning, teaching and assessment of several classes. Gemma described how her confidence in incorporating ICT into her teaching led to overuse. As the sophistication of her understandings about pupil learning developed, her mentor began to push her to question the ways in which her use of digital technology was contributing to learning:

> Around about Easter time, once I was really proud of myself and we were doing loads of PowerPoints and loads of stuff on the board, I started getting comments on my observation sheets, which were things like that I was too teacher-led. You know, presentation was great but they didn't do anything, they just sat there and watched the pretty colours and the pretty lights and . . . You know, how can you involve them more? And I thought back and I thought actually that is true, because if only one person can come and match the picture with the word, that's 29 other students who aren't doing anything. Even if they are looking at the board, they are probably not concentrating. So I had to think of ways to get them all doing stuff, still using ICT on the one board.

This high-level thinking about learning led Gemma to integrate ICT with non-digital resources to optimize learning. Gemma gave an example of one way she did this, a 'simple thing' as she called it. To allow more thinking time for the class, she decided to have everyone jot down a response to the question in their books, before calling on one pupil to come to the IWB to do a match-up, thus engaging more of the pupils in the learning. She described herself as moving from a position where she was 'keen to get on' towards focusing more on each individual's learning. This also had the effect of removing the focus of attention from the front of the room. She asked herself at one point why she was so tired, and concluded that she was not using ICT as effectively as possible since she was teaching in a too teacher-centred way. Although she still had not come up with many solutions to the problem at the point of interview, she had begun to reflect on ICT's strengths and weaknesses and experiment with adaptations to her teaching. Gemma was finding a blend between the pedagogy and the tool that was leading to improved learning outcomes.

Michaela, too, was concerned that there needed to be some balance in the range of resources and activities, and that it was important to focus on what you were trying to achieve in a particular lesson:

> But I also think it is very important, as I said before, not to be over-reliant, over-dependent upon it. That we need to still make sure that there are other aspects, especially in the modern-languages classroom. The speaking needs to continue, you need to practise active skills. And if you can incorporate that into sort of using video, which then uses the

whiteboard and things like that, that's fantastic. But as long as students are practising language it's key.

Louis articulated similar concerns about the possible use of technology for its own sake, and how the learning objective must come first and then appropriate approaches found to ensure good learning:

> The novelty can detract from the linguistic objective and just become a tool for its own sake. We tend to forget the simplicity of what the object-ive was.

Claire agreed that overexposure can be a problem and felt that the chil-dren still need to have things on the desk to *do* as well as watching the board. Gemma noted pupil passivity in some lessons observed, and calls to mind the primary pupils she observed at the beginning of the course, who instead of making music were required to sit and watch an attempted presen-tation on it:

> Also I've talked about the fact that it can be too teacher led, but I also think you can go into overkill with this stuff. If they do have whiteboards and PowerPoints and internet games five hours every day, there's absolutely no point in doing it because it loses its effectiveness and you know they won't focus and things like that. I am worried about that . . . Because I do worry that they don't actually do anything anymore. The concern from the pri-mary placement is still there that the children are not as active.

Hennessy et al.'s (2005) empirical study conducted in 2000 examining how secondary mathematics, English and science teachers integrated tech-nology into their teaching was carried out in the schools in which these trainee teachers were working. They found that there was a great deal of caution among teachers about the benefits of ICT for subject teaching, as well as about how ICT might best fit with their learning objectives. It is clear that practice in most of these schools has moved on considerably, as a key concern for most of these trainees in this cohort was to do with over-exposure to technology, not only in languages lessons but also across the curriculum, as Hannah explains:

> Well I just don't know, you kind of wonder in any one week how . . . how many lessons each pupil is exposed to it. Because we don't know. We are not in their classrooms. And it would be interesting to find out just how

much they had. If I'm thinking you know ICT is brilliant and I tend to use it in all my lessons. If every teacher is doing that then there is a danger and erm . . . some . . . Every so often when I have gone back to just . . . kind of non ICT strategy, whether it is . . . kind of like word associations or board slapping or something like that, they have been successful for the novelty factor. So I do think it is . . . It is like anything it is just about the balance and realising that ICT does very much enhance pupils learning but we can't depend on it exclusively.

Interestingly, Michaela quoted a pupil who, arriving in her lesson and seeing the IWB set up, said 'Oh, another IT lesson!' Selwyn (1999), analysing different subject communities' ICT use, draws on the idea of 'cultural transparency' (from Lave and Wenger 1991). The idea here is that for good integration ICT must be highly visible as a learning tool, but should be invisible in its role as a mediator of the subject matter. Where this is not successful ICT can get in the way of learning, becoming visible as a mediating tool but invisible as learning tool. In this context it would appear that to pupils, either through over-exposure to digital technology or through insufficient marrying of technology and learning outcomes, the ICT had become very visible, and they had begun to react against it.

Related to the visibility issue, several trainees raised the effectiveness of whole-class timetabling in a computer suite as a final caution. In the computer suite the technology itself is highly visible, with the danger that the teacher might adapt the learning to fit the tools available, rather than privileging the learning aims. In this situation the technology can operate as a constraint rather than an opportunity. Trainees felt that working in the ICT suite *had* benefits; in particular, it allowed pupils more independence. Gemma, for example, cited doing surveys and making graphs, producing revision lists and developing reading through websites as useful computer-suite activities. She noted, however, that timetabling in the ICT suite led at times to feeling coerced into using the technology: 'Sometimes the ICT lessons came at the wrong time, like what am I going to do in there with them.'

It would seem that by the end of their first year of learning to teach, the trainees had developed an understanding about the affordances of digital technology that comes close to that articulated by John and Sutherland:

However, we need to be cautious when we speak of the affordances of new technologies and even more cautious about assuming that a given medium of technology will automatically afford particular learning outcomes. In reality, learning is always distributed in some form between the technology, the learner and the context and there is nothing inherent in technology that automatically guarantees learning. (2005: 406)

Using ICT to develop subject knowledge and for personal organization

Digital technology had another role to play in supporting the trainees in the maintenance and enhancement of their subject knowledge. The use of online dictionaries allowed them quick and easy access to reference materials that were useful for planning. Claire bookmarked a number of news sites in French and German that she could watch to keep her own language up to date. Louis found that he could enhance his second and third foreign languages through creating his own dictionary:

> In my personal development I had to work a bit on my German knowledge. So what I started doing is put up a kind of Excel, create some sort of full-language dictionary, French, English, German and Spanish.

Gemma felt her own foreign languages benefited from trialling some of the materials she would be using with her classes:

> Because you can often find games, and then you go on and play them yourself just to make sure they are beneficial for the students. And then you discover things that you'd forgotten.

She also noted that teaching with ICT pushed her to be highly accurate in her own written language, remarking that the preparation of presentations on PowerPoint made her take a lot of care with checking genders and so on. This was especially the case as a lot of resources were shared in her second placement, and she felt more pressure to pass on accurate and well-prepared resources to colleagues. As noted earlier, the subject subculture in this department, where it was the norm to share digital resources, was influencing her practice; as part of the team she needed to share and felt obliged to make her contribution as high in quality as possible. Related too to the idea of the subculture, Claire found the method of sharing resources among the teachers, namely via email, very helpful and she liked the climate that this created: 'And it was . . . really reminded me of working in an office when you were sharing things.'

While not peculiar to modern languages teachers per se, trainees noted the benefits of using digital resources for personal organization:

> It is quick, it is fast. It's also you're saving a lot of paper, ink and . . . You know, you don't have . . . to have massive shelves of, you know, resources all the time. You can create portholes and . . . Again, . . . working as a staff and as a department, this is I think something that should be considered in the future. *Louis*

For Hannah, using spreadsheets for her marking made it much easier, and she noted that personal organization of resources is much easier in a lesson, where one can have resources ready digitally on screen without dealing in numerous pieces of paper.

Conclusions

The stories of these five trainee teachers learning to teach using digital technology suggest an openness to explore innovation in MFL teaching and learning. Their initial reluctance was often to do with a lack of confidence as well as lack of understanding as to the potential of the tools. When they witnessed good classroom practice where the technology was benefiting learning, they were quick to begin to assimilate it into their own work and indeed often adopted methodological approaches where ICT played a central role:

> Yeah I got carried away at one point. [laughs] Which I would never have thought, ever. And I was really worried about the ICT Skills Test and I practised, and I bought a book, and it was easy, I could do it all. [laughs] Yeah. It's been good. Definitely. It is one of the areas I think that has come on the most this year, and I impress people now. *Gemma*

The trainees certainly were influenced by a number of factors, but mainly, it seems, by the understanding that there was a fit between the learning aims of their lessons and the ways that these could be achieved through digital technology. At some point in the teaching year, they tended to step back and evaluate the effectiveness of their use of ICT and make changes that led to better learning:

> Obviously, the whole point is don't overuse it and understand that it enhances . . . the pupils' learning rather than, you know, their learning

is dependent on ICT. It is like anything; it is just about the balance and realizing that ICT does very much enhance pupils' learning but we can't depend exclusively. *Gemma*

When they worked in departments where there was a culture of using technology, they quickly developed into enthusiastic and ICT-competent users and moved from a position of distrust of it for language teaching and from personal concerns about competence to absolute confidence and conviction that it offers a lot for the learner and teacher.

In talking about how they saw themselves working with ICT in the future, all expressed a commitment to keep using it and to continue to develop their practice in this area. Several mentioned wanting to develop their use of video further, and Louis was keen to create an online databank for listening on an intranet. Both Hannah and Gemma felt that their competence and confidence with ICT had been factors in their getting appointed to their first teaching jobs. Gemma mentioned that in her interview the selection panel were very interested in her work with ICT and the skills she would bring to the department. Hannah was recruited by the school in which she had her first placement and in which there had been little use of ICT. She described her passionate commitment to developing the department's use of ICT:

> Obviously every teacher has her own style and you don't want to infringe upon that. But I have said to my Head of Department that I am going to make sure that in the next year or two the whole Department are using ICT all the time, just because of my positive experience with it this year and from what I've seen in other schools.

Naturally, these accounts reflect only a small number of self-selected trainees on one training course. Nevertheless, there are commonalities in their stories that suggest that they are convinced by the fit with the pedagogy of the subject, that they can see the benefits of the use of digital technology for pupil learning and their own learning as teachers. John and Sutherland maintain that 'the pragmatism of teachers has to merge with a "pedagogical cultural agenda"' (2005: 409). It would seem from these accounts that this agenda is in place and is likely to be taken forward by these beginning teachers.

References

Condie, R. and Munro, B. (2007), *The Impact of ICT in Schools – a Landscape Review.* Coventry: Becta.

DfES/QCA (1999), *The National Curriculum; Modern Foreign Languages,* London: HMSO/QCA QCA (2007) *The National Curriculum; Modern Foreign Languages Programme of Study for Key Stage 3 and attainment targets,* London: QCA.

Eraut, M. (1994), *Developing Professional Knowledge and Competence.* Abingdon: Routledge Falmer.

Hennessy, S., Ruthven, K. and Brindley, S. (2005), 'Teacher perspectives on integrating ICT into subject teaching: commitment, constraints, caution and change'. *Journal of Curriculum Studies,* 37, (2), 155–92.

Hoban, G. (2002), *Teacher Learning for Educational Change.* Buckingham: OUP.

John, P. (2005), 'The sacred and the profane: subject sub-culture, pedagogical practice and teachers' perceptions of the classroom uses of ICT'. *Educational Review,* 57, (4), 471–90.

John, P. and La Velle, L. (2004), 'Devices and desires: subject subcultures, pedagogic identity and the challenge of information communication technology'. *Technology, Pedagogy and Education,* 13, (3), 307–26.

John, P. and Sutherland, R. (2005), 'Affordance, opportunity and the pedagogical implications of ICT'. *Educational Review,* 57, (4), 405–13.

Lave, J. and Wenger, E. (1991), *Situated Learning: Legitimate Peripheral Participation.* Cambridge: Cambridge University Press.

Lortie, D. (1975), *Schoolteacher: a Sociological Study.* Chicago: University of Chicago Press.

Ofsted (2005), *Embedding ICT in Schools: a Dual Evaluation Exercise.* London; Ofsted.

Selwyn, N. (1999), 'Differences in educational computer use: the influence of subject cultures'. *Curriculum Journal,* 10, (1), 29–48.

TTA (2003), *Qualifying to Teach,* London: TTA.

Chapter 4

Digital technology as a tool for active learning in MFL: engaging language learners in and beyond the secondary classroom

Rachel Hawkes

Introduction

I am a full-time teacher of modern languages and Head of Department in an 11–16 rural comprehensive school in Cambridgeshire. This chapter is an account of my department's teaching and its 'story' as it has developed and continues to develop in its use of ICT; how it has built up its strengths and how it is still to develop. It is in essence an action–research ethnography as I am part of the context and integral to it. As the Head of Department I am completely engaged and involved in the processes of learning, development and training that we are involved in. This account lays out an analytical narrative of the ongoing development of ICT use in one modern-languages department. It charts how over time we have developed a pedagogy in which ICT plays a crucial, integral role. I will give examples of excellent practice, supported by data from lesson observations and pupil and staff interviews.

The context and need for change

In the last ten years in the modern-languages department, we have examined critically every aspect of our teaching methodology with two aims: first, to improve the achievement of students as measured by GCSE results at age 16 and NC levels at age 14; and second, to improve motivation for language learning among students across the age and ability range. On arrival as a new Head of Department in 1999, I found that the modern-languages department had the unenviable position of results at GCSE A*–C that were 30 per cent below the whole-school results. The recent school-inspection report by Ofsted had identified many aspects of practice that were barely satisfactory, and staff morale and pupil motivation were low. There was clearly a lot that needed to change.

In that process of change and development, we were influenced by a range of governmental initiatives and structures including the KS3 Framework, the NC, changes to the GCSE examination, Learning Styles, Assessment for Learning and Thinking Skills, but we also responded to the perceived needs of learners in our classrooms. This led to a high level of experimentation and the trialling and reviewing of innovative practice that was instrumental in the development of a new language teaching and learning pedagogy.

Eight years later the results at GCSE in modern languages are in line with the whole-school results. Ofsted judged in 2004 (and 2007) that overall provision in modern languages was outstanding and the school now holds a second specialism status as a Language College. Pupil motivation towards language learning is high as, understandably, is teacher morale. It is not difficult to show that the department's successful integration of ICT into subject teaching has been instrumental in the changes over the last eight years. I want to suggest, more fundamentally, that our use of ICT is a central tool in our developing pedagogy of active learning in languages.

Active learning in the secondary modern-languages classroom: a developing pedagogy

The figure below shows my attempt to describe the model of active learning that we adhere to in the modern-languages department:

FIGURE 4 Strategies to promote active learning

You will see that this learning model is described in terms of what pupils do and are able to do. This is not to say that the role of the teacher is minimal or less active that that of the pupil. In the strategic modern-languages classroom, learning is co-constructed through and within the oral interaction. The teacher's role is central in this dialogic interaction that is predominantly and optimally in the target language.

The way this pedagogical approach is operationalized in the interaction gives rise to several key features that typify teaching and learning in our department. The following two tables list key aspects of oral and written communication:

Features of oral interaction in the active-learning classroom

Feature	Rationale
Thinking time	To recognize that pupils need processing time in oral interaction and that their responses can be longer, more complex and more thoughtfully developed if they have this time
Pupils talk in pairs	To reduce the anxiety and fear of risk-taking by sharing the responsibility for answering
'No-hands-up' policy	To extend the need for all pupils to continue thinking
Suspend IRE/IRF sequence (teacher initiation–pupil response–teacher evaluation/feedback)	To delay the evaluation from the teacher that often closes the interaction and ends the thought prematurely. Asking several pupils their opinion before judging the response includes more pupils in the interaction
Prolonged interactions with pupils	To favour several longer interactions with a few pupils rather than a one-phrase answer from every pupil in the class
More paired and group activity	To increase the overall quantity of the oral interactions
Pupils respond to answers of others	To recognize the opportunity for and benefit of peer learning within the oral interaction and to try to engage pupils 'outside' the interaction by inviting responses and further comments
Teacher responds to content more than form	To avoid the focus exclusively on form and respond first and foremost to the message expressed
Spontaneous interaction encouraged	To foster pupils' desire to communicate and make their own meaning in the target language
Lots of 'I think that' and 'because'	To try to prolong interactions by asking pupils to give and justify their opinions
Teacher position in class	To stand back and form 'wedge' shapes to 'draw out' the oral interaction and include all pupils within it

Continued

Continued

Feature	Rationale
Gesture and eye contact to promote active listening	To keep eye contact with the pupil talking but also exaggerate 'listening-mode' gestures to draw all listeners in
Pupil talk scaffolded	To encourage pupils to make meaning, the teacher helps them to formulate their message in a meaningful, yet structurally reproducible way
Teacher modelling role-play partner	To provide a model for the pupils to emulate, often by playing dual roles in the interaction
Time for memorization: practice and mastery	To give pupils the opportunity to practise the language and memorize it so that they experience a sense of mastery that comes from automatization

Features of written communication in the active-learning classroom

Feature	Rationale
Modelling	Pupils are clear about the task objectives and what makes a good piece of work
Levels of attainment	Pupils understand the descriptors
Learning objectives and outcomes are the focal point for teacher's written feedback	The tick grid is used at the outset to set the objectives for each task
Feedback shows what students have done well and how to improve	Teacher uses the tick grid that is understood by all and a marking code initially
Feedback promotes further independent thought on next steps	Pupils are able to act on the feedback to improve their work
Progression	Teacher is clear about this and ensures that pupils are also clear
Self- and peer assessment	Students develop the skills needed to reflect critically on own and others' work

The teaching and learning of languages that I describe above occurs predominantly, though not exclusively, in the target language. Pupils not only engage actively, regularly taking the initiative, but do so operating routinely in the target language. I want to suggest that the use of ICT in whole-class teaching, independent learning and interaction beyond the classroom is crucial to the creation of the learning environment I have described.

Part 1: whole-class teaching using technology

Early in 2003 the modern-languages department was using overhead projectors with acetates to introduce and practise vocabulary, model role-play dialogues, explain grammatical structures, facilitate the correction of tasks and explain homework. At this time, there was a lot of talk of interactive whiteboards and their potential for use in the classroom. For us the cost of this was prohibitive but I was fortunate enough to be at a conference where I saw a subject teacher from a different discipline using a data projector in conjunction with PowerPoint software. I saw the potential in this software for language teaching and we replaced two overhead projectors with data projectors almost immediately. A colleague and I began to explore the potential of the PowerPoint software for presenting new language, and within a year our practice had developed to the point where we were routinely using PowerPoint in our teaching and were storing and sharing the resources centrally.

With the benefit of hindsight, I can say that the development was not simply a matter of replacing the functions of the overhead projector with newer, smarter, faster technology. The possibilities of the new software were met by the incessant questions of reflective, enquiry-driven practitioners and it was this productive fusion that generated new practice. The question–answer cycle, akin to an action–research cycle, is still ongoing and our practice is therefore still developing.

Effecting sustained change in practice across a whole department relies on more than the experiments of two teachers, however. As the changes were so unplanned and dynamic, it is perhaps quite surprising that the practice spread so quickly through the department. In terms of ICT policy there was no top-down decision from me as the Head of Department to force through any change of practice. Resources that were being developed and used were simply shared at departmental meetings and made available to all. As it became clear that other teachers wanted to make use of these resources, more data projectors were provided, initially as stand-alone machines that needed to be set up for each lesson, and subsequently as ceiling-mounted devices so that each classroom had its own projector for ease of access.

It is not that there weren't some difficulties adapting to the new technology. These arose most memorably when two colleagues, who had both been on maternity leave during the period of greatest change in terms of use of data projectors, arrived back to find that overhead projectors had disappeared from some classrooms, teachers were regularly using PowerPoint presentation in their lessons and Ofsted had decreed that the department's use of ICT was outstanding. Coupled with the usual difficulties a return to work after maternity leave can bring, the radical change in practice brought a high level of additional strain to these teachers, who felt under pressure to catch up and begin to produce lots of interactive lessons but felt ill-equipped for the task. It was only necessary to make it clear that there was no compulsion to write their own materials or even to use those made by others, but that all resources were to be freely shared and were just there as an additional resource for them to take advantage of. Looking back, it is clear that this was a pivotal moment for the department, and the acceptance that there would be writers and developers as well as users in the first phase was crucial. Recently, a research student from Finland, Bára Jonsdottir, carried out a case study of ICT use in subject teaching in our MFL department. Through in-depth interviews with five teachers in the department, she found that the use of ICT for whole-class teaching was thoroughly embedded and that all teachers regarded themselves as confident users:

> Beatrice stated it had been a push for her that everybody agreed to work in this way, and Wendy described how much using data projectors had changed her teaching: 'That just has changed my teaching a lot . . . it used to be the . . . old fashioned . . . what are they called . . . overhead projector.' Jennifer claimed that one of the reasons why she decided to apply for a job in the department was that she had known they were using ICT a great deal. All three asserted that they had become quite confident and advanced ICT users from working in the department and following its policy about ICT usage. It was rather obvious that Megan and Helen were considered to be leading the way in the use of technology, and Wendy pointed out the importance of having someone in a reasonably senior role keeping up with changes and showing people how to use new technologies. (Jonsdottir, 2007)

It is now true to say that all teachers in the department write their own material in PowerPoint, but it is also still the case that some colleagues take a lead in the writing of new material that others then use and adapt to suit the learning needs of their own classes. The contribution that whole-class teaching using ICT makes to the active-learning pedagogical approach to language teaching in our department is described and documented here using several sources of evidence: videoed lesson observations; lesson observation notes; teacher self-report from interviews conducted as part of an MPhil case study; and 'pupil-voice' feedback from questionnaires and discussion with staff. As a point of departure for this analysis, I have identified aspects of teaching crucial to the active-learning pedagogy and I then detail the way in which our use of ICT underpins it.

PowerPoint as planning tool for language lessons

One interesting aspect of the department's approach to using ICT for whole-class teaching, which emerged from the recent case study findings, was the shared understanding that PowerPoint remains just a tool at the disposal of the 'expert' teacher, who retains responsibility for planning, crafting and authoring the lesson. One colleague interviewed expressed this view as follows:

> You don't want to fall in the trap of thinking, 'oh I'm gonna make that PowerPoint and they are gonna love it', you know, you still have to plan it well, it has to be . . . you know, the level has to be right for them, and you have to have your learning objectives clear in your mind, you've got to know what level they're working at and what you want them to achieve, so you've got to keep all of that very fresh in your mind, because at the end of the day it's only technology and you still have to be a very good classroom practitioner in order to use that method I find . . . so yes, great, ICT usage is wonderful. However, it has to be treated as a tool and you still have to put a lot of your personal input into it.

Another colleague 'noted that having written a PowerPoint presentation for a lesson meant that the teacher would be very well prepared, and had thought of the learning process in advance'. This function of PowerPoint as a tool for lesson planning has been something we have often discussed as a department. The act of laying down the thinking for a specific lesson sequentially as a series of PowerPoint slides that can be viewed at a glance, previewed in 'presentation mode' and then easily edited, has the effect of clarifying thought during lesson planning. It makes plainer the progression within a lesson and even within a sequence of lessons, and can aid the teacher in ensuring that the lesson outcomes meet the lesson learning objectives. But, as the previous quotation points out, the effectiveness or otherwise with which this is achieved depends entirely on the expertise and thought processes of the teacher.

The findings from the case study that was based on teacher self-report during individual interviews with the researcher also confirm that teachers in the department believe that using ICT in whole-class teaching means pupil-centred and well as teacher-led lessons. One of the reasons for this lies in the fact that having the whole lesson prepared in advance using PowerPoint makes for less stressful, more effortless teaching in the classroom. The teacher is able to rely for pace, transitions, explanations and examples on the pre-lesson-prepared PowerPoint material, leaving a lot more space to react to individual pupil needs as they arise during the lesson:

It makes for effortless teaching where you can actually concentrate on the learning, I think I make better relationships with pupils because . . . you know, your brain can only do so much at once, and so if I can leave the actual presentation bit over to the computer and over to the data projector . . . and I know that they're all ready for me and I'm not having to go, 'oh where is that sheet and where is that, or whatever', then I actually am more alert, I'm more aware of the needs of the pupils within the class . . . I think I'm able to give them more individual attention, I think I'm able to notice them more . . . so I think it frees up quite a lot of your brain to do other things.

I turn now to examining some key aspects of our teaching that are supported by our use of ICT for whole-class teaching.

Target-language interaction

It is part of the department's practice to present and explain the learning objectives for the lesson in the target language. This is supported by a written version on a PowerPoint slide projected to the whole class using the data projector, which gives the pupils a visual focus and a means to support their request for clarification if necessary. Pupils are encouraged to do this and are willing to do so, as this excerpt from a departmental lesson observation shows:

This is a lesson which introduces new language (i.e. some character adjectives) but it is carefully and intrinsically grounded in previous learning in terms of the explicit links made with the pronunciation of vowel combinations. The planning is exceptionally good and made explicit to the pupils in German at the beginning of the lesson – the teacher explains using mime, examples, gestures and facial expression all of the lesson objectives and pupils are asked to respond to the question 'Alles klar?' A pupil feels secure enough (and interested enough) to ask the meaning of the word 'Thema' – it was explained by the teacher with an example in TL [target language] and all were then clear. *Lesson observation, 2 March 2007*

This visual backup that using PowerPoint provides extends well beyond the explanation of learning objectives. It is exploited at every stage in the lesson to provide 'modelling' to pupils. For example, in the explanation of a pair-work activity, a slide showing an example of the two roles and the question-and-answer format to be used serves to obviate the need for a wordy exposition from the teacher, who needs do little more than interact with the slide, demonstrating the activity itself. An example of such a pair-work activity is shown below:

FIGURE 5 ¿De dónde eres?

Activities that typically require L1 explanations are possible in the TL thanks to the visual support that a well-designed PowerPoint slide provides. The role of the teacher in the interaction is not reduced by the use of ICT. It is rather that meanings are communicated through a three-way dialogic interaction involving pupil, teacher and ICT. The teacher needs to rethink and restructure his or her communication with pupils, often reducing the number of words he/she uses and incorporating, through gesture and emphasis of key words, the visual support provided by the use of PowerPoint. The fact that pupils understand the explanations and what is expected of them, and are able to participate fully in this interaction, demonstrates its success. Lesson observations conducted in the department show the high proportion of TL use in lessons, as well as the low proportion of teacher time giving task instructions.

Grammar teaching

Although I stated previously that we have been influenced by governmental policy changes and initiatives over the past ten years, I believe that with respect to the teaching of grammar we have developed our own approach, based on a belief that we want pupils to become independent users of the target language, able to express their own thoughts and opinions. For this aim to be realized, we needed to teach pupils across the age and ability range about structures, how to use them, reuse them and adapt them to make new meanings. This means that we have needed to find ways to make grammar explicit, accessible and memorable for pupils of all abilities. Our use of ICT has been fundamental to this teaching aim. I would go further than this, however, to suggest that the possibilities offered by ICT, and in particular PowerPoint, have worked in synthesis with the creativity of some teachers in the department, to produce a higher level of innovation than would have been realized without its use.

As an example, I cite one particular grammatical feature of German: the use of the accusative or the dative case following a group of prepositions, depending on whether the action of the verb implies movement or not. This is an awkward grammatical concept with which A-Level candidates still often struggle. It is not easy to avoid introducing it at GCSE level, however, as it occurs when relatively straightforward sentences are constructed. One particular teacher in the department, one of the most creative and experienced users of PowerPoint in the department, came up with a way of demonstrating this grammatical construct using the image of a mouse, who moves to various positions on the screen to show examples of accusative-case usage. For instance, the mouse runs behind the sofa, or remains stationary on the screen to show dative-case usage as in the sentence, 'The mouse sits on the chair'. This use of PowerPoint has proved highly successful in teaching this grammar point. The slides below show parts of the lesson sequence:

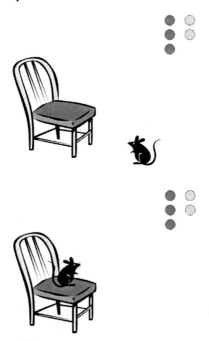

FIGURE 6 Mouse prepositions

In the first slide shown, the mouse is animated so that he jumps onto the chair, modelling use of the accusative case. The second slide shows the mouse already sitting on the chair, showing use of the dative case.

Visual, auditory and kinaesthetic (VAK) and memory: meeting the needs of all learners

In our discussion so far, much has been made of the visual support offered by whole-class teaching using PowerPoint and a data projector. Two years ago, I began to reflect on our progress so far in terms of our dual aims of improving attainment and motivation in modern languages. It was clear that we had made a lot of progress towards these aims. Results had risen by 25 percentage points at GCSE and the low number of pupil referrals to me as Head of Department was a key indicator that pupil motivation had greatly improved. However, it did seem to me that in our teaching and learning developments we had prioritized the needs of visual learners, and had not yet explored how we might best meet the needs of learners with auditory and kinaesthetic learning preferences. We began to explore the role that music, song, rhythm and movement might play in our language teaching.

This began in the form of songs to learn key verbs and structures, but has since extended into using actions to music to memorize patterns and structures; music for pronunciation practice; songs for fun and culture; as well as movement for accelerating memory and synchronizing right- and left-brain functions. The use of music and song to fix learning is as old as the learning of nursery rhymes and the transmission of folk songs from generation to generation, but the benefits of singing together in a group have recently received new impetus with the government's appointment of a singing ambassador in this country, Howard Goodall, who asserts that singing 'is a basic, human activity as fundamental to our well-being as, say, laughter' and highlights its importance as a learning method by claiming that 'music puts things in your memory'. Since his appointment earlier this year, several articles and interviews on the subject have highlighted the physical, mental and social benefits of singing. I summarize below the views expressed recently on the subject:

Alleged benefits of group singing

Physical benefits	Mental benefits	Social benefits
boosts immune system	stimulates higher levels of concentration and focus	connects people effectively with others
strengthens heart and other muscles	accelerates memory and speed of recall	provides social reassurance and support
reduces blood pressure	improves self-esteem and confidence	provides coherent community activity in a non-competitive way
improves breathing	improves group behaviour	is a powerful and creative form of self-expression
is therapeutic for speech impediments	enhances ability to work with others	
releases endorphins and produces feeling of well-being	teaches performance skills	
produces relaxation and release	works as an anti-depressant	
improves posture		

As a department we now use music, song and movement as an integral part of our language teaching. We have found that pupils of all ages and abilities respond very positively to learning in this way, and that it is effective in helping pupils to memorize key structures that pupils of similar ability levels had previously struggled to learn. An excerpt from a departmental lesson observation shows how motivating such learning opportunities can be:

> The lesson moves on to whole-class revision of 2 x verbs *haben* and *sein*. I wonder how many classes boast pupils that at this point in the lesson exclaim, 'Oh great, I like doing this!', as I heard when this activity was announced. The teacher used video of Year 9 pupils singing the two verbs to two well-known Queen songs. Then the class rehearsed the verbs, but simultaneously, which increased the challenge on their powers of concentration. *Lesson observation Year 8 German, 2007*

The use of ICT here is key as it provides, first, the visual support in the written form of the verbs and, second, it displays the video of older pupils singing the verbs, which serves to heighten the interest and motivation of pupils.

Assessment (for Learning)

The department has embraced the main tenet of Assessment for Learning, believing that pupils need teaching to make explicit the learning objectives, to show examples of good work at each stage, to provide personalized feedback that makes clear what the pupil has done well and to demonstrate for each individual the next steps in the learning process. I have already described the way in which teachers explain the learning objectives in each lesson. In the examples from our practice that follow, it will be clear that whole-class use of ICT has also facilitated the other three aspects of our teaching, namely modelling good work, providing personalized feedback and highlighting the next steps for progression.

Using PowerPoint, it is routine practice in our teaching to include some modelling of good practice. The teacher can show an example of what would fulfil the task criteria simply by including a model answer to display to and discuss with pupils before they embark on the task itself. Figure 7 below shows such an example from a Year 8 German lesson:

Wir bilden Sätze!

NC Level 3

Ich mag das.
Es ist gut.

NC Level 4.5

Ich mag Tennis,denn ich finde es lustig, aber
ich mag lieber Fußball,und mein Bruder findet
Skateboardfahren aufregend.

Meine Mutter, die Linda heißt und 40 Jahre alt
ist, mag schwimmen,denn sie findet es toll.

FIGURE 7 A model answer

Making explicit for pupils the features of a good answer by specifying the linguistic structures as well as the content is now fully embedded in departmental practice and is included in our Schemes of Work as well as our PowerPoint lessons. The following example from a lesson in which pupils prepare for a piece of writing on themselves, their family and their free time shows how the means by which pupils are going to be assessed are made clear. The use of this tick grid is now embedded across all languages at both key stages. Pupils are involved at every stage. They negotiate with the teacher at the outset the number of examples of each feature that they think they should include.

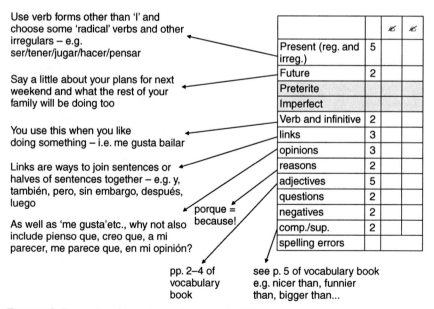

Use verb forms other than 'I' and choose some 'radical' verbs and other irregulars – e.g. ser/tener/jugar/hacer/pensar

Say a little about your plans for next weekend and what the rest of your family will be doing too

You use this when you like doing something – i.e. me gusta bailar

Links are ways to join sentences or halves of sentences together – e.g. y, también, pero, sin embargo, después, luego

As well as 'me gusta'etc., why not also include pienso que, creo que, a mi parecer, me parece que, en mi opinión?

porque = because!

		✎	✎
Present (reg. and irreg.)	5		
Future	2		
Preterite			
Imperfect			
Verb and infinitive	2		
links	3		
opinions	3		
reasons	2		
adjectives	5		
questions	2		
negatives	2		
comp./sup.	2		
spelling errors			

pp. 2–4 of vocabulary book

see p. 5 of vocabulary book e.g. nicer than, funnier than, bigger than...

FIGURE 8 Preparing for a piece of assessed writing

They have a copy of the tick grid in their books to refer to and complete as they write and, when the teacher has marked their first draft, they receive a completed tick grid showing both their successful and unsuccessful attempts at each feature. Their first draft is usually also coded for mistakes and pupils then redraft their own work before a NC level or GCSE grade is awarded.

To help pupils to understand the process of marking more fully, it is often the case that teachers will scan in examples of pupil work to include in their PowerPoint lessons. Projected to the whole class, the teacher is able to help pupils identify aspects of successful and unsuccessful TL writing. Practice in the department is continually developing in this respect and one teacher recently made a short video of herself marking a piece of Year 9 German writing using the tick grid and coding the mistakes. Projecting the video to the whole class and involving them in commenting on the mistakes made, inviting them during the lesson to anticipate and pre-empt the errors by strategically pausing the video, the teacher was able to involve pupils actively in the assessment process. After videoing this lesson, I was able to ask pupils for their feedback, and all those asked confirmed that they had found it helpful and felt more confident about their ability to redraft their own work more accurately as a result. Figure 9 below shows an example of a piece of Year 9 German writing that had been coded using the marking code on the same slide:

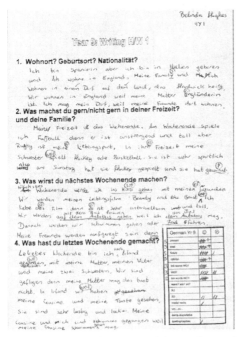

Marking code for writing

A	Auxiliary verb required/incorrect
Adj	Wrong position or agreement error
G	Gender error
I	Infinitive verb required
M	Meaning unclear
P	Plural required
PP	Past participle required/error
Sp	Spelling error
T	Tense incorrect
V	Verb required/incorrect
WO	Word order incorrect
@	Incorrect use of à/de

FIGURE 9 Year 9 German writing and use of the tick grid and marking code

It would not be possible to include these Assessment-for-Learning strategies so effectively in whole-class teaching without using PowerPoint in conjunction with a data projector.

Classroom management: pace and transition

In one of my most recent lesson observations in the department, I saw pupils learning all parts of the verb *ir* (to go) and using it to formulate plans for the weekend in the future. During the course of the Spanish lesson, which was in the target language throughout, pupils had the opportunity to practise and memorize the parts of the verb, supported visually by pictures, aurally by a song ('Baa, Baa, Black Sheep'), and kinaesthetically by gestures, to emphasize the correct person of the verb, to listen to and understand future plans and identify correctly the meaning by matching the utterances to pictures, to correct their answers, to see and have explained in the target language how to structure sentences in the future using *ir* plus *a* plus an infinitive verb, to practise forming sentences orally about future activities using all parts of the verb *ir*, to watch a video clip as stimulus for the teacher to model a description of her own plans for the weekend and finally to formulate their own plans for the weekend.

This was achieved in a forty-minute lesson, usually fifty minutes long but shorter this time to allow a student teacher time to do her starter activity with the class. I videoed the lesson as well as observing it and on viewing it subsequently, I noted that there was no transition time needed between activities because they all flowed on through the same PowerPoint presentation. There was no need to pause to give paper out, to change to a different piece of equipment or to write on the board. The pace of the lesson was quick without seeming rushed as the teacher did not need to move in order to change from one activity to another. All teacher movements were solely introduced for the explicit purpose of teaching and learning, i.e. clarifying a particular word or structure using mime or gesturing to the appropriate place on the PowerPoint slide for emphasis. The teacher was able to face the pupils at all times and maintained eye contact with them during the whole lesson. This seemed to be reassuring to the pupils and might be interpreted as a positive counterbalance to the effect of having a whole fifty-minute lesson entirely in the target language. There was certainly no sign during the lesson that pupils were lost or unable to follow. There was clear evidence that the teacher was in a position to give her whole attention to the action of the lesson, having the backup of her PowerPoint presentation, which made each activity readily available at the click of her cordless mouse.

The fact that all teachers in the department see whole-class ICT as a crucial element in maintaining pace and flow and facilitating transition between learning activities emerged strongly in the teacher interviews from the case study. As the researcher summarizes:

In fact, they were unanimous that using PowerPoint in lessons meant more effective use of time, and most stated that classroom management became easier as everything would be prepared in advance and inclusive in the clear, bright, interesting and motivating multimedia presentations. They claimed that with less transition time the pace had been quickened, resulting in more freedom for the teacher to go around the class, facilitated by a remote mouse as well. The PowerPoints would help to structure the lesson, there would be no time wasted looking for things, giving out too many work sheets, sticking in books or writing on the board with their back to the class causing pupils to lose concentration.

Authenticity: making it 'real'

One further key aspect of language teaching that has developed in the department directly as a result of our use of ICT for whole-class teaching has been our attempt to bring in more authentic material into the classroom to engage learners and make their learning experiences more real. Although this aspect of our teaching does not rely on PowerPoint, it does rely on using a data projector in conjunction with the internet. In this way, we are able to include material such as adverts, video clips, websites, music videos and songs, and integrate them easily within our lessons. The source material can be exploited in any number of ways, depending on the ability level and interests of the pupils themselves. One way in which film trailers on the video-sharing website YouTube have been used with all ability levels has been as stimulus for personal response and giving opinions. Figure 10 below shows an example of a simple proforma we use to scaffold pupil responses to authentic video material.

Conclusion

In these examples of materials, lesson observation notes and teacher quotations, I hope to have shown the strategic importance of ICT in whole-class languages teaching in our department. With it, all teachers have been able to embrace an approach to teaching which demands a high level of activity from the learner. Our use of ICT facilitates this at every stage: in planning, by

¡Vamos a mirar algo!

Nombre: ....

Clase: ....

Fecha: ....

Nombre del programa/de la película: ....

1. ¿Qué tipo de programa es?
- ☐ película
- ☐ dibujo animado
- ☐ telenovela
- ☐ noticias
- ☐ programa de deporte
- ☐ telecomedia
- ☐ concurso
- ☐ programa de música

2. ¿Para quién es?
- ☐ adultos
- ☐ niños
- ☐ todos

3. ¿Dónde tiene lugar?
- ☐ afuera
- ☐ en la ciudad
- ☐ en el campo
- ☐ adentro
- ☐ en el estudio
- ☐ en un edificio

4. ¿Cómo es?
- ☐ divertido
- ☐ cómico
- ☐ triste
- ☐ informativo
- ☐ serio
- ☐ interesante
- ☐ emocionante
- ☐ aburrido

5. ¡Añade tu opinión!
- ☐ me gustó
- ☐ no me gustó

6. ¿Has entendido algunas palabras? Pues, escríbelas aquí.

_____

_____

_____

_____

_____

_____

FIGURE 10 ¡Vamos a mirar algo!

making the teacher thought processes more logical and the learning outcomes more tightly focused on the learning objectives; in teaching, by enabling the teacher to focus more attention on the learner and on the interaction in the classroom as it unfolds; and in learning, by enabling lessons to take place in the TL, by making grammatical concepts clearer and more memorable, by facilitating the inclusion of a variety of learning activities to meet the needs of those with different learning styles, by signalling clearly the expectations of each task and facilitating personalized feedback and target setting and by allowing access to a range of engaging, authentic materials. The fact that all teachers in the department have been allowed to develop at their own pace in their use of ICT seems to have helped us to arrive at a shared understanding of the benefits of ICT in whole-class teaching. It is believed by all of us to have played a significant role in the raising of standards across the department and in raising the profile, status and popularity of the subject.

I turn now to consider the ways in which we are developing our use of ICT beyond the classroom, an aspect of our teaching that is not as yet fully embedded across the department. I will also look ahead to further ways in which we may seek to develop our use of ICT in the future.

Part 2: beyond the classroom

Guided by our aims of raising attainment and pupil motivation in language learning, we have come to believe that the higher the level of pupil activity in lessons and the higher the level of pupil autonomy in learning, the better. My evaluation of teaching in the department shows that pupils learn more actively in lessons than previously, achieve better and are generally well motivated. The next steps in terms of development, both of teaching and learning and of ICT use, signal the need for pupils to have the impetus and opportunity to become both more autonomous and more creative in their learning. Several developments in our use of ICT support these aims and we are beginning to see the impact on a small, but significant, scale.

Use of email and electronic marking

Pupils also develop writing well thanks to teachers' outstanding use of ICT. Excellent assessment also contributes to pupils' success; teachers' thorough testing, marking, and constructive comments give each student exact information on how to improve. *Ofsted report for Modern Foreign Languages, Comberton Village College, March 2004*

Building on the positive judgements from the inspection report in 2004, I wanted to take all that was good about our formative assessment of written work, but use technology further to enable me to mark work electronically, to streamline the process of redrafting for pupils and to make submission of work easier and more manageable. Further inspired by an idea in an issue of the *Language Learning Journal,* I adapted Microsoft Word to code mistakes in superscript, insert explanatory comments or footnotes, track corrections that are made and indicate examples of good writing. I then began a small-scale project whereby pupils in one class submitted their written work electronically via email.

One benefit to the pupils seemed to be the clarity of the correction, the fact that the codes are placed next to the error and the comment boxes are contrastive in colour and placed to the side of the main body of the text linked to the error by a dotted line. A second benefit was that the redraft could be achieved by editing the first draft and it was no longer necessary to copy out of the whole piece of work.

In addition to the coded errors, ticks for good examples of foreign-language usage were given and in the explanatory comments pupils were all given their average sentence length (or ASL) and their accuracy percentage, calculated by giving the percentage of words which appear correctly in the text. They were then given a further target or targets as a specific focus for the revised draft. Pupils were also able to submit work as soon as it was done, and I was able to mark a few pieces at a time and return them, which avoided a build-up of marking which occurs when a class of 32 all hand their extended written work in at the same time. Although the process took the same amount of time as marking by hand, I felt I was able to give a far greater level of detail in the comments than would be feasible with handwritten assessment. The example in Figure 11 below shows a piece of work marked using this method.

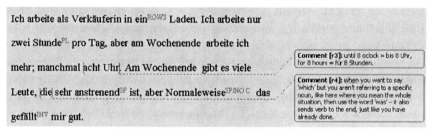

FIGURE 11 Ich arbeite als Verkäuferin

The reaction from pupils in the trial groups was highly positive. Pupils in both Years 10 and 11 mentioned the ease of reading and understanding the corrective feedback and the increased facility with which they were able to locate and correct errors. Specific comments pupils made included the following:

It allows me to identify more easily where errors are occurring, i.e. in R1/R2/R3.

It's easier because it is sent back to you as soon as it is marked.

It motivates me with my German homework.

This method of written assessment proved effective with the groups who trialled it and it was shared with the department. It has not become embedded in departmental practice and teachers currently prefer coding pupils' written work on paper. Given that the most important aspects of our approach to assessment are fulfilled by our use of the tick grid, coding and redrafting practices, I am not motivated to promote strongly the use of electronic marking currently across the department, but I do see the potential for its use in the future.

Using video

As previously mentioned, video made by pupils has begun to form part of whole-class teaching, as for example in the use of Year 9 pupils recorded singing the verbs for Year 8 lessons. This has proved highly motivating for both 'performers' and 'audience'. Recent reflection on our teaching in the department has led me to focus on the notion of audience and how it relates to pupil work and motivation. The knowledge that, when a pupil produces some written (or spoken) work, it typically has at most an audience of two people, the pupil and his or her teacher, highlights a limitation in current classroom practice. We know from experience ourselves that if we are producing something for a larger audience we will take greater care in its production, put more thought into the planning and spend more time thinking about how it will be received and its 'fitness for purpose'. When we have asked pupils to present orally to the whole class, it has made a qualitative difference to the effort they have made with pronunciation and intonation. In the same way, we have begun to look at ways in which we can find a larger audience for our pupils' work.

One project that has been tried over the last two years is a video tutorial project. Four volunteers formed a video group who met regularly with their teacher at lunchtimes to write, produce and film short videos on aspects of German grammar. The format that they used was two characters, one strong in German and one weak, plus a narrator who, off camera, provides the background structure to the sequence. The videos produced were then used in lessons for pupils in lower years as they learnt these grammatical concepts. While I have no way of comparing the effectiveness of these videos for learning with alternative teaching methods, I am able to describe the motivational effects they had. The pupils in the video group found themselves endowed with a sort of celebrity status whereby pupils who had watched the videos in lessons went on to greet them in the corridor and even ask for their autographs. The interest that was raised for future involvement in making more videos was also a clear indication of the motivational effect.

**Email: extending the dialogue, providing
one-to-one differentiated support**

Although this is by no means a strategy confined to language teachers,
we have found as a department that broadening our communication to
include email from our school accounts to parents and to pupils is having positive effects on the levels of engagement of individual learners. In
2006, I was teaching a class (set 4 out of 5) which consisted of 30 learners
of French in Year 9. I knew that this was a crucial group in terms of options
for Key Stage 4, as languages were at this point optional in my school and
I really needed to convince as many as possible to continue on to GCSE
French. I launched an email communication project with parents through
which I aimed to keep all parents updated as to progress, targets for the
class and homework tasks through the year. I also made it clear, however,
that this communication could be two-way and that I would welcome the
opportunity to respond to parents and pupils on an individual basis. Those
opting to continue with French to GCSE numbered 23 of the 30 pupils.
This was a very high proportion given the optional status of the subject
at the time and the ability level of the pupils in the group. The following
shows an example of parental communication during the email project:

From: xxx xxx [xxx_xxx@yahoo.co.uk]

Sent: 16 January 2006 14:14

To: Rachel Hawkes

Subject: Re: Happy New Year and brief overview of this term

The CD is really useful – many thanks Rachel. Julia is considering
a language as part of her GCSE curriculum. She enjoys French,
but is talking about perhaps Spanish. We would be grateful for any
feedback/suggestions you may have in this regard.

   Thanks for the guidance re grades. Hopefully – with the help of
your CD and revision she will pull a grade 5 out of the bag by the end
of Year 9 (she's current 4.5 I think.)

With regards

Rachel Hawkes wrote:

Dear Parents/pupils in 9y4

Happy New Year and I hope you had a good Christmas. During
this term we will continue to work to make sure pupils are able to

⇨

---

say/write/understand French in 3 time frames, past, present and future, as these are essential to real communication in any language. We have started Module 3 this term, which begins with talking about plans for the forthcoming weekend. The whole class has made a really positive start to the term. Progress-wise the group is ahead of equivalent groups that I have taught both last year and the year before. It would be good to know from you as parents if it has been possible (or not) to look at any of the material from the CD with your child or even if you have had a conversation about how French is going with your child. Please remember that I am not expecting anything from you – it is just useful to know!

Homework from me this week is for Wednesday and is to translate into French five future sentences that pupils have in their books in English and then to write five more sentences in French. There is an A5 sheet with language to support this loose in their books. Obviously this is a crucial term as we near the end of Key Stage 3 and in early May the final KS3 levels in French will be assessed. An overall level 5 indicates that pupils have achieved a good enough level to achieve a C grade or better at GCSE, so this might be useful when talking with your child about their GCSE options. Early in February the options evening will take place and forms will be issued and the process of choosing options will begin, so this is a good time to start discussing.

As always, please email me with any feedback or questions.

Best wishes

Rachel Hawkes

Since the completion of the project, it has become usual for us to make our email contacts available to all pupils and parents – it is printed on the vocabulary books that we give all pupils at the start of each academic year. Pupils do email teachers to ask specific questions about homework, about grammar, sometimes even about specific vocabulary.

Blogging

Following on from the aim to create a greater audience for pupil work, the department has embarked on a project with four other local schools to create a blog. We will use it to upload examples of pupil work that pupils from other schools will read and respond to. We also plan to engage our foreign-language assistants in the production of some authentic material for pupils to read and respond to, with the aim of encouraging higher levels of attainment in reading. Once we have successfully established the blog as a host page for our pupils' written work, we hope to extend it to include podcasts made by our pupils that pupils in other schools will listen and respond to.

This is our newest development and is fully in line with our aim of greater pupil autonomy and creativity. This is necessary to enable pupils to access the higher levels of attainment at Key Stage 3. Level 7 in the NC for writing states that 'pupils produce pieces of writing of varying lengths on real and imaginary subjects, using an appropriate register. They link sentences and paragraphs, structure ideas and adapt previously learnt language for their own purposes' (1999: 45). It is sometimes difficult to create the opportunities for this to occur within the classroom context, but it is our belief that the blog will provide the right stimulus for the more independent approach to writing that is implied in the higher-level descriptors.

Conclusion

This chapter tells the story of ICT use in one modern-languages department, as it set out to improve pupil attainment and motivation several years ago, and began to develop an approach to language teaching and learning that centralizes pupil activity and engagement. This approach harnessed the positive aspects of new government initiatives such as VAK and Learning Styles, Thinking Skills and Assessment for Learning, but did not not adhere too strictly to any one individual policy, preferring instead to experiment with a variety of different strategies, being led always by the needs of the learners in our classrooms. ICT use in whole-class teaching has been at the heart of this department's journey. It has answered many questions posed by creative, enquiring and resourceful teachers who have used it as a powerful tool in the development of an active-learning approach to language teaching.

I do not think that this point in time marks any particular arrival or conclusion to the journey. It is simply where we currently are on route to better language teaching and learning for our pupils. As the second part of this chapter identifies, there are many aspects of pupil-centred activity using ICT that we have yet to develop and much still to do before learners achieve the levels of autonomy and creativity in language learning of which we believe them capable.

Reference

DfEE (1999), Modern Foreign Languages. *The National Curriculum for England.* London: DfEE.

Chapter 5

Engaging pupils in bilingual, cross-cultural online discourse

Michael Evans

Introduction

One of the most radical ways in which the digital revolution can impact on foreign-language learning is through the medium of Computer-Mediated Communication (CMC). The potential of this medium for school learners of languages is strongest in the extent to which it provides contexts and perspectives of learning which represent alternatives to the conventional classroom framework of teacher + class that prevails in most schools. A CMC platform allows for alternative configurations of teaching and learning including, for instance, pupil + pupil; pupil + pupils; teacher + pupil; teacher + pupils. What this environment makes possible is the diversification of sources of input and learning support; diversification of modes of L2 output; diversification of purposes and types of learning; and an interplay between private and public dimensions of linguistic and communicative processing. The extent to which a language learner is required to draw on and to switch between inner resources and public interaction is heightened through the medium of CMC. Of course, the vision I am depicting is an ideal one and teachers who have already tried to incorporate such a dimension into their teaching programmes will be familiar with the organizational, pedagogical and technological obstacles and difficulties that exist. One of the main problems is the difficulty of maintaining continuity and sustained use of the medium, given organizational and other pressures. However, despite these difficulties and with the increasingly transparent use of online technology in the years to come, it is important to consider this potential for language learners in the instructional context. This chapter, therefore, provides a rare account of a CMC programme that ran for several years and involved language learners in secondary schools located in different countries. What can be learnt from the Tic-Talk experience?

Tic-Talk was a project I began, with my colleagues Edith Esch and Linda Fisher, at the Faculty of Education, Cambridge University, with the aim of developing pupil foreign-language learning through the use of the CMC medium. We were interested in seeing how school-age foreign-language learners could learn from each other through systematic and sustained online contact. How do English learners of French and French learners of English interact with one another through this medium? Does this interaction lead to mutual support and learning? What are the cultural, linguistic and strategic dimensions of this learning?

Principles of design

The programme extended over a period of five years, including a pilot study from May to July 2001, in which the activities and approaches were trialled. The main period in which the project ran was as follows:

Year of project	No. of pupil participants	No. of groups	Approximate no. of pupil messages
2001–2	152	24	2,000
2002–3	134	20	1,600
2003–4	100	15	1,000
2004–5	94	10	885
Total corpus	480	79	5,485

The planning of the pupil involvement in the programme was done with the collaboration of at least one key teacher in each of the schools involved. This collaboration was mainly twofold: the selection of pupils and the management of use of the programme in lessons. In the first case, the teachers organized the completion of a participants' grid, providing details of age, interest and an indication of the L2 competence of each participant, which was returned to me as programme director and which I used to construct the Tic-Talk groups. Most of the pupils were from Y10 and Y12 classes in England and from *troisième* and *première* classes in the francophone countries. As well as grouping on the basis of compatibility of interests and linguistic ability, a further criterion was to ensure as far as possible a balance of L1 speakers in the two languages and a spread of participants from the different schools in each Tic-Talk group. As far as the role of the teacher was concerned, though the project was primarily pupil focused it became clear that the teachers had an important role to play. However, pressures of time and professional commitment meant that there was a limit to how far they could contribute to the coordination of the project. The programme therefore relied entirely on external coordination of the activities and feedback to the pupils. The teachers' support was in motivating and monitoring the participation of the pupils at their own school. It became clear in the feedback from pupil interviews that they saw their teacher in this context mainly as a kind of walking dictionary, in place of a conventional or online dictionary. A degree of flexibility was also necessary in allowing the individual teachers to decide how they were to integrate the programme in their lessons. Pupils had password access to the bulletin board through the internet and therefore could log on both during lesson time and independently from home or elsewhere. A decision was taken by the project team to give the pupils access only to their own Tic-Talk group rather than to enable them to view all the groups. The reasoning behind this was that group cohesion and identity seemed more likely to be enhanced if they could only view and interact with each other. In terms of regularity of contact and participation, the project worked best with participants at schools where the teacher timetabled at least part of a lesson each week to writing messages on Tic-Talk.

As far as the principles underlying the task design are concerned, the key ones were 'variability' (new activities were uploaded on a weekly or fortnightly basis, and different types of activities and topics were included, see below); 'topicality' (where possible the participants were encouraged to draw on current issues or aspects of their daily lives); 'interactivity' (this took different forms: where practicable the groups were provided with feedback on their previous week's comments and opinions; games encouraged interaction between members of the group); 'flexibility of language choice' (different emphases toward the use of L1 or L2 were made in the different activities; in all cases the focus was on meaning and communication rather than language as form, though as will be seen below there were many examples where the pupils spontaneously focused on each other's language use); and finally 'comparativity' (pupils were required in different ways to compare both explicitly and implicitly the languages and cultures associated with English and French). These principles are illustrated in the following description of the three main types of activities outlined below.

Conversations strand

In this section of the bulletin board, participants were asked to communicate with each other on topics of their choice related to their daily lives.

The idea here was to give them space to bond as a group by discussing and sharing common interests and opinions. The linguistic requirement here (at least as a starting point, since it was not 'policed') was that they should write in the L2. The following is an example of the opening message I uploaded at the start of each year as a way of setting the parameters for this strand of activity:

Hello everyone ☺ and welcome to TIC-TALK! We hope you will enjoy using this conference to make new friends from different countries and to discuss topics of interest to you. We also hope that your English and French will improve as a result. You can learn from each other – almost as much as from your teachers! This project will only work if you regularly log on to read your messages and to send messages to the others in your group.

Members of this group are: Chris, Natalie and Tania (from AA in England). Aissatou (from BB in Senegal), Charlotte, Florian and Chloe (from CC in France), Steph (from DD in England) and Laura (from EE in England).

In this part of the conference you should start by introducing yourselves and by asking questions to the others in the group. After that you should answer each others' questions and talk about your interests and daily life at school and home. Try to do as much as you can in the foreign language but don't worry if you switch into your own language – the main thing is to communicate.

Topic discussion strand

As well as engaging in more independent conversations, the participants were urged to contribute to discussions around a 'topic of the week' which was kick-started by an opening message often supported by visual stimulus. The topics were chosen mostly on the basis of topicality in the news and seasonal relevance, as issues capable of eliciting divergence of opinions or a comparative focus (especially between French and English). The first topic used in most years (see below) attempted to trigger thinking about language identity and the role of language as a medium of international understanding and harmony. It also had a biblical theme which framed the topic as a narrative. We found that biblical themes often served as an effective vehicle for discussion on Tic-Talk.

The Tower of Babel

Would the world be a better place if we all spoke one language?

Do you know the story of the tower of Babel? In the Bible, the story goes that the tower was built by men (speaking the same language) who wanted to reach heaven. To stop them doing this, God 'confused their language' so they couldn't understand each other. The people then abandoned their city and scattered to different parts of the world speaking different languages.

Do you think the world's problems are partly due to having different languages? Why are you studying a foreign language? Which languages do you speak? Would we be better off if everyone spoke English (or a new invented universal language)?

By the way, do you know which country the tower of Babel is supposed to have been built in? Ask your teacher or look it up on the Web.

During the course of the Tic-Talk project the issue of catering for both French and English as media of communication in the initial presentation of each topic discussion was dealt with either by providing a message in both languages or alternating between French and English for each topic. The following is a list of some of the topics discussed during the programme:

- *Pour ou contre la guerre en Irak?* At the time of the outbreak of the war in Iraq, this issue elicited strong views on both sides of the argument on the decision to invade.
- *Mars* In the context of American, Canadian and UK efforts and pronouncements related to travel to Mars, arguments for and against exploration of space were presented in French and pupils were asked to give their own views.
- *Fox hunting* With the passing of the law banning fox hunting in the UK, this was another topical issue. It was also an opportunity to reflect on differences with other countries involved in Tic-Talk (e.g. France, Canada, Senegal) on the legality of hunting.
- *Mother's Day* This topic, posted on Mothering Sunday in England, was presented in both languages in the initial message (addressing the anglophone participants in English with a summary of traditions in England, and addressing the francophone participants in French with a summary of how the day is spent in France).

- *Easter* As the Easter holiday break approached, the topic was presented in relation to *The Da Vinci Code* theme which was in the news at the time. The posting included pictures of Da Vinci's Last Supper, and the notorious clothes advert parodying it which was banned in France. Participants were asked to compare the two pictures and to comment on the ban.
- *Friday the 13th* This posting (coinciding with the date on the calendar) consisted of a list in English of example superstitions and a passage in French on symbolic references to 13 and Friday in the Bible. Participants were asked for their views on this date and other superstitions.
- *Végétarien?* This posting, written in French, presented comparative statistics about numbers of vegetarians in both France and England and asked participants for their views on the issue and why they did or did not eat meat.
- *Le diable, existe-t-il?* After a brief profile, in French, of Lucifer as represented in the Bible, participants were asked to say if they believed in the existence of the Devil and to suggest which man or woman in history most resembles him.
- *Animal testing for medical research* The topicality of this subject related to the controversy in England regarding the closure of a research centre conducting animal research into brain diseases. The posting consisted of a text in English presenting arguments in support of the use of animals for medical research (taken from the Association for Medical Research), and a text in French presenting arguments against (from an animal rights association in France).
- *Les Oscars* Timed to coincide with the Oscar ceremony in Hollywood, this discussion was organized around two posters of films that received a nomination for an award (one French film and one American) which participants had to identify; they then had to go on to describe, in French, the best film they had ever seen and, in English, one they thought was very bad.

More playful tasks

In order to inject more light-hearted interactive tasks into the project, it was decided to engage the pupils periodically in less serious tasks instead of the topic discussions. The following are some examples:

- *Photoquiz* This required them to guess the odd one out from a selection of four famous faces and to give their reasoning in the L2.

- *Caption/légende* This required them to write as many captions as possible (in French and English) to go with a cartoon posting, and the best captions from all the groups were reproduced in future weeks.
- *Guess the film* The text consisted of a brief summary of a nameless famous film which the participants had to identify and then follow up with their own description of a film which the others in the group had to identify.

Analysis of CMC interaction

Peer scaffolding

The Tic-Talk data reveals interaction of different kinds and at different levels of discourse. One of these features of interpersonal interaction relates to the spontaneous instances of peer scaffolding that were generated. There were frequent occasions in every year of the project in which participants requested help from other members of their group who were native speakers of the target language. One can also define these as 'language related episodes' (Swain 2000: 111–12) since the focus of the interaction is the quality of the target language produced by the participants. The environment seemed to have been viewed by the pupils as uninhibiting in this respect, particularly once a degree of familiarity was established within the group. The help provided takes different forms as is shown in the following example, taken from part of a thread of discussion stimulated by a 'guess the film' task.

Date: 17 March 2004 10:15 p.m.

Ahhh! C'est *Finding Nemo*. Je n'ai pas vue le film, mais mes amis ont dit que c'etait fantastique. Il est un film de Disney, est ce-que vous avez un film de Disney que vous aimez le plus? *Le Roi Lion* pour example? J'adore ca film! Simba est adorable!

Translation: Ah! It's *Finding Nemo*. I haven't seen the film, but my friends said it was fantastic. It's a film by Disney, do you have a Disney film you like the most? *The Lion King* for example? I adore that film! Simba is adorable![1]

(Please, by the way, when I make mistakes in my French, please don't hesitate to correct me, as otherwise I'll keep on making the same mistakes. Thanks.)

Siobhan

xxxx xxxx

Date: 23 March 2004 12:09 p.m.

Ahhh! C'est *Némo*, je n'ai pas vu le film, (en fait c'est un dessin animé) mais mes amis ont dit qu'il était fantastique. C'est un film de Disney, quel est le film de Disney que vous aimez le plus? *Le Roi Lion* par exemple? J'adore celui-là! Simba est adorable! Voila, j'espére que moi non plus je n'ai pas fait de fautes . . .

Marie

Translation: Ah! It's *Nemo*, I haven't seen the film (in fact it's a cartoon) but my friends said it was fantastic. It's a film by Disney, which film by Disney do you like the most? *The Lion King* for example? I adore that one! Simba is adorable!

There, I hope that I too haven't made any mistakes . . .

Marie

Date: 23 March 2004 12:14 p.m.

Me to, I found it was *Némo*, I seen it at the cinema, and I have it in DVX: I love *Nemo*, he is super!! If someone don't seen it, you must run to watch it!

Marie

Date: 23 March 2004 12:18 p.m.

Moi aussi j'ai trouvé, c'est bien *Némo*!!!!!!

J'ai vu ce film avec une de mes amies qui en est folle!!! C'est SUPER!!!!! Je vous le recommande si vous voulez voir quelque chose qui change des films normaux lors desquels on devine facilement la suite!! Car, là, on ne s'attend pas à ce qui va se passer!!! En plus c'est assez drôle enfin ça dépend de l'humour de chacun mais c'est marrant. Bref même si certains pensent que c'est vraiment gamin, moi je ne le trouve vraiment pas.

Tu me demandes un autre film de Disney que j'aime?? Bien, à vrai dire, je les aime presque tous mais mon préféré est *Cendrillon*. J'adore ce conte, les souris, les oiseaux et tous les animaux qui aident Cendrillon pour aller au bal et tout . . . c'est trop beau et une trop belle histoire je pense!!!

Sinon, j'aime bien *Le Roi lion* aussi, comme toi Siobhan. C'est sympa, quand le babouin (je me rappelle plus de son nom) le montre à tout le monde!!!! waaaa!!

Pour tes fautes d'orthographe: *je n'ai pas vu* il n'y a pas de *e* à *vu*.

Au lieu de dire *il est un film de Disney* on dit *c'est un film de Disney* (= *cela est un film de Disney*).

Voilà, tu n'as pas fait beaucoup de fautes!!!!!

Gros bisous à tous!!!! J'espère pouvoir reparler de films avec vous!

Quel est votre film et votre dessin animé préféré??

A la prochaine!

Charlène

Translation: Me too I've worked it out, it's *Nemo!*

I saw this film with one of my friends who is crazy about it! It's great! I recommend it to you if you want to see something different from the usual films where you can guess easily what's going to happen next! Cos here you can't say what'll happen next!

What's more it's quite funny well it depends on your sense of humour but it's cool.

Well even if some people think it's childish I don't find that at all.

You ask me which other Disney film I like? Well, to tell the truth, I like almost all of them but my favourite is *Cinderella.* I adore that story, the mice, the birds and all those animals who help Cinderella to go to the ball and everything . . . It's really beautiful and a really beautiful story I think! Otherwise, I really like *The Lion King* too, like you Siobhan. It's nice, when the baboon (I forget his name) shows him to everyone! Wow!

As for your spellingmistakes: *je n'ai pas vu* there's no *e* in *vu.* Instead of saying *il est un film de Disney* we say *c'est un film de Disney* (*that is a film by Disney*)

There you are, you didn't make many mistakes!

Kisses to everyone! I hope I can talk again about films with you later! What is your favourite film and cartoon?

Till next time!

Charlène

Siobhan makes an explicit request (in L1 English) for correction of errors in the text of her message (in L2 French) in which she identifies the mystery film. The appeal is first met by Marie, a French native speaker, who responds by reproducing Siobhan's text with corrections discreetly made without commentary. Interestingly, Marie does more than correct the spelling mistakes. She adds one or two little touches that provide add-itional scaffolding. The insertion of the parenthesis '(en fait c'est un dessin animé)' provides extra help in terms of vocabulary acquisition by pointing out that *Finding Nemo* is not just a film but a cartoon film. Marie signs off with a modest, semi-joking, self-deprecatory comment that she hopes she hasn't made any errors (even though she is writing in her L1). Subsequently, Charlène, also a French native speaker, responds to Siobhan's request for help in a different way. Her style of support is more direct and explicit than Marie's; she picks out two errors and provides the corrections, even add-ing an indication that *c'est* is a shortening of *cela est*. Whilst Marie provides implicit corrective feedback in the form of a written recast of Siobhan's text, Charlène provides more explicit corrective feedback (Ellis et al. 2006) which is more explanatory in style: but both undoubtedly reveal precocious talent as teachers. The same can be said by many other participants in the different cohorts of Tic-Talk, which suggests that the collaborative solidar-ity engendered within this virtual environment encourages the pupils to take on roles of language teacher and learner.

Cross-cultural interaction

A second form of interaction that occurred at times in the project con-sisted of patterns of attempts at interpersonal or cultural connection between different members of a group. What is clear from these episodes is that the communications go beyond requesting linguistic support for what they want to express in a message (though request for such help is often included). These episodes are ones where possibilities of common ground are explored within the cross-cultural context. An example of this is a fairly extended string of messages within the conversations task. The chain of 28 messages is too long to quote here so I shall provide a brief outline of the communications in order to illustrate how this is suggestive of the participants' interpersonal moves and reactions. One might describe these episodes as group-related episodes as they are con-cerned with socialization processes within the fledgling online group community.

After the initial, fairly standard, stream of introductory messages from most of the members of the group in which the individuals give some information about where they live, their background and their interests, Adeshola (a pupil with an African background enrolled in a school in London) inserts a comment which can be taken as a gesture of interest in the sociocultural background of the French participant: *I have done some research about Coutances. The population is 11,827. It is in the region of Basse Normandie.* This is followed immediately by a message from Rachel, an English student at a different school, which also can be interpreted as a bonding gesture with the francophone members of the group. She reveals that she has lived in France and in the USA: *Alors, je peux parler un peu de français mais je ne suis pas bilingue ou quelque chose comme ça* ('So, I can speak a bit of French but I am not bilingual or anything like that'). She then makes an interesting comment in relation to the name of her pet dog: *J'ai un chien qui s'appelle Copain. Les anglais ne connaissent pas ce mot alors ils disent 'Copper'. Ça m'énerve vraiment, mais c'est la vie!* ('I have a dog who's called Copain. The English don't know this word so they say 'Copper'. That annoys me really, but that's life!') By referring to *les anglais* in this way, Rachel positions herself more closely with her French interlocutors. A few days later, Toby joins the group. He is an older, bilingual student at a school in Montreal. He immediately takes a fairly dominant role within the group and deploys his fluent English and French appropriately in addressing different members of the group. Eventually, Camille, based at a French lycée in Dakar, begins to contribute to the conversation. Both Toby and Rachel attempt to relate to her by asking questions about Senegal. Toby comments: *salut Camille! Comment ca va? Quel age as-tu? I wish I were in Africa now! Here it's -5C, and it's snowing! Ah, Quebec! No, seriously, I'm happy that it is, because soon I will be able to play hockey and go skiing, and all that winter stuff! What kind of stuff do you do in December? I was wondering: what is your first language?* Rachel also tries to draw Camille into the group by showing an interest in her country: *salut Camille! Pardonnez-moi mais je ne sais rien! Dakar, c'est grand? Est-ce qu'il y a beaucoup de choses a faire? Tu aimes habiter la? Moi, j'habite dans un petit village.* ('Hi Camille! Excuse me but I don't know anything! Is Dakar big? Is there a lot to do? Do you like living there? Me, I live in a little village.') Camille responds to Rachel with a fairly lengthy message not only exchanging information as requested about Dakar, but also conveying it in a markedly expressive and friendly style: *réponds-moi vite, j'attends ta réponse avec impatience: on apprendra ainsi à mieux se connaître, qu'est-ce que tu en penses?☺ Je te fais de gros bisous +++.* ('Answer me quickly, I look forward to your reply: that way we'll get to know each other better, what do you think?☺ Lots of kisses.') The next message that appears in this thread is from Adeshola, who has been absent from the conversation during all this interaction between Rachel, Camille and Toby. Her brief message distinctly conveys a sense of feeling excluded from the interaction: *Camille et Rachel, il faut savoir que le tic-talk est pour tout le monde. In other words 'don't leave me out!'.* Rachel replies with an ironical comment that indicates she has noted Adeshola's complaint but is unrepentant: *Adeshola, Liberté, Egalité et Fraternité – il n'y a pas de régles. Rachel.* ('Adeshola, Liberty, Equality and Fraternity – there are no rules. Rachel.') She then posts a few days later another message specifically addressed to Camille. That is followed by a move by Toby that (whether consciously or subconsciously) serves to restore communality by raising a new topic, the capture of Saddam Hussain, which provides the focus of the remaining messages in the thread.

What this example indicates is that the communication that takes place between these participants is to some extent dependent on interpersonal interaction. The valuable aspect of this from a language learning point of view is that most of the interactions involve writing in the L2. For many of the participants such opportunities, set in the cross-cultural context, are more or less absent from the conventional classroom. The extent to which the participants dominate and steer the discussions (or at least are able to deploy a larger repertoire of interactional moves) seems to correlate with their use of questions in messages. The table below shows that although Toby posted fewer messages in this thread than Rachel or Adeshola, he formulated many more questions than the other two:

	No. of messages	No. of questions
Adeshola	7	0
Rachel	10	6
Toby	6	10

Codeswitching

A third important feature of the interactions is the language used by the pupils, in which they express themselves. This choice of language (English or French) was largely made independently by each participant, despite occasional requests from me at the start of a new topic thread for messages to be written in one or other of the languages. Other external pressures were also sometimes made by their classroom teachers encouraging them to write in the target language. It is evident that in most cases pupils switched between the languages of their own accord and for different reasons (see Evans forthcoming); often, as in the case below, language switch between messages by one pupil seemed to mirror the switches made by their interlocutor.

From: Michael Evans

Date: 30 Nov 2003 05:36 p.m.

Should school uniform be abolished?

Do you have to wear a uniform at school? If so, describe the uniform and say what you think of it. As you know, people have strong views either way. Does compulsory uniform eliminate personal expression or is it a way of making sure everyone looks smart and equal?

This time we'll make this discussion also a survey. So at the end of your message on this, please also choose one of the two statements below:

1. Yes, school uniform should be abolished.

2. No, school uniform is cool.

From: Tiphaine

Date: 02 Dec 2003 12:34 p.m.

Dans mon collège nous ne sommes pas obligés de porter un uniforme. Mais je suis ni pour ni contre. Je pense qu'il permet de ne pas faire de différences entre les classes sociales bien que l'on puisse voir à cause de la qualité du vêtement.

Par contre c'est aussi bien de pouvoir choisir son habillement car cela peut être le moyen d'exprimer ses goûts.

Je pense que je suis plutôt pour l'abolition du port d'un uniforme.

Translation: In my school we don't have to wear a uniform. But I am neither for nor against. I think that it helps to avoid showing differences between people from different social classes based on the quality of their clothes.

On the other hand it's also good to be able to choose what to wear as that is a means of expressing one's taste.

I think that on balance I'm in favour of banning uniforms.

From: Elin

Date: 11 Dec 2003 07:24 p.m.

Yes, I have to wear a school uniform. We wear 'knee-length box-pleated dark navy' skirts, white shirts and blue wool jumpers. There is also a school coat but it is not compulsory to wear it so no one does. Most people at my school hate our uniform but we have to wear it. We also have to have black shoes, our hair clips have to be plain brown or navy, and if you have long hair it has to be tied back. Although I think it is good that everybody wears the same, as it is smarter, I think that we shouldn't have to wear a uniform.

Yes, I think school uniform should be abolished.

From: Tiphaine

Date: 02 Dec 2003 12:34 p.m.

I think your school is a bit strict. You always have to wear a skirt!!?? It's cold in winter!

From: Elin

Date: 20 Dec 2003 02:05 p.m.

Oui, je sais que c'est tres froid en hiver, mais nous devons les porter tout le temps. C'est horrible quand il pleut aussi.

Translation: Yes, I know it's very cold in winter, but we have to wear them all the time. It's horrible when it rains as well.

The first pupil message in this exchange, written by Tiphaine, a French native speaker, is in the L1 (French). This is followed by a reply from Elin, an English native speaker, also written in the L1 (English). Tiphaine then writes her next message in the target language (English) and this is mirrored in Elin's response which is also in the target language (French). What seems to be happening here, there-fore, is that the English pupil, Elin, is taking her cue from Tiphaine, the French participant, as to which language to use in each of these two postings. Similar codeswitching patterns occurred in other inter-actions in different Tic-Talk groups. From a language-learning point of view, one can argue that the pupils benefit linguistically from this kind of exchange from the points of view of both reading and writ-ing. From an interpersonal point of view, codeswitching may have been a reflection, as the following pupil's comments in an interview indicate, of the participants' desire to be accommodating: 'I think because they were writing in English it seemed logical to write to them in French.'

Analysis of pupil perceptions

Questionnaire data

Pupils' views of different aspects of the Tic-Talk programme were gathered through questionnaires and interviews with sample participants at different schools involved in the project. They provide a useful indication of preferences related to issues such as task design, learning value and dimensions of interaction. Let us begin by looking at the responses to a questionnaire completed by 16 pupils at a London comprehensive school and 14 pupils at a *lycée* in France.

What is the most interesting aspect of Tic-Talk?

The majority of respondents referred to the experience of communicating with others as the main focus of interest for them. Some pupils phrased this as an interesting encounter with 'difference' in the shape of different views and different experiences. Others emphasized more that it was the fact of peer communication ('communicating with youngsters like us') that they valued most. Some pupils specified that it was the global dimension of this communication that interested them most. One French respondent referred to the supportive environment that fostered this communication: 'communiquer avec tous ces gens dans une autre langue, dans cette bonne ambiance'. Other aspects that were mentioned included expressing one's own opinions, writing in the L2, discussing news items and correcting people's mistakes.

What is the most interesting topic on Tic-Talk?

The most popular topic among both groups of pupils was that of the existence of the Devil. This was mentioned by 13 of the 30 responders. The reason for its popularity is partly a reflection of the religious and moral interest of the pupils and partly because it was seen to generate debate and differences of opinion. The religious motif generally was popular among pupils as it seemed to provide a narrative backcloth and a common point of reference for cross-cultural discussion. The next most popular topic seems to have been the discussion around the use of animals for medical research as this seemed again to touch on existing views, often strongly held, but where clear positions can be identified on both sides of the argument.

Have you learnt any new words or phrases in the target language?

The following table lists the target-language words and phrases that the responders gave in response to this question:

London group		French group
how to say 'what do you think?'	fully	anyway, that's about it
le diable	nonetheless	loads of love
les humains	mainstream	theme
chrétien	disabled	I will introduce myself in brief
vas-tu	Mars stuff	terms
vacances	probe and buggy	what more can I say?
en voyage	fluently	unexpectedly
je crois en Dieu	currently	guys
je peux te demander de m'aider	worldwide happiness	hope
rester sur place	otherwise	acute
	evil	perfumes
	mainstream culture	personality
	worrisome father	cripple
	seagulls	pressure
	peers	smart and equal
	perhaps	cosmetic research
	however	skin ointments
	earth	chemotherapy
	dull	leukemia
	freedom	
	also	
	as for the butler	
	shocked	
	upon	

If one compares the two lists, it is interesting to note that the London group (linguistically less proficient and confident than the French group) seem to be much less conscious of acquiring specific lexical items through the project. The examples they do provide also seem to cluster around the main themes that interested them (namely, religion and travel). Furthermore, the list includes three cases of questions. In contrast, the French group are able to put forward a much longer list that spans a wider range of vocabulary and more complex idiom. Interestingly, despite the longer list the only question included is not a real one but a rhetorical question used by a Canadian bilingual student in one of the groups: 'What more can I say?' It may be that this gives us an indication of the kinds of linguistic gains that are registered with participants operating at different levels of linguistic and intercultural competence and confidence. Yet the London pupils' perceived gains in the practice of question formulation may be a reflection of the relative lack of focus on this linguistic feature in conventional lessons.

Has the project helped your French/English?

Perceptions of specific lexical gains merit comparison with the pupils' comments on how the programme helped their learning of the language more generally. In a way, reversing the patterns of responses to the question about words and phrases, here it is the London group who almost unanimously stated that the project did help their French. Of those that elaborated on how it had helped, the most common references were to improvement in writing. Others referred to 'understanding', 'confidence', 'asking', and 'grammar and vocabulary'. In contrast, half of the French group said that the project had not helped them with the learning of their English. Of those that did find it helpful, one pupil made the comment that it was a form of 'language learning on the job' (*sur le tas*) which is a perceptive metaphor of language learning through having to use it in sustained and structured interaction.

Suggestions for improvement

Many of the respondents expressed satisfaction with the programme and did not offer suggestions for improvement. However, echoing feedback from pupils in other studies on their use of online technologies, some of those who did make suggestions wanted more graphics and pictures. It would seem that the quality and attractiveness of the visual and other design features of the virtual environment play a key role in the motivation of users in this age range. Some would also have liked a faster turnover of discussion topics and a faster pace of interaction. Others suggested including more people in each group, especially in groups where only a small number contributed.

Interview data

The second base of evidence on pupils' perceptions of Tic-Talk and their participation in it was gathered from semi-structured interviews with a sample of pupils at two participating schools in England, and a focus-group interview with a selection of the participating students at a Canadian *lycée*. In order to probe the positive motivational and learning benefits of the forum, interviewees were selected on the basis of the volume of messages they posted.

Reading input

The most prolific of the UK 'posters' made an interesting comment, when asked which discussion topics he found most interesting: 'especially the

French ones. It was interesting to find out what they were saying.' Rather than pointing to a specific topic, as most of the other interviewees did in answer to this question, Ovie refers to the language and to the textual input. This echoes a more general comment he makes about what he considered to be the most valuable aspect of the whole project:

> I think it would be the French. When French people speak French it's different, it's more, it's not as standard as how we learn. I think that's the main point. You learn lots of new phrases that are quite useful when you're speaking not just writing.

One of the issues emerging from this comment is the importance of reading others' messages. From the Tic-Talk evidence, it would seem that only a minority of the English participants dwelt sufficiently on the messages written by their French counterparts, and therefore did not exploit the texts sufficiently as reading stimulus. Some perhaps weaker students or those who were less fully engaged within their group tended to focus simply on their own contribution and therefore failed to contribute to the development of threads of discussion in any meaningful way. One of the potential implications of this from a pedagogical point of view is the involvement of the classroom teachers in exploiting extracts from the CMC discussions as stimuli for language teaching in the classroom, and, more indirectly, as material for developing their pupils' reading strategies. At the interview Ella explained her use of questions in the group discussions as a way of generating responses in French which would help develop her French reading competence: 'Yes. I thought interacting with people and stuff, if they were to reply in French, would help me with my reading.' This suggests that personal interaction can play a special role in enhancing the pupils' receptivity to textual input. Perhaps messages addressed to oneself are likely to trigger more intensive attention than textual material addressed to others or to a general audience.

The asynchronous character of the interactions meant that the more confident or more focused of the participants were able to produce fairly lengthy and considered textual messages which were rich in linguistic as well as content material.

Learning value

One of the recurrent comments made by different interviewees was that the 'genre' of written communication generated by the forum was different to the type of written exercises they were normally required to do in lessons. Ovie describes this genre as 'conversational writing'.

> I think it's a bit more difficult writing in French about ideas cos we haven't really done much conversational writing. When we have writing tasks it's like write about your holiday, things like that. So I think it is something different . . . it's just practice really. As you do more of it you get better.

Similarly, Amy describes this form of writing as being different to the meaning-deficient writing activities in lessons, and therefore as seeming to provide a new and valued learning benefit in her eyes:

> *I:*   What about the language-learning aspect of it? Do you feel your French has improved in any way?
>
> *A:*   Yes, at first we weren't ready to write in French except in the conversation ones. Then because you were properly describing yourself – when you are writing in tests I suppose you can make up whatever you want because, well, you're not really going to know – but when you were writing on there, you wanted people to know actually about you so you were writing proper things that were interesting. You've got to write properly.

The distinctness of the linguistic experience is described by Tejumade as 'I've used words I've never seen before'.

Many interviewees also commented on the learning value of some of the content of the messages. Ovie pointed to some of the content learning in the topic discussions: 'I think for some of them – again Mother's Day, you explained how it is in France. It was quite interesting to find out about that.' For others, like Juliet, the experiences of exchanging messages about their cultural backgrounds were viewed as interesting vehicles for learning:

> I find that really interesting. Share ideas with someone. I had a conversation with one of the girls. She asked me to speak about my culture and everything. I really enjoyed talking about it. She wanted to know everything about my culture and I wanted to know about hers. Even though I didn't know her.

Exploring strategies used in writing

The exchanges can provide useful material for discovering the participants' thinking and strategies used when confronted with linguistic obstacles in the process of communicating in the target language. The following is an example of a stimulated recall technique used during an interview with Tejumade in which we looked together at an extract of a sequence of messages in the discussion on the topic of the existence of the Devil. The first message in this extract is from Gwenaelle, a pupil at a French *lycée*, and the second from Tejumade, a pupil at a school in London:

Gwenaelle

Date: 16 December 12:30 p.m.

Bonjour,

pour repondre à votre question je pense que le diable existe!! Oui parce que je suis chrétienne et dans le monde dans lequel on vit on voit le mal partout. Le diable c'est le mal!! On voit du mal dans toutes les guerres qu'on voit sans arrêt, dans ce que l'être humain devient!!!!

Je pense aussi qu'après la mort il y a l'enfer et le paradis, ce serait impossible que notre vie s'arrête quand on meurt, il y a forcément quelque chose apres la mort; L'enfer existe sûrement mais on ne peut pas le prouver!!!

Je pense que les hommes qui représenteraient le plus le diable sont les chercheurs pour le clonage et tout ce qui va avec!!! Car ils se prennent pour Dieu, ils veulent créer des hommes et cela vient surement du diable!!! Je ne vois pas d'autres hommes possibles, mais je pense pas qu'il y ait beaucoup de monde d'accord avec moi mais c'est ce que je pense!!

Translation: Hi,

To answer your question I think the devil exists! Yes because I am Christian and in the world in which we live we see evil everywhere. The devil is evil! You can see evil in all the wars we see all the time, in what human beings are turning into! I think also that after death there is heaven and hell, it's not possible that our life stops when we die, there has to be something after death; hell definitely exists but we can't prove it!

I think the people who resemble the devil most are scientists who research cloning and everything that goes with that! Cos they act as if they are God, they want to create humans and that definitely comes from the devil! I can't see other possible humans, but I don't think there are a lot of people who agree with me but it's what I think!

From: Tejumade

Date: 19 December 2003 10:41 a.m.

Bonjour, je pense que le diable existe car je suis aussi chrétienne. Je crois que le diable existe dans la société que nous humains habitent dans ces jours et qu'il est toujours en forme d'homme. Je pense vraiment qu'il est toujours au travail donc il faut faire attention.

C'est tout.

Translation: Hi, I think the devil exists because I too am Christian. I believe that the devil exists in the society which we humans live in these days and that he is always in human form. I really think that he is always at work so we have to watch out.

That's all.

At the interview, Tejumade was asked to talk about how she processed Gwenaelle's message and about decisions she made in her own production:

T: It was OK there was a word I didn't understand you know.

I: Such as?

T: At first I didn't know what *chrétienne* was. Then I learnt it was 'Christian'.

I: How did you find out it was 'Christian'?

T: It sort of looked like 'Christian'. Just to make sure, I asked my teacher . . .

I: *Je pense que le diable existe car je suis aussi chrétienne.* That's an interesting sentence because you said that *chrétienne* you didn't understand what it was. It was a new word for you and yet you were using it here.

T: What I tend to do is that I use their text too to help me. If they say 'I am a Christian' then I also write 'me too, I'm also a Christian'. So basically, I use their text to help me and sometimes I add a bit of my own so they understand me.

I: So you deliberately used some of the words that you found from them to help you.

T: Yes.

I: So the fact that you are a Christian and she says she's a Christian, is that interesting, something you've got in common?

T: Yes it's interesting but I'd also like to hear the opinions if the others replied. Maybe they weren't Christians and they had their opinions about the Devil. I'd also like to hear their opinions as well. But there was also, I felt I could connect with her, she was Christian and I was Christian. We have the same beliefs, etc. It was OK.

One of the striking aspects of Tejumade's rationalization of her language use here is that she uses the native speaker input as a kind of model or writing frame for her own production: 'I use their text to help me.' This modelling is both textual (producing similar sentences) and conceptual (we're both Christians). Tejumade describes her own contribution as an addition: 'I add a bit of my own.' What seems to be happening here is a process of learning that is naturally Vygotskyan, in the sense that the learner here may be pushing herself to move up a step within her zone of proximal development through scaffolding provided by the native speaker peer. But what she focuses on in this instance is a word which has conceptual resonance for her. In other words, in this instance the zone can be defined as both linguistic and conceptual.

Conclusions

The role of the teacher and the programme administrator

One of the key questions that arises from a project like this relates to the nature of the role of the instructor (in the classroom and in the virtual environment). Though Tic-Talk was designed as a forum for naturalistic encounters between the participants with minimal intrusion from teachers and administrator, the full pedagogical potential of such an environment can only be realized by developing the roles of the teachers involved. As stated earlier, my own role as coordinator consisted primarily of keeping the ball rolling. Beyond the initial organization of the groups and the ongoing management of the logistics, I restricted my pedagogic role to that of feeding the discussions through selecting and carefully designing the sequences of topics and activities that changed more or less on a weekly basis. Interestingly, some of the Canadian participants who took part in a focus-group interview with the project teacher commented on the limitations and benefits of my relatively constrained presence:

I: Est-ce que ce que Michael a fait comme animateur, c'est suffisant? (Is what Michael did as coordinator sufficient?)

P1: Bien moi, je préférerais qu'il donne son point de vue lui aussi pour voir qu'est-ce qu'il pense. C'est tout le temps intéressant de savoir. (Well I'd prefer him to give his point of view also so we can see what he thinks. It's always interesting to know.)

I: Son point de vue par rapport au sujet de la discussion? (His view on the topic of discussion?)

P1: Oui exactement, vu que c'est lui qui dirige. (Yes exactly, since he's the one directing.)

I: Toi, ta réaction? (Your reaction?)

P2: Par rapport à ce qu'elle dit que l'animateur donne son point de vue, dans un forum de discussion peut-être que ce qu'on peut dire . . . international quand il montre c'est intéressant, mais si jamais c'est pris dans la classe ici c'est le professeur l'animateur, moi je pense que c'est pas une super de bonne idée que le prof donne son point de vue au début. (In relation to what she was saying about the coordinator giving his opinion, in a discussion forum which is perhaps international when he shows something it's interesting, but if it is the class teacher here who is the coordinator, I think it wouldn't be a great idea for the teacher to give his point of view at the start.)

I: Ça va enlever la liberté. (It would take away the freedom.)

P2: Puis l'élève il va dire 'ah bien le prof pense comme ça, c'est mieux que moi je réponde comme ça. Alors le prof va être content que je pense la même chose que lui'. (Then the pupil will say 'oh well the teacher thinks this, it's best if I reply like this. So the teacher will be happy that I think like him'.)

I: Donc ça va être moins libre. (So it will be less free.)

The pupils taking part in this exchange are clearly aware of the importance of maintaining a balance between having the freedom to communicate independently in the forum on the one hand, and a structure which will allow them to do this. What the pupils seem to want to avoid most is teacher input regarding opinions and views on the topics of discussion. Other evidence from the project would indicate that what pupils were on the whole very happy to turn to their class teacher for is support with the language. Interestingly, one of the pupils makes a distinction between the class teacher and the project coordinator on the basis that the latter, based at a different country, is providing a more global perspective on a topic.

Limitations of the project

An account of a project such as Tic-Talk would not be honest if it did not include an acknowledgement of the ways in which it was not successful. The division of participants into separate, self-enclosed groups can have the consequence of poor levels of discussion due to lack of participation. There were several pupils each year who contributed very little and in some cases nothing to the exchanges. In some cases this was due to insufficient promotion and encouragement from their class teachers; in other cases it was a personal decision on the part of the pupil, possibly through lack of self-confidence or motivation. For those who did contribute in such groups, lack of an audience and of responses was a frustrating and disappointing experience. Cohesion can to some extent be anticipated but never entirely so, when groups are composed of people of different ages and nationalities. In the latter years of the project, having fewer but larger groups meant that even where there were passive group members, there was still a sufficient number of contributors to keep the forum alive.

A second potential inhibitor of the success of the project was of a structural nature. The international breadth and diversity of the participating schools and pupils was a source of motivation and interest for the pupils (some at interview suggested we include more schools and countries) but this plurality led (especially in the early years of the project) to confusion and therefore breakdowns in communication. This problem was in some cases exacerbated by the asynchronous framework. Given that participants were scattered in different time zones and were constrained by different school timetables, this mode of CMC is the natural choice for any project that wishes to stretch over several months. A negative consequence of this mode, however, is that delays of several days or more can intervene between a message and its reply from interlocutors, thus taking the edge off a lively exchange of views and debate.

Key lessons learnt from Tic-Talk for future projects

Tic-Talk was devised and implemented in an era that predated Facebook and the other social networking sites. With more sophisticated technologies continuing to become available to teenagers, some at least of the limitations and hesitancies experienced by users of Tic-Talk may diminish with similar projects in the future. However, the challenges facing the reluctant pupil and especially the reluctant language-learning pupil in this age range will no doubt remain with us in some form for a long while yet. Added to this, pupils will continue to need help and opportunities to overcome the linguistic and cultural barriers. The lessons from Tic-Talk are that projects of this sort provide a valuable experience of real communicative dialogue involving two languages ('someone is actually going to read this so it has to be good', said Ella at interview about how writing on Tic-Talk differed from normal writing in lessons).

A second main pointer from this project's experience is the importance of structuring such discussions and interactions around opinions and topics of interest. The two criteria are clearly interlinked since pupils will generally have opinions primarily on topics that interest them. Opinions, furthermore, are valuable mediating tools because they are safe zones for pupils to explore, since on the whole there are no right or wrong opinions.

Finally, an important feature of the success of participant interactions generated by Tic-Talk is due to the fundamental principle underlying the project's conception: namely, that the dialogues, interactions, learning and other communicative processes it facilitated were liberally dependent on the use of two languages: French and English. Where pupils wanted to express themselves in their own tongue and not worry about their lack of sufficient competence in the target language, they were free to either codeswitch or simply to use the L1, as Ella explained at interview:

No, I thought I've got a definite opinion about this and I'm sharing my opinion. I wasn't sure how to do it in French and we've only got 20 minutes to write this because it was at the end so I thought it's best I don't faff around trying to sort out . . . I thought it would be more useful if I actually get my ideas out.

Note

1 All translations are my own. They did not appear in the original texts written by the pupils.

References

Ellis, R., Loewen, S. and Erlam, R. (2006), 'Implicit and explicit corrective feedback and the acquisition of L2 grammar'. *Studies in Second Language Acquisition*, 28, (2), 339–68.

Evans, M. (forthcoming), 'Code-switching in CMC: linguistic and interpersonal dimensions of cross-national discourse between school learners of French and

English', in M. Turnbull and J. Dailey-O'Cain (eds), *First Language Use in Second and Foreign Language Learning: Intersection of Theory, Practice, Curriculum and Policy*. Clevedon: Multilingual Matters.

Swain, M. (2000), 'The output hypothesis and beyond', in Lantolf, J. (ed.), *Sociocultural Theory and Second Language Learning*. Oxford: Oxford University Press, pp. 97–114.

Chapter 6

SIDE by side: pioneers, inventors and the tyranny of educational distance

Cal Durrant

Introduction

Australia is a vast land of contrasting climates and topography. Stretching from ten degrees south at the northern tip of Cape York to 43 degrees south at the bottom of Tasmania, its nearly 8 million square kilometres span over three and a half thousand kilometres from north to south and approximately four thousand kilometres from east to west. In relative size, the United Kingdom could fit within this space some thirty-two times over, yet it has a population of just over twenty-one million. Added to this, however, Australia is also the flattest and driest of the continents, with the exception of Antarctica, and it is one of the oldest. And it is its age that has provided such a distinct geography, with a unique set of flora and fauna, characteristics that have attracted large numbers of tourists for over three decades.

Yet Australia's geography and resultant harsh climate have also been determining factors in population settlement since Captain Arthur Phillip established the first European colony at Sydney Cove in 1788. Australians are, in the main, coastal plain and urban dwellers. Almost 70 per cent of Australia's population live in the major cities of Australia, which are pre-dominantly situated along its coastline and concentrated along the eastern seaboard. Of the rest, only just over 2 per cent of the population still call remote or very remote Australia 'home' (ABS 2008). Yet Australians still like to hold on to images of themselves as being larger than life, rugged, outback figures – much like the *Crocodile Dundee* character created and pro-moted by former Sydney Harbour Bridge painter turned film-maker Paul Hogan. Individualistic and self-reliant, yet maintaining a simple philoso-phy of life, perhaps sums up one way of interpreting the 'typical Aussie', though as some media commentators have observed, for Australians to think of themselves as having any single 'national identity' is in many ways just a myth, given its distances between major population settlements and its multicultural diversity, particularly since World War II. According to Graeme Turner, our national identity is 'in a sense a "national fiction" Australians collaborate in producing every day' (Turner 1993: 247). So where do such impressions come from, and how do they relate to teaching languages via technology over vast distances?

In this chapter, I want to examine some of the ways in which Australian identities have evolved and how these are perhaps surprisingly interconnected with the manner in which distance-education provision has been pioneered in this country using the languages department at the Western Australian (WA) Schools of Isolated and Distance Education (SIDE) as a specific example.

Settlement and the pioneer legend

One of the most enduring of all the myths about Australian identity is that of the 'pioneer'. The term 'pioneer' – referring to the European men and women who first arrived and helped tame the landscape – gained currency in the 1890s. Over time, the term was generalized to include not just the early explorers but all those who turned their hands to the land (Hirst 1982). The influential writers Henry Lawson and A. B. (Banjo) Paterson helped in part to establish and perpetuate this myth of a better, classless society inhabited by the pioneers. Painters like Frederick McCubbin also built on this perspective; his *The Pioneers* contains three panels depicting the toil and victory of the selectors from their first arrival in the forest to their established selection and finally the triumph of the harvest scene. This version of Australia's past reached its pinnacle with the eventual inclusion of convicts as pioneers. The celebration of pioneers met its challenge with the outbreak of World War I and the emergence of the ANZAC legend. As Hirst observes, after 1916, Australian schoolteachers were encouraged to 'link diggers, explorers and pioneers together' and so the 'digger' myth was born (Hirst 1982: 33). It took until just before World War II for these myths to be closely interrogated. Xavier Herbert (*Capricornia*) was one of the first writers to do this with his explicit alignment of pioneers with 'the enemy' as far as Indigenous welfare was concerned. More recent connections between early white settlers in Australia and some of the more devastating ecological challenges to what is often called marginal farming land, brought about by clearing practices that paid scant regard for the future welfare of the soil, lend further support to such a critique.

One of the other interesting aspects of Australian-identity formation has been the changing attitude towards convicts. During the convict era, this cohort was very much at the bottom of the social scale; now, Australians turn to formal organizations devoted to searching for convict heritage, and if there is an Irish connection identifiable, then status is even further enhanced.

Nevertheless, the view that Australians take of themselves is still more closely connected to notions of 'the bush pioneer' than to those of the 'city slicker'. Australia's remoteness, isolation and economic reliance on the land have helped sustain such views, even though population trends have nearly always denied it. What has finally emerged from the pioneer legend is the idea that, while the original definition of pioneer may have had a military connotation and referred to a soldier who, much like a scout, went ahead of the main force to 'prepare the way', the meaning has now been extended to refer to anyone who invents something or shows the way forward for others. Thus the explorers were pioneers in the sense that they opened up the land by surveying and mapping it; the settlers became pioneers in that they developed the land traversed by the explorers, though, as Hirst so aptly asks, for whom apart from themselves? Theirs became a pioneering for the future rather than their own generation. Convicts have more recently been included in the pioneer bracket because of their involvement in building towns and cities as well as the arterial roads that connect them. The term is now popularized to the extent that we hear references to people such as 'pioneers of aviation' in Australia, which merely refers to those who helped develop and adapt the principles and opportunities of aviation to this particular landscape, and one that has a particularly close connection to the distance-education focus of this chapter via the Royal Flying Doctor Service (RFDS). Whatever its current meanings, those who inhabited Australia kept pushing further and further away from the heavily populated centres in order to find land that would help sustain them, and as they set up their families in homesteads and on large cattle runs or established small rural communities, two things became apparent: first the sheer inventiveness required to survive, and second the recognition that their offspring needed schooling.

Inventions

The harsh environment in which many of the early settlers, pastoralists, selectors and prospectors found themselves meant that in order to get on, they had to find solutions to problems not faced in their country of birth. Self-reliance and ingenuity became key factors in their survival. Consequently, inventiveness is another one of those characteristics that is often identified with being Australian. Such claims are not without some foundation; Australians have been instrumental in some important discoveries and in developing a surprising number of inventions, and by no means has this been restricted to European resourcefulness; Indigenous Australians developed unique and highly successful hunting weapons like the woomera and the boomerang long before the white man's arrival. More recent Australian successes have included the following:

- the world's first pre-paid postal system in 1838
- the grain stripper that cut and removed the grain into storage in 1843
- the underwater torpedo – Louis Brennan in 1874
- the stump-jump plough in 1876
- ship refrigeration allowing meat exports from Australia to Europe in 1879
- the first electric drill by Arthur Arnot in 1889
- free-style swimming – called the 'Australian Crawl' during the early 1900s
- the first feature film (*The Story of the Kelly Gang*) in 1906
- the first automatic totalizator by Sir George Julius in 1913
- Aspro pain relief by George Nicholas in 1917
- the RFDS by the Rev John Flynn in 1928
- the Hills Hoist rotary clothesline by Lance Hill in 1945
- the Victor two-stroke rotary lawnmower by Mervyn Richardson in 1952
- R. N. Morse's solar hot-water system in 1953
- the Black box flight recorder by Dr David Warren in 1958
- the Orbital engine by Ralph Sarich in 1972
- the Cochlear implant by Professor Graeme Clark in 1979
- the baby safety capsule for infant car travel in 1984 and
- the first multi-focal contact lens by Stephen Newman in 1992

(Convict Creations [n.d])

Inventiveness, then, has also been identified as being yet another aspect of identity formation and a significant factor in taking on the tyranny of educational distance in the harsh and relentless Australian landscape.

Pioneers of correspondence

At the time of the 1881 census in the colony of New South Wales (NSW), some 20,000 children were being educated at home, representing almost 13 per cent of the total student population. As examinations assumed a more important role in colonial schooling during the 1890s, it was recognized that students educated in formal school settings performed better than those receiving domestic tuition. With the extension of settlement into the farthest reaches of the state by 1901, many private and state-funded schools were established in inland regions and the percentage of students relying on tutors, governesses or their mothers began to decline (Barcan 1965).

Early attempts to address the issues of distance and schooling included the appointment of itinerant male teachers who were allocated a district where they visited children living in remote locations at least twice a year. The teacher delivered a number of lessons, swapped used books for more advanced ones, set work to be done by his next visit and then left the parents to act as tutors until next time. Victoria, while the smallest of the mainland states, was the first to use the itinerant teacher system from 1874. Queensland picked it up after the turn of the century, but because of the long gaps between visits, the system was deemed to be far from efficient (Higgins 1994). As for secondary schooling, the principal pathway for children in remote areas remained the long and costly absences at boarding schools in the major cities or regional centres across the country.

By 1922, Queensland had exchanged the itinerant teacher system for the Primary Correspondence School. While it provided a cheaper education provision for the State Education Department, students and parents lost the human contact of the itinerant teachers, apart from the exchanges of written information. In addition, the turnaround time and the inconsistent delivery of mail to remote parts of the country made it more difficult to maintain a sense of continuity, despite the acknowledged quality of the actual materials. Students and their parents were caught on a perpetual merry-go-round of waiting for the next set of lessons to arrive, completing the ones already received and trying to pick up the threads of responses on returned work submitted many weeks before.

Queensland's Correspondence School conducted this type of schooling for the next fifty years, though technological innovations were introduced along the way, including the addition in 1923 of travelling domestic-science railway carriages followed by manual training ones in 1925 (Queensland Department of Education, Training and the Arts 2006). During its peak in World War II, over 7,000 students were enrolled at the school.

Other state systems also took advantage of an expanding and ever more reliable mail network in Australia. Correspondence schooling commenced in NSW in 1916, and by the time Queensland had converted from itinerant teachers to the Primary Correspondence School, NSW had nearly 600 students enrolled in primary-level correspondence schooling (Barcan 1988). In WA, the largest state in terms of area but as yet sparsely populated, correspondence classes commenced soon after in 1918 and rapidly progressed to offering some secondary schooling, due in part to the fact that students in the far north of the state were so removed from Perth (Mossenson 1972). By the outbreak of World War II, correspondence lessons were being provided for children with special needs who lived in Perth and also for Indigenous children living in pastoral districts or on Aboriginal Mission stations that did not have schools.

NSW also embraced secondary correspondence work in 1922, just before the Correspondence School was shifted to the site of the old Blackfriars Teachers' College. It gained international recognition when the founding Principal, Walter Finigan, delivered the opening address at the First International Conference on Correspondence Education held in Canada in 1938. Some claim that Blackfriars served as the model on which other countries based their own distance schooling programmes (Sydney Distance Education High School [n.d.]).

Australian Schools of the Air (SOTA)

In line with the ingenuity displayed by the list of inventions outlined above, attempts by Australians to overcome the remote nature of the outback have led to significant educational innovations. These include 'the use of itinerant teachers, mobile tent schools, the use of VHF radio for lessons, satellite teaching for remote properties, interactive television teaching' and, more recently, high-speed broadband IP-based provision (Higgins 1994: 57). The standard of the learning packages developed for children living in isolated and remote areas of this country has long been recognized as being among the highest in the world.

The first real impact of technology on distance-education provision – apart from the improvement in transport access via motorized technology – followed the improvements in radio broadcasting that came about during World War I. In NSW, after some rather disappointing experiments in 1924, the Australian Broadcasting Commission (ABC) broadcast a number of educational programmes in 1933. It was slow to grow, mainly because teaching methods were not always appropriate for the medium and also the cost of purchase, upkeep and licences for radio receivers had to be carried by the users.

The RFDS began operations in 1928 and in a few years was part of an extensive radio network across Australia's outback regions. At that time, the network relied on pedal-powered radio transmitters invented by another Australian, Alfred Traeger, in 1929 (Traeger's pedal sets were still being sold to developing countries in the 1960s, and in 1970, his company provided an educational radio network for Canada (ADB 2006)). He and the RFDS founder, the Rev John Flynn, often talked about other potential uses of the radio network. In 1944, a female member of the Council of the RFDS of South Australia made the suggestion that two-way radio might be a useful method of providing education to children living in remote areas. In 1951, three half-hour broadcasts a week commenced from the Alice Springs RFDS centre; it was the beginning of the Alice Springs School of the Air, the first of its kind anywhere in the world (SOTA Alice Springs).

Other states with school-age children living in remote areas were quick to pick up on the idea. In 1953, Victoria introduced short-wave broadcasts that allowed students to hear their teachers' voices. It also allowed for teachers to hear their students' voices for the first time; it was a new pioneering experience for remote rural students (Distance Education Centre, Victoria).

A SOTA was opened in Broken Hill in 1956. It began with a single teacher offering three hours of two-way radio contact for pupils scattered across the outback in NSW, Queensland and South Australia (NSW Department of Education 1980). WA had commenced radio broadcasts for correspondence students in 1940, but this was expanded with the establishment of the first WA School of the Air at Meekatharra in 1959. Once again, it was achieved by using the RFDS's two-way radio network, though the transmissions were from a classroom in the town (SIDE 2008b).

Australian SOTA received international attention during the 1960s through the success of the Australian television programme *Skippy the Bush Kangaroo*. By 2005, over sixteen SOTA had been established around Australia. This network connected students scattered across over 1.5 million square kilometres. Of course, the largest and most remote areas are to be found in WA, and it is to this part of the continent that we now shift our attention.

WA

WA makes up one-third of Australia's land mass and is some three and a half times the size of Texas. The capital Perth is recognized as being the most remote capital city in the world; in fact it is closer to Singapore than it is to the national capital, Canberra. Because of its two and a half million square kilometres, WA experiences quite dramatic shifts in climate, particularly between the tropical northern extremes of the state and the temperate south. As with the rest of the mainland, the greater the distance from the coast, the more extreme are the temperature variations. Marble Bar in the north holds the world record for the most number of consecutive days (160) with temperatures in excess of 37 degrees Celsius, while the hottest place in Australia is Wyndham with an annual mean temperature of 29 degrees. It is unsurprising, then, that the most concentrated population centres are located along WA's 12,000 km coastline, with over 70 per cent of the population living in the south-west corner of the state where temperatures are milder (Wilkins 2006). But it is the remote, more sparsely populated parts of the state that have presented the greatest challenges to education authorities in WA.

Distance education in WA

The first SOTA in WA was established at Meekatharra in 1959. The original Teacher in Charge remained under the jurisdiction of the Correspondence School in Perth, and that's how it stayed for the next twenty years until it was established as an autonomous school on removal to Meekatharra District High School in 1975. As with other Australian SOTA – as outlined above – a close relationship existed between the school and the RFDS. It made use of the flying service's radio frequencies until its transfer to the high school. In 1995, the building was further extended and refurbished (Meekatharra SOTA 2008).

A year after the Meekatharra SOTA started, the Kimberley SOTA was established at the RFDS base in Derby, later transferring to the Derby District High School in 1981. Twelve months later, it gained its own radio frequency, reducing the amount of interference to lessons from RFDS traffic. Other users were not the only problems encountered by radio users of the time:

> The radio reception was very poor with students and teachers often frustrated by severe static, and misunderstandings of what was being asked. Bad weather and sunspots, interference from Indonesian fishing vessels and batteries used to power the radios often going flat or being used in vehicles, made teaching and learning in this environment extremely difficult. (Kimberley SOTA 2008)

Lessons were conducted by the class teacher at approximately the same time every day and they ran for about thirty or forty minutes. The Kimberley SOTA received further additions to its operation in 1987 and 1990, before getting a new purpose-built construction of its own in 2002.

Kalgoorlie SOTA commenced broadcasting 'air lessons', as they are still called, in 1962. Like its sister organizations, the Kalgoorlie SOTA was built around the RFDS radio network. In 1991, it relocated to the historic Boulder Technical School site erected in 1905. Most of the students served by the Kalgoorlie SOTA live on pastoral stations but there are some whose parents are employed in more exotic occupations such as prospecting for gold or cutting sandalwood. Still others provide essential services to some of the region's remote locations (Kalgoorlie SOTA 2008).

Though it is the second smallest of the WA schools, the Port Hedland SOTA services the largest area of over half a million square kilometres. It began transmitting radio lessons to the Pilbara in September 1964. Twenty-four years later, a new building at the International Airport was opened to house both the RFDS and the Port Hedland SOTA; despite their close association at all SOTA sites, it is the only remaining joint venture of the two organizations in WA (Port Hedland SOTA 2005).

The final school to open was the Carnarvon SOTA in 1968. According to the first Principal, Frank Atkinson, the accommodation was a converted washroom next to the toilets at the Carnarvon Primary School:

We opened with about 32 children from Years 1 to 5. The following year, numbers increased to just over 40. A number of these were on rented sets which were subsidized by the lotteries commission. The greatest numbers of children were in grades 1, 2 and 3. (Carnarvon SOTA 2008)

Distance-education programmes went through a number of restructures in WA during the latter half of the last century. In 1983, the then state Minister for Education, Robert Pearce, launched the Distance Education Centre that was an amalgamation of the WA Correspondence School, the Isolated Families Early Childhood Correspondence Scheme and the Isolated Students Matriculation Scheme. Twelve years later, the SIDE were formed out of the merger of the Distance Education Centre in Perth and the five WA SOTA. The expansion of communications media in the Perth centre enabled the fast tracking of alternative delivery modes via technological advances across the state (SIDE 2008b). And it is to this delivery mode that we now turn.

SIDE and language study

I want to examine a number of aspects of the SIDE operation in relation to language learning as realized through its publications, reports and media exposure. In particular, I want to look briefly at the following areas that appear to be of most relevance:

1. clientele
2. subject/language offerings
3. partnerships
4. supporting languages instruction delivery
5. impacts of technological change and
6. results

Clientele

One of the interesting realities of modern-day distance education in WA is that the clientele is changing, just like everything else. In fact, in 2008, remote students are no longer the largest of the student cohorts. SIDE now caters for a great number of students who come from a range of circumstances; this new clientele comprises traditional full-time students who are not able to attend because of their geographically remote locations, children who call WA home but who are on extended interstate or overseas travel with their parents, regular school students who through timetable clashes or staff shortages are unable to take their subject of choice at their own high school, those who are dealing with serious or extended illnesses and even adults who want to improve their education or employment prospects by studying school subjects part-time.

Subject/language offerings

As a consequence, SIDE attempts to offer the full range of subjects available at most primary and high schools, including a comprehensive selection of Tertiary Entrance eligible courses; it provides a large number of audio and visual resources specifically prepared for distance learning and has a fully equipped Resource Centre from which students may borrow items. In more recent times, with advances in technology and pedagogy, the emphasis has shifted to more interactive lesson delivery via radio, television and digital technology (SIDE 2008a), advances that open up ways of supporting students who choose to study languages other than English.

In 2007, the languages department at SIDE had twenty-seven language teachers who taught across Indonesian, French, Italian and Japanese in Years 3–12. The department services over 1,800 students who are either without language teachers or who, for other reasons, are unable to access a language at their own school (SIDE 2007a; SIDE 2006).

Partnerships

SIDE has had to reconsider the way it operates in order to foster partnerships with a number of other schools and institutions (Chamberlain 2007). This involves liaising with school systems as well as individual schools. Trying to maintain quality delivery across such geographically and culturally diverse regions remains a challenge to any provider, but SIDE has attempted to address this in relation to its languages programmes by signing a Memorandum of Understanding with both Primary and Secondary State Government Schools in WA (SIDE 2007e).

In 2007, John Willcock College in Geraldton, a rapidly growing city over 400 kilometres north of Perth, joined the SIDE languages programme. Over 200 Year 8 and 9 students who were new to the language, unfamiliar with SIDE processes and with no knowledge of how to engage with Centra – SIDE's interactive online delivery software package – enrolled to study Japanese. Significant additional enrolments such as these require skilful coordination amongst the Japanese teachers, the Learning Development Support team at SIDE, the remote supervisors, the new school and its administration as well as the students themselves (SIDE 2007c). Another consideration for partnerships is the requirements of specific communities. For instance, Useless Loop primary school situated south of Carnarvon completed a range of activities centring on Japan during a language teacher's visit in late 2007. One of the reasons for the school choosing Japanese as the language for their younger students commencing in 2008 is that the large salt mine in the area is owned by a Japanese company (SIDE 2007d). Similarly, more formal partnerships developed with large companies can be of mutual benefit; during 2007, BHP Billiton covered all costs for SIDE personnel visits to Leinster primary school, a mining community situated some 650 kilometres northeast of Perth (SIDE 2007e).

Supporting languages instruction delivery

From its early beginnings with itinerant teachers, Australia's distance-education providers have relied on teachers visiting their students at least twice annually in order to provide a human face to what can be a lonely experience. Despite its associated costs, SIDE has maintained this principle in WA, and teacher visits are regular parts of the distance-education schedule. With more of SIDE's student cohort now being made up of students living in rural and remote districts, but attending schools rather than living on remote cattle stations, teachers often plan their visits in teams. The languages team does regular visits to schools in specific regions; in 2006, 95 per cent of the SIDE languages department participated in school visits to over fifty schools in Western Australia. In a 2007 report, a new staff member hailed one such visit 'The Great Southern Odyssey'. It involved two language teachers travelling in excess of 2200 kilometres in a departmental vehicle and visiting five country schools over three and a half days (SIDE 2007b). School visits are designed to be both educational and interesting, and teachers attempt to immerse their students in the language being studied as well as cultural aspects of their learning. For example, a visit to a district high school (Years K–10) that has just joined the SIDE Italian programme might involve organizing games, preparing Italian food like pizza, ravioli, lasagne, gnocchi and tomato sauce and perhaps conducting a quiz about the regions of Italy and Italian cuisine.

In addition to school visits and maintaining online contact with their students, the SIDE languages department does regular term reports to students and parents via the SIDE journal *Inside Views*. Aside from general information about the study of languages at SIDE, there are regular tips for students about how to achieve success when studying a language by distance. Here's an example from Volume 1 of the 2007 SIDE journal:

- Stay organised. Your language teacher has given you timelines, deadlines, work calendars. Use these tools to help you stay organised.
- Plan for regular study time in your week. This time needs to include revision time too.
- Stay in contact with your Language teacher. Speak to your teacher on the phone or via the post or email, at least every week.
- Enjoy your Language studies! Make the most of every opportunity to speak to other people who speak your Language. Read and listen to as much as you can in your Language.

(SIDE 2007a: 13–14)

Apart from getting involved with their students in celebrating National Languages Week every August, the languages team also focuses on encouraging students to take every opportunity to participate in cultural exchanges such as the Réunion Island Exchange programme for French students, to host students from other countries, to attend cultural events such as film festivals and exhibitions (often held in Perth during term holidays) and to join organizations such as the Alliance Française.

Impacts of technological change

Because of the nature of its work, SIDE has attempted to stay abreast of the latest technologies and their applications to teaching and learning languages in the distance-education mode. Changes have been both regular and rapid, particularly since online course delivery became possible with advances in digital technology. As Head of the Online Teaching and Learning unit, Ross Manson says: 'SIDE is fast becoming a totally "wired" school' (Manson 2008: 8). Traditionally, SIDE students received correspondence or air lessons that were supplemented by telephone tutorials, but in recent years, the move has been towards a more classroom-like learning environment. Alternative delivery systems include:

> the transmission of voice, data or images using a satellite, microwave or terrestrial mechanism. Generally there is no particular technology that is eminently suited for educational purposes, and a mix of telephone, electronic and voice mail, audio teleconferencing, teletext, radio, audio graphics, television, facsimile and videoconferencing is used according to location and circumstances. Other innovations include the production of materials on electronic disks, the development of a number of quality videos, and regular broadcasts via GWN and Westlink throughout regional Western Australia. (SIDE 2008b)

During 2007, SIDE embarked on a major professional development programme for its staff that revolved around the replacement of the Microsoft Conferencing software used by SatWeb students with Centra Symposium. The advantages of the new software include an improved interface where all the required tools are on the one screen; the ability to hold discrete areas for each separate school in the SIDE network; the capacity to use any PC with internet capability to access SatWeb lessons without having to be connected to a satellite dish; and more efficient use of the bandwidth available (Bromage 2007).

To achieve this type of change requires significant time, energy and expertise, and it is clear from SIDE reports that for both the Online Teaching and Learning team (formerly the Learning Delivery Support unit) and the teaching staff, this is still a project in progress in 2008. As with any school, there are frequent changes to staffing at SIDE, though some teachers eventually return to the centre. One such teacher had taught Indonesian at SIDE for six years before returning to a primary school near Dampier in the far north-west of the state. In 2007, she was reappointed to SIDE after two and a half years away; previously, she had taught using telematics, videoconferencing and live television, but on her return faced the challenge of using Centra 'and the other technological advances which have happened while I was away', admitting that it was 'a bit of a learning curve' (Manson 2008: 8).

One of the advantages of Centra is that it is a synchronous or 'live' workspace that can be shared. In some ways, it can be thought of as a visual version of what the early two-way radio transmissions achieved – immediate, personal and interactive connections between teaching staff and their students. With Centra, students and their teachers can both hear and see one another on the same screen-space while sitting at their computers, so that answering questions, demonstrating, explaining concepts or sharing visual images is much as it would be for a standard classroom teacher. Students are also able to interact with their teachers and classmates as though they were right there with them (Manson 2008). Another advantage of the 'virtual classroom' enabled by Centra is that its interactive capacity makes it far easier to engage students for the full lesson of up to fifty minutes than was possible with previous technologies. Head of English, Gerry Lane, suggests that Centra promotes interaction on three levels: with materials, between learners, and between learners and teaching staff (Lane 2008).

As with any significant change, not everything runs smoothly; at the time of this book going to press, SIDE's Centra system was not working with computers using the Vista operating system or with Apple Mac computers. Clearly such glitches make life difficult for those living in isolated places with little technical support, however, the software suppliers were hopeful of these problems being solved before the beginning of Term 3 (Manson 2008).

The languages department at SIDE has embraced the new software as an additional resource, though acknowledging the effects of such innovation in one of their regular reports in *Inside Views*:

> This has been especially the case in our weekly lessons (in Indonesian) with students via *Centra, Janison*, Videoconferencing and Teleconferencing. We've had a number of courses on upgrading our online delivery to make things more 'zippy' and 'hippie-hippie shake' for our students . . . We bid a sad farewell to the SIDE TV show, but never fear, there are more digital 'goodies' coming your way in 2008! (SIDE 2007d: 19)

In general, it would seem that SIDE teachers are extremely happy with the way this software is being applied:

> *Centra* allows us to communicate with our students by talking over the internet, using a head set with microphone, and both student and teacher can draw on a whiteboard that we both can see. I can also show work samples, discuss designs and demonstrate how assessment is completed. (Garnett 2007: 14)

Results

The size of the geographical region that SIDE services, as well as the number and age ranges of its student body, present genuine challenges to all of its teachers, but particularly to those who are engaged in languages education. Yet SIDE students continue to perform remarkably well both in state and national competitions as well as in Tertiary Entrance Examinations (TEE). Until recently, private-school students have tended to dominate state language awards and honours, but in 2006 and 2007, awards to SIDE students have included:

- an Endeavour Fellowship through the Federal Government's Department of Education, Science and Training to travel to France
- an Advanced Diploma in French Language Studies (the only certification recognized by the French Government)
- a Teach and Learn Programme scholarship from the Japanese Consulate to study at the Japan Foundation Institute in Urawa
- the top Year 12 student of French award in the Alliance Française Examinations
- a University of Western Australia Fogarty Foundation Certificate of Excellence in French
- a Western Australian Curriculum Council Certificate of Distinction in Indonesian, based on results gained in the state-wide TEE
- the French Consulate Prize
- the Best Country Student of French award
- outstanding results in the TEE, leading to the Special Subject Award for Italian
- the top Year 10 student in the WA Alliance Française examinations
- four distinctions for primary SIDE students of Japanese in the Australian Language Certificate

Results of this nature constitute one way of measuring the success of a programme, but on what basis might we measure the overall strength of the SIDE's approach to languages education in WA?

Conclusion

In 2001, the Australian government funded extensive research into languages education in Australia through the Department of Education, Science and Training (DEST) under the National Asian Languages and Studies in Australian Schools (NALSAS) Strategy. One of the tasks that the project team, comprising Lindy Norris, Tracey Jones and Ross Gerring, set itself was to examine the operations of a number of distance-education providers of languages education across four Australian states. Out of this research, the project team developed a series of professional development modules designed to demonstrate what constitutes 'best practice' in the distance delivery of languages education. The project is called Facilitating the Learning of Languages Other Than English or FLOTE and the website can be accessed at the following address: www.flote.edu.au/index.htm.

The FLOTE project identifies two key dimensions of a languages-learning environment in a distance-education context: the personal/interpersonal dimension and the pedagogical dimension. One of the challenges for distance educators is that they are once removed from their students, and this makes establishing connections with them particularly difficult. Teachers describe the moment of teaching becoming frustrating, when they realize that problems of understanding and comprehension have arisen, but can't deal with them as easily as they might if the students were sitting in front of them in a classroom situation. Pedagogically, distance educators also need to understand what equipment their students have and the limitations of the tools at their disposal, in particular the lack of body language and verbal cues when students can't see their teacher or their classmates.

In addition to these two dimensions, the project team suggests a number of other essential ingredients for establishing an effective languages learning environment:

- positive attitudes towards language learning
- active support for the learner at both the delivery site and the learning site
- a language-rich environment
- a strong focus on learners learning how to learn and learning how to direct their own language learning

- ready access to the teacher and
- strong relationships between all concerned – teacher, learner, significant other(s)

(FLOTE 2001)

In looking at the SIDE provision of languages education in WA, two things stand out: first, the amount of enthusiasm generated by the languages department itself about learning a second language and some of the benefits of discovering the cultural attachments of that language – and this is evident in their print and online reporting; second, the lengths to which SIDE personnel go in establishing, maintaining and expanding relationships among students, staff at the different SIDE campuses, schools and community organizations, once again evidenced by the growth in student numbers and participating industry partners. Each of the essential ingredients suggested by FLOTE is one that the SIDE administration appears to have addressed, and the current roll-out of the next generation of online technology in the form of the Centra Symposium software promises to provide richer ways of closing the traditional gap between students and their tutors that has dogged distance educators since the days of the pioneers. As one SIDE language teacher suggested at a recent student awards ceremony:

I teach the students over the phone and through online courses and teleconferences . . . We still get to do group work over the phone or on the computer so they don't miss out on much . . . Not having face to face contact with people to practise can be a barrier to learning a language through distance education, but it has not been for these motivated students. (Department of Education and Training 2007)

What SIDE students experience during the first decade of the twenty-first century would be unrecognizable to Correspondence School students a hundred years ago. In many ways, the tyranny of educational distance has already been conquered by educational 'pioneers' with inventive minds and technological ingenuity. National identities are also changing as Australia becomes less monocultural and more identifiably South East Asian rather than Eurocentric. And the languages department at SIDE is also helping to 'pioneer' such change. Nevertheless, it is worth reminding ourselves that today's innovations and inventiveness will also rapidly fade into the past, to be identified as both quaint and old fashioned by future users who will look back with nostalgia on the pioneers of their trade.

Australian historian Russell Ward has suggested that national character 'is not, as was once held, something inherited', but neither is it entirely
the imagination of 'poets, publicists and other feckless dreamers' (Ward
1958: 1). For Ward, national identity is 'a people's idea of itself' which is
something that is generally rooted in some form of reality (ibid.). We might
apply the same principle to the work of distance providers of languages
education in Australia: it is not enough that one has successfully provided
such instruction in the past, but neither is it sufficient to rely on all the
hype about technology alone having the capacity to solve every problem
and meet every challenge presented by the future. Rather, there appears to
be an ever-shifting meeting point along the continuum between history and
futuristic hype; a place where committed educators find a space to blend
traditions of the past with the practicalities and demands of the present
along with visions of the future. Taking the best of these is what the languages department at SIDE appears to be doing, but what that means for
the next generation of Australians who gain their languages education in
distance mode remains to be both seen and investigated.

References

ADB (Australian Dictionary of Biography) (2006), 'Australian dictionary of biography: Traeger, Alfred Hermann (1895–1980)'. Available at www.adb.online.
anu.edu.au/biogs/A120280b.htm (accessed 21 June 2008).

ABS (Australian Bureau of Statistics) (2008), 'Population demographics'. Available
at   www.abs.gov.au/AUSSTATS/abs@.nsf/Lookup/3218.0Main%20Features32
00607?opendocument&tabname=Summary&prodno=3218.0&issue=2006–
07&num=&view (accessed 24 June 2008).

Barcan, A. (1965), *A Short History of Education in New South Wales*. Sydney: Martindale
Press.

Barcan, A. (1988), *Two Centuries of Education in New South Wales*. Sydney: University
of New South Wales Press.

Bromage, J. (2007), 'Online learning – SatWeb'. *Inside Views*. 3, 6.

Carnarvon SOTA (2008), 'A brief history of Carnarvon school of the air'.
www.carnarvonsota.wa.edu.au/SOTA%20History/default.asp#1 (accessed
25 March 2008).

Chamberlain, N. (2007), 'From the principal: ongoing improvements and change'.
Inside Views, 7, 1.

Convict Creations ([n.d.]), 'Australian inventions'. Available at www.convictcrea-
tions.com/culture/inventions.htm (accessed 28 June 2008).

Daymond, K. (2007), 'Languages department report: Indonesian'. *Inside Views*, 6,
12–13.

Department of Education and Training (2007), 'Achievements: le SIDE est mag-
nifique'. *School Matters*, 11, 9.

FLOTE (2001), 'Essential characteristics of an effective learning environment in a distance education context'. Available at www.flote.edu.au/modules_detail. htm?SID=89 (accessed 14 December 2007).

Garnet, P. (2007), 'Design and technology report'. *Inside Views*, 6, 14.

Gilmore, M. (1979), *The Passionate Heart*. Sydney: Angus and Robertson.

Higgins, A. (1994), 'A background to rural education schooling in Australia'. *Journal of Research in Rural Education*, 10, (1), 48–57.

Hirst, J. (1982), 'The pioneer legend', in J. Carroll (ed.) *Intruders in the Bush: The Australian Quest for Identity*. Melbourne: Oxford University Press.

Kalgoorlie SOTA (2008), 'History'. Available at www.emerge.net.au/~kalsota/ information.htm (accessed 25 March 2008).

Kimberley SOTA (2008), 'Sat web lessons'. Available at http://members.westnet. com.au/ksota/radio.htm (accessed 25 March 2008).

Lane, G. (2008), 'English learning area report'. *Inside Views*, 1, 10–11.

Manson, R. (2008), Online teaching and learning'. *Inside Views*, 1, 8.

Meekatharra SOTA (2008), 'About the Meekatharra school of the air'. Available at http://myweb.westnet.com.au/msota/index.html (accessed 25 March 2008).

Mossenson, D. (1972), *State Education in Western Australia: 1829–1960*. Perth: University of Western Australia Press.

NSW Department of Education (1980), *Sydney and the Bush: A Pictorial History of Education in New South Wales*. Sydney: NSW Department of Education.

Port Hedland SOTA (2005), 'Brief history'. Available at www.porthedlandsota. wa.edu.au/www/pages/opening.htm (accessed 25 March 2008).

Queensland Department of Education, Training and the Arts (2006), 'The department of public instruction 1875–1957'. Available at http://education.qld.gov. au/library/edhistory/state/brief/primary-1875.html (accessed 28 June).

SIDE (2006), *SIDE Secondary School: 2006 Annual Report*. Leederville: SIDE.

SIDE (2007a), 'Languages learning area report'. *Inside Views*, 1, 13–14.

SIDE (2007b), 'Languages department report'. *Inside Views*, 2, 11.

SIDE (2007c), 'Languages department report'. *Inside Views*. 3, 18.

SIDE (2007d), 'Languages department report'. *Inside Views*, 7, 18–20.

SIDE (2007e), *SIDE Secondary School: 2007 Annual Report*. Leederville: SIDE.

SIDE (2008a), 'Schools of isolated and distance education overview'. Available at www.side.wa.edu.au/side_overview.html (accessed 25 March 2008).

SIDE (2008b), 'The SIDE story'. Available at www.side.wa.edu.au/side_story.html (accessed 25 March 2008).

Sydney Distance Education High School, 'The history of distance education'. Available at www.sydneyh-d.schools.nsw.edu.au/school/about/history/ (accessed 25 June 2008).

Turner, G. (1993), 'Media texts and messages', in S. Cunningham and G. Turner (eds) *The Media in Australia: Industries, Texts, Audiences*. Sydney: Allen and Unwin.

Ward, R. (1958), *The Australian Legend*. Melbourne: Oxford University Press.

Wilkins, P. (2006), 'Some facts about Western Australia'. Available at www.wilmap. com.au/wa.html (accessed 18 April 2008).

Chapter 7

Teacher and student perceptions of e-learning in EFL

Miranda Hamilton

Introduction

The exploration of technological possibilities to support language learning has moved on apace since the early days of the technological gold rush, where computer-based grammar games and exercises held the key to all linguistic truths, and interaction with the computer was largely a solitary experience. As our burgeoning technological culture leads us toward a utopian vision of a 'network society' (Castells 1996, cited in Hawisher and Selfe 2000: 278) with English as the lingua franca of the internet, the social dimension of electronic exchanges between learners promises to 'foster the building of a learning community' (Arnold and Ducate 2006: 44) thereby liberating the language learner from the constraints of the classroom. If institutions are to aspire to and invest in the dream of normalizing technology (Warschauer 1996), there needs to be a broader understanding about issues surrounding the effective appropriation of technology in EFL teaching. A hiatus currently exists between the technological expertise of the teacher and the techno-confident student, and teachers and learners straddle a digital divide in technological proficiency, which in turn upsets the familiar classroom-learning environment. The diversity of student, teacher and institutional technological understanding raises questions about the disparity that exists between the values and expectations each group places on technology.

This chapter describes teachers' and learners' responses to two projects that involved the integration of CMC in the context of the teaching and learning of EFL to young adult learners within a VLE. The school described is an English-language school in the UK and is part of an international organization, providing English-language education for adults and young learners as well as training EFL teachers. Both young and adult learners come from across the world to the school to learn English, spending up to twelve months learning and improving their language skills both by living in the target language community, and by coming to a school that specializes in the teaching of English as a foreign language. The teachers are native speakers of English, and all classes are taught in the target language. The school is forward thinking and well resourced with purpose-built computer rooms. It also has an established technology-enhanced language-learning (TELL) directive, where new technologies are evaluated for their pedagogical merits and subsequently introduced where deemed appropriate. The two projects described in this chapter formed part of the school's TELL directive.

By way of foregrounding the technology used by the responders in the projects described in this chapter, I will begin by taking a general overview of the development and range of applications of ICT tools in recent years in EFL teaching, so that we can locate the teachers and the learners described in this chapter within an evolving electronic landscape. The subsequent sections of the chapter will then reflect on the responses of the teachers and the learners during two four-week CMC teaching programmes. I will draw on individual interviews conducted before, during and after the teaching programme, examining and contrasting the possible relationships between:

- priorities for language teaching and learning
- previous experiences and perceptions about the value of using technology to support language learning
- the effect of the intervention programme on beliefs and attitudes to the technology used during the intervention programme

With increasingly widespread access to computers in schools and institutions as well as burgeoning technological functionality, it seems that a wealth of opportunities lie ahead for the intrepid ICT pioneer to strike out and explore the pedagogical potential of technological tools that can support language learning. Along with the pace of technological change and the ubiquitous presence of technology it would seem that there is a need for regular re-evaluation, experimentation and investigation into classroom practices with regard to the means by which computers are deployed to support language learning. As we grow in familiarity with the technologies available to us, it seems that boundaries are there to be pushed back, with newly identified needs emerging that would have been previously undreamed of, and are subsequently characterized by improvements in ICT design. Yet despite the pace of technological change, there has been

no systematic analysis of the value teachers and learners attach to its integration in the language classroom. Considering the pace of change and
development, what can be learned from teachers and learners about the
means by which they interact with, appropriate and embed the newly familiar into their pedagogical tool box?

In recent years, we have seen a move away from the static ICT tool in the
form of the CD-ROM, and a transition towards an increasingly dynamic
model that offers online language development and support practice activities. Online activities and teaching resources are now available and are regularly updated by publishers so that they work alongside their course books, as
well as 'open-source' materials that are contributed to and modified by the
language teaching community (for example, Dave's ESL Café, www.eslcafe.
com/). Over the years, teachers and learners have exploited generic Office
tools in the classroom to support the development of language skills. The
advent of word processing has enabled many of our learners to leave behind
the messy, inky process of constructing text. Increasing familiarity with this
technology has seen both teachers and learners building and electronically storing personal banks and records of work. Furthermore, beyond the
challenges that face the learner in the construction of text in the target language, electronic and online dictionaries, spellchecks and phonemic charts
are just some of the tools that have emerged in recent years, offering the
learner quick-fix linguistic solutions. Although these tools create other difficulties for the learner, in the first instance they alleviate the sheer incon-
venience of simply not knowing. Similarly, PowerPoint has led to a wealth
of imaginative classroom activities (see Chapter 4) making it possible for
learners to construct presentations in the target language. Technological
improvements and upgrades mean that projectors and screens are beginning to be replaced by the IWB, adding yet another technological dimension to conventional projector-based presentations, as well as opening the
classroom door to the world beyond with big-screen access to the internet.

In its natural state, the internet seemed in its infancy to be an unruly
creature for teachers and learners that required careful manipulation so
that effective teaching and learning could take place. Teachers exercised
caution as they set learners free to roam in hitherto-uncharted electronic
territories. The ubiquitous presence of the internet at work and at home has
to some extent helped to dispel early suspicions, and we have become more
trusting and tolerant of its random quirks and foibles. Increased familiarity has brought with it the lure and promise of untold internet riches
for exploitation in class as well as in the computer room. In its status as a
resource centre, tailor-made materials can be sourced from the internet,

provided by both the publishers and the online community. At the press of a button the internet can deliver instant and authentic access to the target language. The bold and imaginative create ingenious internet lessons so that learners can explore and linguistically exploit the Web. Although as a resource the internet is still in its infancy with its pedagogical functions still to be understood, it has opened up unimaginable opportunities.

For many teachers, the communicative promise of an express exchange of letters between pen pals through electronic mail has seemed ripe for exploitation in the language-learning classroom. Intrepid pioneers challenged unfathomable logistical obstacles of this form of CMC to expand classroom horizons and set up meaningful electronic exchanges between learners in the target language beyond the remit of the classroom. Although the pedagogical application of email might seem self-evident, reduced technological functionality rendered its exploitation prohibitively complex. Technological improvements have since simplified and extended the range of electronic communicative possibilities, so that we are now witnessing the exploration of the pedagogical potential of chat rooms, discussion forums and online social networking. Improved ICT functionality has eliminated the problem of 'will it, won't it work', although issues of logistics between distant countries and synchronous communication still remain.

Institutions offering distance-learning programmes, where learners and tutors are separated in time and space from one another have, by necessity over the years, appropriated and integrated newly emerging technologies. In recent years, advances and the deployment of a range of communication technologies in the distance-learning community have been described as virtual learning. Yet this is not to say that students who have physical access to classrooms and teachers are not engaging with those same technologies as the distance-learning model. Schools can use the same content, delivered in the computer room. Improved technological functionality raises the threshold of what is pedagogically possible, leading to the emergence of blended learning that might be described as combining the notion of the real-time classroom with virtual learning.

The evolution of the range of technological options that are available for teachers and learners to exploit in the language classroom has led us to the almost inevitable arrival of the VLE. This emergent educational platform promises to alleviate old technological complexities, combining multiple technological elements that have previously functioned as tools in isolation from one another but in the context of the VLE are housed within one technological platform. Language development and support activities can exist alongside links to the internet. Homework can be set, delivered and returned online. Easy access to CMC can generate synchronous and asynchronous discussions between participants. All these tools are located within one platform, with the potential to suit the needs of both the distance and classroom learner.

We have become increasingly familiar with the range of ICT tools we have at our disposal. The presence and development of technological platforms has raised awareness about the multiplicity of applications available to us in the exploitation of ICT to support language learning. We read and hear the argument that we are living in a brave new technological world that promises to transform our learning environments into 'different kinds of centers for learning' (Hawisher and Selfe 1991: 56) and that will revolutionise the teaching and learning of foreign languages (Dunkel, 1987: 254, cited Salaberry 2001: 45). Yet alongside such optimism, concerns have been expressed by People at the Centre of Communications and Information Technologies (PACCIT, an Economic and Social Research Council (ESRC) research programme), suggesting that rapid developments in ICT have not lived up to the promises expressed by early proponents of technology. It is therefore appropriate to turn our attention to teachers and learners, as the lead players in the implementation of the shift towards the integration of technology in learning English as a foreign language.

Priorities for language teaching and learning

The two teachers described in this chapter took part in a four-week ICT project. As part of the project, teachers participated in an intervention programme and delivered a weekly lesson with their students in the school computer room. The technological focus was synchronous and asynchronous CMC in the form of chat rooms and electronic bulletin boards. Synchronous lessons involved students working from their own terminals, chatting to students from another language school in response to pre-determined topics. Asynchronous lessons culminated in students contributing their thoughts and ideas to the school message board. The data that I am describing and reflecting upon has been drawn from their interviews with me before, during and after the intervention programme.

In the first lesson, students chatted synchronously in pairs, online. Before the lesson, they prepared questions and then interviewed students from another language school. The target structures were question formation and superlatives. Students gathered information before writing a profile of their online partner on the message board.

In the second lesson, the target structure was the second conditional and the language of negotiation. Students were paired synchronously with students from another language school and were asked to imagine they were stranded on a desert island. They were provided with a list of seventeen items from which they had to select eight that they agreed would be the most useful. In the final task the students described the choices they had made with their partner on the message board.

The third lesson was asynchronous. Students were provided with a discussion thread and short news story on the message board, before talking about the issues arising from the topic. They were each given different individual readings that represented the points of view of people who had posted their opinions to a public message board. Students mingled and compared their readings before writing and posting their personal response to the topic on the message board.

The final lesson was a jigsaw reading. Using synchronous technology, individual students were paired with students from a different school and exchanged information about their readings before discussing emergent issues. In the final task students wrote a personally reflective piece in response to the topic before posting their work to the message board.

Teacher 1: Anne

Anne was a conscientious teacher with five years' experience in the classroom. She was highly committed to supporting her students' linguistic requirements and expectations, and this was reflected in the organized way in which she approached her lesson planning. She adopted a similarly strategic approach in terms of her priorities for language teaching. In describing her pedagogical preferences, Anne explained that she could be flexible and adapt her approach depending on the students and the focus of the lesson.

> I will do a conventional PPP class, particularly in an exam class, where accuracy is prized so highly, but on the other hand, repeated fluency tasks will back up any kind of accuracy work. There has to be a working towards closing the gap between control and fluency . . . The jump.

A 'PPP class' could be considered to be a more didactic approach where the teacher *presents* the language point, provides the learners with an opportunity for controlled *practice* before encouraging learners to *produce* the target language point in freer practice. Anne discussed her interest in Task-Based Learning (TBL) with the researcher and experimented with this approach during her teacher training. In TBL the teacher doesn't pre-determine the linguistic focus of the lesson, but students collaborate in order to complete a task. The language that forms the basis of the lesson emerges from the task.

Despite her engagement with the two diverse pedagogical approaches, Anne explicitly expressed her concerns about the merits of TBL. In refer-encing Krashen's Monitor hypothesis, where the student consciously notices the language he or she produces, scanning and self-correcting errors, she considered that those students with a less 'well-developed monitor' would be less capable of independently focusing on linguistic accuracy without any additional support from the teacher:

> In the context of Task-Based Learning, if the student is encouraged to produce, produce, produce and there's no correction, no focus and there's no correction afterwards or during, then they won't necessarily improve. Their mistakes are fossilized.

Anne expressed a preference for lessons where the focus was on accur-acy, identifying fluency tasks as a useful support to accuracy work in class. Her comments suggested that she was more comfortable with the more teacher-led PPP approach to language teaching. This was also apparent when she described her perception of the role of the teacher in helping learners to become more accurate language users:

> You have to, in order to gain respect, have a higher level of knowledge than your students, a far higher level . . . Sometimes it's a barrier to them if the teacher doesn't act as an expert.

Furthermore, Anne prioritized meeting the needs and expectations of her learners, which led to a concern about the extent to which learners val-ued more communicative fluency-based lessons. Her priorities were based on her perceived notion of learner expectations and their beliefs about good language learning:

> In terms of student expectations . . . a lot of students feel they should be corrected, so if they are talking to another student, they sometimes feel it's wasted time . . . they don't understand that the aim of the lesson is collaboration.

Teacher 2: Ben

Ben had taught EFL for four years, and was a thoughtful and creative teacher, adopting an easy-going but considered approach in the classroom which made him very popular with his students. Although he did not have the same level of awareness about the range of methodological approaches to language teaching as Anne, Ben also expressed a preference for the PPP model of EFL teaching, as he liked to work more closely to a lesson plan when addressing a new language point, identifying that this was the time to attend to issues of linguistic accuracy: 'I think when you are presenting a new language point, and they're getting it wrong, that's the time for you to . . . model the correct answer.'

However, in discussion he indicated that he valued the principles that lie behind communicative language teaching where there is an emphasis on learners creating meaning and understanding in the target language, mediated by a variety of contexts, rather than simply focusing on form and grammatically accurate linguistic structures. Ben explained how he liked to work with 'freer' language that emerged from the lesson: 'If I'm doing more of a vocabulary thing, then the language tends to come out of the lesson, it's sort of freer.'

In describing the reasons for his preferences in adopting a communicative approach to language teaching, Ben took care to locate himself and his role as the teacher within the classroom: 'Well to, umm, to provide a correct kind of input that's going to get them communicating . . . to generally lubricate the process of communication . . . I like a noisy classroom.'

His perspective on collaboration in the classroom provides an insight into a preference for a more constructivist approach to language learning where by creating the right conditions the learner 'cognitively engages with the meaning' (Esch 1996: 48):

> Because it implies working something out as a group together. So if you don't know something, maybe your friend helps you, and maybe the teacher collaborates as well, so rather than imposing the language point, you're sort of all working together to get to a point of understanding.

The extent to which Ben prioritized the value of communication in his classroom and his teaching was reflected in his observations about the significance of issues of accuracy over fluency. His views were significantly different from Anne's:

> It [accuracy] doesn't bother me a great deal, because I think that the mutual understanding, working out the meaning and talking to one another is part of the process that leads to increased accuracy.

A relationship appears to emerge between the priorities and beliefs Anne and Ben attached to language teaching, and their approach and thoughts about working with technology. Before the CMC intervention programme, they discussed their experiences integrating technology into their teaching of EFL. It appears that the teachers' thoughts about language teaching and technology informed the value they attached in their response to working with a new technological platform during the CMC intervention programme and subsequently in their reflections about the experience.

Responses to using technology in the classroom before the CMC teaching programme

Connections to priorities for language learning

Teacher 1: Anne

Anne considered taking learners into the computer room to be motivating and that it provided learners with both variety and a change of scenery from the classroom, and therefore was a useful technological tool that could be used to encourage learners: 'The novelty factor is quite a large part of it . . . in the computer room it's like an automatic lift in there.'

In terms of approaches to using technology in the classroom, Anne was less clear not only about how it might be effectively exploited but in terms of her perception of how the experience might be of value to the learners. This seems to be related to the priority she attached to her concerns about learners achieving linguistic control and accuracy:

> I will do controlled exercises, but there's a certain 'so what' element, in the sense that I don't know why it's better to do it on the computer than in their books. But free writing, there's a reason to it, it's to do with editing, I find it's easier to edit.

Beyond the classroom Anne felt technology to be of value in terms of making language accessible to learners after class, both in terms of 'backup' as well as supporting work completed in the lesson, and for students who were unable to attend an English language class.

Teacher 2: Ben

Ben felt that technology was a part of his students' world and as such thought that it was an element that could not be ignored. With this in mind, Ben identified two criteria that indicated to him the value of integrating technology into the EFL classroom, both related to technology as a platform for communication. In the first instance, he considered that working with electronic communication had a practical application for his students: 'cos the odds are that they are gonna come into contact with email English.' However, he was unwilling to integrate technology for technology's sake, and he considered it was important, in using technology, 'to be able to see that there's a genuine outcome for the students' which he could identify.

The second criterion was pedagogical. Before the CMC teaching programme, Ben had used a wide range of technological applications in his weekly computer lessons, and had experimented with 'varying degrees of success' with a synchronous chat-room lesson. Despite the difficulties Ben had encountered, he identified with this form of CMC as a means by which students might focus on fluency. By printing off the students' electronic chat he felt that students could then focus on accuracy and reflect on their language:

> I think they can see the value of something like a chat lesson, where you are asking them to have basically a conversation, but have it written down . . . 'cos you can focus on the accuracy, especially if you take a quick print-off.

The early difficulties Ben had experienced in manipulating unfamiliar technology before the CMC teaching programme had not overwhelmed the way in which he identified with the potential application of the technology to the learner. Ben's priorities for language learning in relation to the value of collaboratively arriving at meaning and understanding, and the importance of fluency before addressing issues of accuracy, seem to have influenced the way in which he conceptualized the value of integrating technology in the EFL classroom.

Concerns about working with technology in the EFL classroom

Before the CMC teaching programme, the teachers were asked about the issues that concerned or deterred them about working with technology in the classroom. Both teachers expressed concerns related to confidence particularly with reference to their lack of technological expertise.

On a practical level, Anne and Ben both expressed their anxiety about problems relating to technical failure, because they would neither be able to diagnose nor to fix the problem, particularly in a live classroom. Their fear was that they might find themselves with a group of expectant students without a lesson, as Ben described: 'Sometimes the computers just go down, and that can really bring a lesson to a halt . . . you feel the rug has really been pulled from under you.'

Anne explained that her fear of technical failure was a major cause for anxiety, because it represented such a challenge to her preferred approach in the classroom, which was to meticulously plan each stage of the lesson: 'When something goes wrong and how to deal with that . . . so frightening . . . I'm not very good at winging it, I don't like winging it!'

These concerns seemed to challenge how Anne and Ben perceived themselves through the eyes of their students. Anne felt that, in order to gain respect, the teacher should be seen as an expert with a 'far higher level' of knowledge, so that in the computer room her fears about experiencing technological difficulties acted as a deterrent: 'Problems and restrictions stop me experimenting to the extent that I'd like to.' When things went wrong, Ben explained how he had a tendency to become more authoritative and that it 'brought out the sort of dictator in me!'. Ben had previously described how he felt that his learners needed to trust that the teacher knew what he was doing. Ben's description of his dictatorial response when things went wrong for him upset his natural preference for a collaborative, communicative and 'noisy' classroom.

On a pedagogical level, Anne and Ben both felt they lacked the depth of experience of teaching in the computer room, with Ben suggesting that this had an impact on his level of flexibility and his ability to respond instinctively to events as they emerged during the lesson:

> If you were very often in there, then you'd have a lot of computer lesson plans up your sleeve, in the same way that you have fillers in class with the board, you know 'back to the board'. You'd have a lot of techniques.

His observation reflects his pedagogical preference for responding to the emergence of 'freer' language and events in class.

Anne felt that she could anticipate and prepare for difficulties by taking more time to plan her computer lessons, but simultaneously this strategy also deterred her because of the amount of time the additional preparation represented: 'I'd need time to experiment to see its restrictions, to anticipate any technical hitches that might take place, and that takes an awful long time.' Despite the confidence with which Anne and Ben approached their teaching, and their enthusiasm to participate in the CMC teaching programme, fear of the unknown and potential failure filled them with 'anticipation and nervousness' (Ben) and 'a little bit of trepidation' (Anne).

Nevertheless, they remained committed to offering their students the opportunity to engage with technology to support language learning. They felt encouraged and inspired by the support of their colleagues, the sharing of expertise. Ben explained how he would be more likely to venture into new technological areas if he knew that 'someone has done it before successfully'. Ben described a colleague's in-service session with the IWB: 'Actually a session like that will take away some of the fears, you know, fears of the unknown.'

Anne explained her preference for more formal training and support because it gave her a framework and the confidence to experiment. Her preferred structured teaching style seemed to emerge in the way she addressed her concerns about working with technology. Formal and informal peer support provided the teachers with the opportunity to reflect on the pedagogical value of working with new ICT tools, as well as providing expertise and reassurance about the technical challenges of working with the unfamiliar.

With past experience in mind, the teachers embarked upon a new technological experience with the CMC teaching programme. The next section describes their reflections immediately after their lessons, and how they conceptualized the value of integrating this technological platform in terms of how they perceived its value to the learner.

Response to the CMC teaching programme

Working with less-than-familiar ICT tools can represent a significant challenge in the classroom, charged with technological uncertainty and the need to deliver a pedagogically sound lesson. It seems that as the teachers reflected on their classroom experiences immediately after each CMC lesson, a correlation emerged between the teachers' priorities for language teaching and learning, and their response to the CMC lessons.

Anne

In her preliminary interview, Anne indicated her preference for a more didactic model of language learning: presenting the learners with language, moving towards controlled practice and culminating in freer practice. Anne prized accuracy highly, expressing her concerns about the potentially detrimental effect of encouraging learners to 'produce, produce, produce' language in fluency activities without correction. She felt that if students were encouraged to produce language without correction or input from the teacher, then mistakes would become fossilized and they wouldn't improve. This had a significant impact on the way in which Anne responded to the CMC experience, relative to her perceptions about language learning, and her perceptions of her role as a teacher in the classroom.

The inherent characteristics of CMC challenged Anne's priorities for language learning, particularly in the synchronous component of the CMC teaching programme, where the pace of interaction can generate a high level of linguistic inaccuracy between interlocutors. With each synchronous lesson in the programme, Anne found it difficult to rationalize the pedagogical balance between the value of fluency and meaning and the need for linguistic accuracy and form. Although she voiced her understanding of why interactions between learners were 'laden' with grammatical imperfection ('it was to do with the speed of the writing') she found it difficult to tolerate, observing that:

> I saw some really stupid mistakes! I pointed it out to them . . . and I tried to get them to correct it themselves . . . they weren't controlling the language. *Lesson 1*

> I noticed their question forms were absolutely abysmal, so something needs to be done about that. *Lesson 4*

She looked for ways in which she might be able to intervene and to focus on form. It seems that Anne's preference for a more didactic approach to language teaching emerged in the chat room. Teacher intervention is complicated by the architecture of synchronous electronic space. Communication between interlocutors in a chat room might be described as a private affair between those engaged in the interaction. This sense is heightened when students chat with partners who are located in different geographical locations. The fast pace of the interaction makes it difficult for the bystander to step in, eavesdrop on fragments of discourse and pass judgement. This proved problematic to Anne throughout the programme, considering her priorities for language teaching, and was reflected in her final interview after the programme in her reflections about the value of integrating synchronous communication in her own classroom.

While the synchronous components of the CMC teaching programme might have proved to be more challenging for Anne, her response to the asynchronous elements of the teaching programme was quite different. The nature of the asynchronous technology flattered her preferred pedagogical approach. Anne's preference for meticulous planning was challenged with synchronous communication in the chat room because of the need to 'rely on people at the other end'. However, with asynchronous technology, the teacher and student roles are more familiar, with all participants working together in one location: 'This was quite possibly the lesson where I felt most comfortable. I felt that I was in control of the situation.'

With asynchronous communication, the pace of the interaction is more measured and controlled. The teacher can monitor, check and see all her learners, as they plan their message board responses, as they might in the classroom. While planning and preparation is possible with synchronous technology, once in the chat room the urgency to communicate can overwhelm the learners' attention to accuracy. As a technological approach, the asynchronous lesson flattered the priorities Anne attached to language learning: 'You can prepare for it . . . it's also relevant in that it, you know, has a combination of what we've been preparing for . . . they really saw the aim of it, liked the new vocabulary.'

It seems that Anne's preference for order, structure and accuracy inhibited her ability in the 'completely different medium' of chat, to conceptualize and attach any pedagogical value to the fast pace of synchronous online interaction, although she considered ways in which she might be able to address issues of accuracy after the lesson: 'We could keep the dialogue windows open and we could lift particular error-laden phrases so we could look at them afterwards.'

Although Anne valued the 'novelty factor' that students attached to working with technology, she began the project uncertain about the value of integrating technology, and unclear about why it might be better to 'do it on the computer'. However, she also began the study with the view that technology was a useful resource in helping students to write, enabling them to reflect and edit their work as they might not in the classroom. Her perceptions were mirrored in her response to the two forms of synchronous communication during the CMC programme, and while she remained uncertain about the value of 'error-laden' synchronous interactions between learners, she could see the value of the measured and reflective asynchronous lessons.

The concerns Anne expressed prior to the study about the technical challenges of working with an unfamiliar technology did not cause her undue concern during the CMC programme. However, the teachers were provided with support and training and the difficulties of which they had been fearful did not arise during the study. However, Anne was concerned when the online students from the other school arrived late and was unclear about how to manage the time, because she was faced with the proposition of 'winging it'. Her response to the CMC experience was much more closely aligned to the way in which she perceived the pedagogical value of the technology in relation to her own perceptions and priorities for language learning, rather than aligned to earlier fears about the technology.

Ben

Although Ben's response to the CMC programme was different to Anne's, it reflected his priorities for language learning and teaching. In his opening interview, Ben described how he valued collaboration, and while learners might not be using accurate English, they were communicating so that 'you're sort of working together to get to a point of understanding'.

Unlike Anne, Ben felt that providing learners with the opportunity to work out meaning by talking to one another was a part of the process that ultimately leads to accuracy. He identified his role as one that facilitated and supported the process by providing the 'correct kind of input' without overwhelming the communicative process. Ben's sense of his facilitative role as a teacher was reflected in his initial uncertainties about the synchronous medium:

> They kind of went off task a bit and asked whatever they wanted to ask their partner . . . I thought 'gosh, what do I do about this' and decided that actually it was better just to let it go and let them chat . . . it was after all a communication lesson.

Like Anne, Ben was surprised at the brevity and inaccuracy of the students' synchronous interactions, and that 'some of them were even using text language'. Before the CMC programme, Ben considered that it was important that the teacher should provide the 'right kind of input' but that it was 'a matter of how it's done'. This approach informed his interpretation of the value of the technology. Rather than attempt to correct their errors, he considered that teacher input at this stage would 'make the screen look kind of messy and it creates interruptions in the flow of conversations . . . it adds an extra layer of chronology to the questions'.

This observation relates to the priority Ben attached to collaboration between learners, and in rationalizing the high-level linguistic error in the chat room, unlike Anne, Ben indicated a high tolerance of learner error as a part of the language-learning process as indicated by his observation that: 'We as teachers have to accept that they are going to be making a lot of spelling mistakes and whatever, but as long as they're getting their communication over it's OK.'

In his preliminary interview, Ben had expressed concern that he could sometimes be too dictatorial in the computer room, particularly when trying to guide the class through the technology and the lesson plan, making him feel uncomfortable. During the CMC programme the learners' apparent familiarity with the medium meant that he did not have to manage his learners: 'I didn't have to show them how to do it . . . they just kind of found their way there really quickly.'

His preference for facilitating communication between learners was therefore enabled by the technology flattering his preferred teaching style, so that he felt 'empowered' by the experience. By weaving the technology seamlessly into the lesson, communication and language became the dominant force in the classroom, rather than the technology, so that 'you didn't really feel the computers were there at all'.

Like Anne, Ben indicated a preference for the logistical simplicity of the asynchronous lesson, where the students were not partnered with another class in a different geographical location, reflecting the concerns about technical failure that he had expressed in his preliminary interview: 'All I had to concentrate on was what was in my classroom, and not in another classroom.'

It seems, therefore, that the teachers' initial response to their experiences of working with CMC technology during the teaching programme reflected their priorities for language teaching and learning as well as their fears and concerns about working with the unfamiliar. This leads us to consider the way in which the CMC programme might have influenced their perceptions about the value of working with this form of technology.

Changes in beliefs in response to the CMC teaching programme

A month after the CMC programme, I re-interviewed the teachers to ask them to reflect on their experiences, and on whether the programme had changed the way in which they conceptualized the value of integrating CMC technology into their classrooms. Would Anne have resolved her concerns about accuracy over fluency in the chat room, identified a pedagogical reason 'to do it on the computer rather than in their books', and thought about how she might define her role in the altered classroom dynamic in the computer room? Would Ben have overcome his technological uncertainty, and identified a place for CMC in his repertoire of computer-room lessons? It seems that the teachers offset the challenges of learning to work with new technologies with any perceived pedagogical outcome, which related to their priorities for language learning.

Anne

In her closing interview, Anne explained that she had not revisited the technology since the CMC programme. However, she considered that the technology was of value to the learner, observing that: 'It's to do with social benefits . . . you also have a reason to communicate, so much of communication in the classroom is artificial.'

Before the study, Anne had expressed concerns about the meticulous need for planning and preparation required for computer lessons. She became aware during the programme that in the synchronous lessons this was a concern of some consequence and would influence her decision to arrange a chat-room lesson: 'I would probably start off with and do most frequently something which does not involve chatting to people in a different school, just because it's easier.' The linguistic free fall in the chat room in terms of fluency over accuracy persuaded Anne that if she were to revisit the technology she would work with asynchronous technology because: 'I felt their level of language was better . . . I liked the message board!'

The link between priorities for language learning and preconceptions about the challenges of working with technology coloured Anne's views about the value of integrating CMC into her classroom.

Ben

In his preliminary interview Ben expressed concerns about feeling stranded technologically because he lacked confidence that he would know what to do in the event of a technical breakdown. The CMC programme informed Ben about the way in which the technology worked, giving confidence so that: 'I can go in knowing that if any of the students have a problem then I can probably help them out.'

Ben's new-found confidence enabled him to reflect less on technical complexities and more on the pedagogical value of the technology, observing that in the chat room:

It's helping their writing skills, I think it's a valid way to help that . . . their sort of communication fluency . . . never mind the accuracy of what they're saying . . . it takes the stress of that away.

In his reflections about integrating the message board into his lessons, Ben saw asynchronous technology as a way in which to address issues of linguistic inaccuracy from the chat room: 'They pick up on each other's mistakes [in the chat room], it makes them keen to get it right on the bulletin board.'

At the time of the final interview, Ben had not revisited the chat room. However, he had worked independently with the message board, and had written his own materials for two more information-exchange lessons using asynchronous technology. He reflected with surprise that 'actually that's the beauty of it, they didn't take much material writing at all, because I just had the idea . . . I knew it was there and I had access to [the technology]'.

Both teachers taught the same series of lessons to classes of similar levels, but they had responded differently. Although Anne had reflected upon and identified the potential pedagogical value of the technology, the inherent characteristics of the technology overly challenged Anne's priorities for language learning. However, it seems that CMC technology flattered the priorities Ben attached to language learning in terms of its potential to inspire meaningful communication between learners, leading him to exploit the technology independently.

In the next section, we turn our attention to the value that the learner attaches to the integration of CMC technology. The data described relates to students' responses to a series of four asynchronous CMC lessons delivered to a group of twelve Upper Intermediate summer-school adult learners in the UK. As part of the project, students were invited to participate in discussion forums available to them on the message boards outside school, set within the context of a specifically designed VLE called English International. The data discussed in this chapter represents the views of three of the students who were interviewed at the beginning and end of the CMC programme, and contrasted with responses from the whole group who completed opening and closing questionnaires. Three of the lessons from this project correspond with the lessons taught in the first project. The fourth lesson was an integrated skills lesson, where students read an online article for gist and detail, which led to a classroom discussion and culminated in a short writing task on the message board.

The learner

The learners engaged in this short study had chosen to come to the UK to learn and improve their English. During their stay, they were living with

British families, so they were immersed in the language. Unlike the teachers' project, it was apparent that the learners did not express the same levels of anxiety about working with technology, although they did express initial caution, with which they approached something new and unfamiliar: 'The first one, I was less confident . . . this is in my way, sometimes I am like a cat, you know . . . they want to explore first and then they feel better.'

The opening questionnaires revealed that across the class, technology was integral not only to the students' academic and working lives, but also in terms of their free time. They reported that they spent on average between two to six hours daily at the computer screen, exploiting technology extensively because they wanted to rather than because they had to. In this section I will describe the responses of three of the students from the class:

- *Alicia from Italy* Alicia was a 43-year-old woman who was learning English in order to support her young son who was attending a British school in Italy. She had been learning English on and off for several years, had taken private lessons and studied independently at home.
- *Yasuo from Japan* Yasuo was a 38-year-old man who was an English teacher in Japan. He was in the UK to sharpen his English language skills during the summer within the target language community. He had been learning English for twenty-five years.
- *Rami from Qatar* Rami was a 30-year-old man who had been posted to the UK by his company in order to improve his English. His company had a policy of providing English language tuition to their employees, and he had been learning English for two years.

Priorities for language learning

Alicia's perceptions about language learning reflected the choices she and her husband had made about their son's education, and the family's project to learn English. She had clear ideas about how this might be achieved, and valued the notion of total immersion in the language as indicated by the decision to spend the summer in Britain: 'The best way is to stay in a place which, ummm, people speak English, so to live the language.' Paradoxically, Alicia combined the notion of learning by 'just living here' with the structure and guidance of the classroom, the teacher and homework: 'It's very important to revise what you did in the morning or in the afternoon because it's impossible just to learn in the class, we have to revise.'

Yasuo's priorities for language learning were in personally overcoming what he described as a cultural trait: 'The nationality of Japanese is not good at communicating but we have to communicate using English!' He expressed concern that Japan was a long way from the target-language community which only compounded the natural resistance to speak in English by his compatriots. He identified the presence of the English assistant at his school in Japan as a rich resource and he took advantage of took advantage of the opportunity to communicate with her in the target language because she was a native English speaker.

Like many Arab students, Rami was an orally strong student, but language classes proved challenging for him, because although he could intuitively identify whether a sentence was correct, he couldn't explain why. He rationalized the linguistic challenge he faced in learning English by explaining that learners had to be 'patient because they cannot learn English just in one day or one month'. Rami valued tasks that enabled him to monitor and check his progress over time, so that he could reflect on how far he had come from the difficult early days when he first arrived in the school: 'If I try to do workbook like Headway, nice, very nice, you know what's your score . . . the first placement test you have to put it and the date, after you have to practice.' Rami's need to be able to measure his progress reflected his concern about the magnitude of the language learning task, 'cos I have to learn all the tools of the language and connect it together, like grammar, writing'.

Like the teachers, the values and priorities that the students attached to language learning were similarly echoed in their responses to using technology, as described in the next section.

Responses to using technology before the programme

Alicia's preference for a considered approach to language learning was mirrored by her response to working with technology. She willingly engaged with technology so long as she could identify a practical reason for using it, explaining: 'I *use* technology, the technology *doesn't* use me.' Her perception was that as an older learner she was probably less engaged with technology than her classmates, resisting the proliferation of social networking sites, which she viewed with some suspicion because 'we prefer to have a nice talk on the phone [laughs] Yes! I'm an older generation'.

Yet technologically, Alicia also described herself as: 'a little bit of a pioneer' because she used the computer for family shopping, managing household data and digitally storing family photographs, as well as using technology to support self-access language learning at home. Similarities seem to emerge between her practical approach and priorities for language learning and her pragmatic attitude to technology. This suggests that experience with CMC during the programme would help her to identify whether there might be a practical application for this type of technology in her language-learning project.

Where Alicia attached a functional value to language learning and technology, Yasuo attached a communicative value. Technology was fully integrated into Yasuo's life and he used it extensively at home, and to some extent at work, although he pointed out that while the use of technology in the language classroom was beginning to emerge in Japan, it was not yet commonplace. He did not view the proliferation of social-networking sites with the same level of suspicion as Alicia. On arrival in Britain, Yasuo expressed surprise at the confidence with which the European students were able to interact in the target language, and he considered that the communicative inequity between cultures might be redressed by online communication: 'They can be more like other nationalities. They can have like the merits or the good points of the other nationalities.'

High on Rami's list of language-learning priorities was the need to monitor and check his progress. He valued the presence of a teacher to provide him with the knowledge and expertise that he lacked and craved. Similarly, he was very aware that while the computer might be able to help him, it was a tool that he could not always rely on. He had learned from experience that in order to take advantage of computerized language tools, the learner needed to work from well-grounded linguistic foundations: 'They give you more choice, you can't decide which the words is correct . . . if I face the problem for one word . . . if I didn't have a dictionary I cannot use it, I don't know how to spell it.'

In seeking reassurance, Rami therefore valued the presence of a teacher in learning a language, to supervise, and it was immaterial whether the teacher was in class or available online. He had appreciated the relationship he had built up by email with his old teacher because: 'If I need something, or I made a mistake, we have contact.'

A link seemed to emerge between the value the learners attached to the technology in response to the CMC programme, their priorities for language learning and their more general attitudes towards technology.

Responses to the CMC programme

Central to Alicia's response to the use of a new technological tool was the way in which she perceived its functionality. Although at first she was cautious and shy about visiting and having a visible presence on the VLE, her feeling at the end of the four-week project was that:

> I enjoy my experience like this absolutely and I think I show my enthusiasm because I answered the questions that you requested, I participated actively in this project and so it was a good experience for me absolutely. Yes, it's useful, it's modern, it's practical and we can learn a lot from an experience like that.

Alicia valued the discursive nature of the computer-based classroom lessons, with strong topics that were of interest to her. The dynamic nature of the site meant that it was updated with vocabulary that emerged from the lesson, flattering her preference for reflecting on the day's lessons at the end of the day.

Despite Alicia's enthusiasm for the technology, she described herself as a 'passive', albeit regular visitor to the site beyond the classroom. She enjoyed reading her classmates' independent contributions to the discussion forums, particularly those from one of the more vocal students: 'He's a very interesting person because he's going to stay here for 6 months . . . so I read some things he wrote.' However, she felt too shy to contribute to the discussion forums beyond what was asked of her in the classroom. She explained that she felt exposed by the medium because everyone could read her work: 'It's like we stay in a round table and each of them can listen to us.'

Always the pragmatist, Alicia also found it difficult to think of a good reason to open an online discussion with the classmates she saw daily. However she pointed out that this type of technology might be useful to her when she went back to Italy, and wanted to find out whether she might be able to access the site when she went home, when other institutions would be joining the VLE: 'It could be more interesting because you don't know the other people, because every day we see each other in school so why contact you in the site?'

Yasuo's observation in his preliminary interview reflected his response to the technology during the CMC programme. He was aware that he felt communicatively inhibited and had considered that CMC technology might be an ICT tool that could help him to be more confident: 'I mean I can't talk in class, but if I have the chance to talk in the computer, yes, yes.' He valued the communicative potential of the discussion forums because they opened the door for meaningful interaction between learners:

> If someone like Rina or Cyril they submit a topic into the forum, it's a great stimulation. I had to do something it was a great stimulation . . . you

know I had to, I had to, it was not enforced for me but yeah, that was good motivation to read it.

Yasuo participated enthusiastically in each computer-based classroom lesson. He also posted regularly to the discussion forums outside class, which proved to be popular and well received by his fellow classmates. Yasuo described the cognitive merits of revisiting the events of the school day by logging in to the site: 'When I do my homework I was thinking what I did in class and what I talked about in class.'

This observation was reflected in activity reports from the VLE indicating how, after the lessons, Yasuo revisited the classroom materials and postings made to the site. As a conscientious student, Yasuo pointed out that assignments and tasks set on the site gave him an identified reason to log in: 'In my brain I know I have to submit my homework, so that still remained in my brain, so I log on sometimes.' While Yasuo exploited the technology in line with his personal language-learning needs to build communicative confidence, his comments might lead us to think that learners are unlikely to exploit the technology independently, unless they can identify a relationship between what they do in class and what is expected of them by the teacher: 'If we always log in daily to this site, maybe this will be handy, but if we don't have to log in every day, then . . .'

Rami's response to the CMC programme was less positive than Alicia's and Yasuo's. However, like the other students, his interpretation of the value of the technology reflected his priorities for language learning. He found the topics in each lesson stimulating, and enjoyed reading his classmates' responses on the message board: 'I read my classmates work, because I want to see how they thinking and how they write.' However, CMC and the emphasis on interaction between learners did not address his more linguistically specific need to understand how to 'connect' the 'tools of the language', and to have a teacher nearby to check for error:

Yes, I mean also if the students they can use it from their class maybe my subject today, the gerund for example, or the third conditional to talk about grammar, we can use the website and check it during the lesson.

However, Rami liked the VLE because he identified that, as with email, he could use the technology to maintain contact with his teacher: 'Because we can keep in touch. We can talk to the teacher from the class and with you also from my house, I can go back to study.' In his opening interview, Rami explained the difficulties he experienced with the multiple linguistic options technology offered him, which he found confusing. Although the CMC programme within the study did not support Rami's linguistic and pedagogical needs, he identified and valued the potential support offered by two-way interaction mediated by the technology.

Conclusion

The challenges facing teachers and learners in conceptualizing and embracing the value of the technologically new might seem to be quite disparate from one another. It is a disparity that would appear to be driven by the learners' technological competence and their fearless tolerance of ambiguity, leading to the emergence of an 'imbalance between student and teachers, and the differing skill levels of each group', which 'has enabled students to hold the dominant position and determine much of the discourse' (Cuthell 2002: 20).

The result of such an imbalance might be thought, on the one hand, to be a cause for concern for the teacher, while on the other, to thrill the technologically capable student. Yet perhaps this exploration of the disparity between the two groups with its focus on their response to the technology during the teaching programme is too simplistic. It was evident in these studies that both the teachers and the learners ascribed similar values to the merits of integrating CMC into the language classroom, with each group reflecting that they found:

a. CMC was motivating, modern and new
b. CMC was responsive to events in the classroom (for example, recording emergent vocabulary, message-board postings reflecting classroom discussions)
c. CMC helped to develop communication skills, between learners in the computer-based lessons and out of class
d. CMC helped to maintain links between events in the classroom and home

But perhaps the greatest challenge for both the teachers and students in these two short studies lay in the hopes, beliefs and aspirations that they brought with them to the technological classroom. The ability to conceptualize, make sense of and cognitively map the pedagogical merits of their technological teaching and learning environment seems to have been linked most strongly to 'a personally held system of beliefs, values and principle' (Clark and Peterson 1986: 287). If we are to strive towards an increasingly networked learning community, we need to take a step back from our exploration of the pedagogical value of technological functionality, and turn our attentions towards what the teachers and learners bring to the experience in terms of their priorities for and beliefs about language learning. Understanding what teachers and learners bring with them to the technological classroom will richly inform the future of our 'brave new world'.

References

Arnold, N. and Ducate, L. (2006), 'Future foreign language teachers' social and cognitive collaboration in online environment'. *Language Learning and Technology*, 10, (1), 42–66.

Castells, M. (1996), *The Rise of the Network Society*. Malden, MA: Blackwell.

Clark, C. and Peterson, P. (1986), 'Teachers' thought processes', in M. Wittrock (ed.) *Handbook of Research on Teaching*. New York: Macmillan.

Cuthell, J. (2002), *Virtual Learning (The Impact of ICT on the Way Young People Work and Learn)*. Aldershot: Ashgate.

Esch, E. (1996), 'Promoting learner autonomy', in R. Pemberton, S. L. Edward, Winnie Li, W. F. Or and Herbert D. Pierson (eds) *Taking Control: Autonomy in Language Learning*. Hong Kong: Hong Kong University Press.

Hawisher, G. and Selfe, C. (1991), 'The rhetoric of technology and the electronic writing class'. *College Composition and Communication*, 42, (1), 55–65.

Hawisher, G. and Selfe, C. (eds) (2000), *Global Literacies and the World-Wide Web*. London: Routledge.

Salaberry, R. (2001), 'The use of technology for second language learning and teaching: a retrospective'. *The Modern Language Journal*, 85, (1), 39–56.

Warschauer, M. (1996), *Motivational Aspects of Using Computers for Writing and Communication*. Available at http://nflrc.hawaii.edu/NetWorks/NWOl.pdf.

Chapter 8

From textbook to online materials: the changing ecology of foreign-language publishing in the era of ICT

Carl Blyth

The shift from the familiar medium of the textbook and its traditional literacy practices to the medium of the computer screen and its innovative forms of multimodal discourse (Kress and van Leeuwen 2001) corresponds to profound shifts in the ecology of foreign-language publishing. The hegemony of commercial publishing companies is being challenged by the production of open educational resources (Iiyoshi and Kumar 2007). Neither swift nor painless, the transition from textbook to open-access digital materials recounted in this chapter is a case study of conflict, resistance and change.

Digital technology has bestowed power on non-commercial developers who now possess the tools of production (for example, digital equipment and multimedia software) as well as the means of mass distribution (for example, the internet). In other words, digital technology has profoundly changed the traditional relations between producers and consumers of educational materials. Furthermore, changes in professional roles entail a shift in values and beliefs. Foreign-language professionals who employ digital video to capture the language as it is actually spoken in real-life situations often reject the prescriptive linguistic ideology that is deeply entrenched in the fields of pedagogy and publishing. As will be shown, digital video of language-in-context privileges orality over literacy and calls into question the idealized model of the monolingual native speaker so common to pedagogical materials (Train 2003, 2007).

This chapter is a case study of the development and impact of *Tex's French Grammar* (Blyth et al. 2000) and *Français interactif* (Kelton et al. 2004),[1] two websites developed and produced at the University of Texas at Austin that together form a beginners' online French course. The chapter begins with a discussion of the outer layers of the ecology, that is, the context of academic publishing. This section includes a brief discussion of ecological research in applied linguistics before turning to a description of the open-education movement and its impact on academic publishing. Next, the focus turns to the middle layers, the university language programme where the materials were developed. This section gives a brief historical overview of the developmental process in order to highlight the faculty developers' efforts to include student feedback in the assessment and modification of the digital materials. And finally, the chapter ends by examining the inner layer, that is, the students and the materials themselves. A close examination of the digital materials reveals a conception of language as communicative practice.

In general, this case study shows that open-educational publishing includes people who have previously been shut out of the traditional publishing world, namely, the end users – students and classroom instructors (Baraniuck 2007). By opening up the developmental process, digital technology and open publishing can lead to the creation of pedagogical materials that are more learner-centred and user-friendly (Blyth and Davis 2007).

Ecological approaches to applied linguistics

In an article assessing the impact of technology on foreign- and second-language learning, Kern (2006) attributes the slow but steady disappearance of the acronym CALL to the computer's increasing ubiquity. Kern claims that computers are becoming less noticeable to teachers and learners as they become increasingly integrated into foreign-language classrooms and curricula. While computers in foreign-language learning have not yet reached the level of invisibility or 'givenness' that textbooks have achieved, it is generally accepted that computers are becoming 'normalized' (Bax 2003). In support of his thesis, Kern cites Warschauer (1999) who playfully coins the term 'BALL' (book-assisted language learning) to demonstrate that teachers and learners rarely make explicit reference to technology that they take for granted. According to Warschauer (1999), the acronym CALL indexes an outdated conceptualization of the computer as an 'outside instrument rather than as part of the ecology of language use'.

Warschauer's use of the phrase 'ecology of language use' is in keeping with recent trends in applied linguistics. For the past two decades, applied linguists have employed many different metaphors to conceptualize the role of the computer in language learning: the conduit, the tutor, the tool, the community and so forth (Meskill 2005). The multiplicity of metaphors has frequently been taken as prima facie evidence of the complex and dynamic nature of the phenomena described. Recently, applied linguists have increasingly embraced the metaphor of ecology in their attempts to understand language learning in the internet era (Kramsch 2003, Leather and van Dam 2003, van Lier 2004). Kramsch (2003) argues that the rise of ecology as a privileged metaphor has been prompted by globalization and multicultural education, both facilitated by the rapid development of the internet. As a global network of networks, the internet itself constitutes a prime example of a social ecosystem.

The nineteenth-century German biologist Ernst Haeckel is widely credited with coining the term *ecology* to refer to the 'totality of relationships of an organism with all other organisms with which it comes into contact' (van Lier 2004: 3). According to van Lier (2004: 207), the goal of an ecological approach is to discover how the constituent parts of a complex system (be it a biological ecosystem, a computer network or a foreign language curriculum) form a whole. Van Lier (2004: 219) maintains that an ecological approach to language learning is characterized by three primary features:

1. a focus on process and relations
2. a rich view of context and
3. a goal of bringing about improvement of the entities (schools, language programs, classrooms, etc.)

Van Lier cites the research of psychologist Bronfenbrenner (1979, 1993) who conceptualized the ecology of human development in terms of nested systems (e.g. exosystem, mesosystem, microsystem). Adapting Bronfenbrenner's schema to describe the hierarchy of the educational ecosystem (for example, society, school, classroom), van Lier (2004: 208) claims that 'each system has its own set of actors and artifacts, and its own patterns of operations and relations. Also, each ecosystem operates on its own time scale and cycles of events.'

Open education as a 'knowledge ecosystem'

Rich Baraniuk, a pioneer in the open-education movement, refers to academic publishing as a *knowledge ecosystem*, in order to emphasize the interconnections between the *agents* (e.g. authors, students and publishers) and their *artefacts* (such as textbooks, websites, etc.) (Baraniuk 2006). According to Baraniuk (2007b), academic publishing represents a closed system that creates 'shut-outs': 'talented K-12 teachers, community college instructors, scientists and engineers out in industry, and the world majority who do not read and write English' (Baraniuk 2007b). Arguing along similar lines, Blyth and Davis (2007) contend that the structure of commercial academic publishing actually inhibits innovation and results in materials that are not particularly learner-centred or user-friendly. Advocating a more central role for formative evaluation in the publishing process, they criticize publishers as well as foreign-language professionals for largely ignoring the ideas and opinions of end-users, i.e. foreign-language professors and their students:

> Anyone attending a professional meeting hears criticisms of currently available textbooks as being conservative and generic and, thus, ill fitted to a given institution's particular (and actual) needs. This state of affairs is largely an artifact of the complicity that exists among the various stakeholders: commercial publishers, textbook writers, reviewers, and language program directors.

Blyth and Davis (2007) argue that locally produced digital materials represent one of the principal 'engines of innovation' in foreign-language pedagogical publishing because these kinds of materials typically reflect a more open process. The online digital materials described in this case study were the product of intense collaboration between students, instructors, technologists and administrators.

In fairness to publishing companies, today's commercial textbooks are produced using digital technology that allows adopters to customize materials. For example, before adopting a textbook, customers may negotiate significant changes to the textbook, such as the elimination of content or the reordering of a pedagogical sequence. However, while custom publishing allows adopters to adapt materials to their classrooms, it does not fundamentally change the relations between producers and consumers. In other words, custom publishing still leaves the production of educational content in the hands of commercial publishers.

This state of affairs is beginning to change due to ICT, or more specifically, due to the *open-access* and *open-source* movements made possible by the internet. *Open access* refers to content, often of a scholarly nature, that producers make freely available to the internet public. While the democratic ideals of the open-access movement have an intuitive appeal, many publishers and academics have raised serious concerns about the credibility of such 'amateur' materials. The most controversial questions revolve around the issue of peer review, the touchstone of authoritative content. Publishing companies warn that by avoiding the conventional practices of peer and editor review, it is impossible to assure the level of professionalism and authoritativeness that consumers have come to expect.

Despite this very real problem, the open-access movement continues to attract the interest of many universities. One of the earliest and strongest supporters of open-access publishing was the Massachusetts Institute of Technology (MIT). Recognized as a world leader in science and technology, MIT proposed its OpenCourseWare Initiative in 2000:[2] 'MIT OpenCourseWare is an idea—and an ideal—developed, supported, and embraced by the MIT faculty, who share the Institute's mission to advance knowledge and educate students in science, technology, and other areas of scholarship to best serve the nation and the world' (http://ocw.mit.edu/OcwWeb/web/about/history/index.htm). According to the website, MIT's OpenCourseWare has received more than 31 million visitors from virtually every country in the world. These visitors include university students, educators and self-learners.

Another excellent example of open educational publishing is Carnegie-Mellon University's Open Learning Initiative (OLI). According to its website, OLI represents 'a collection of openly available and free online courses and course materials that enact instruction for an entire course in an online format' (www.cmu.edu/oli). Similar to MIT, Carnegie-Mellon is best known for its programmes in science and technology, and the content of OLI reflects this orientation; nine of the ten courses that are currently available focus on scientific and technical subject matter (for example, physics, chemistry, statistics, engineering). The lone humanities course is an interactive video-based French course.[3] Learners may take OLI courses by enrolling as a member of an organized, accredited class through a partnered institution or by enrolling in the self-paced, non-credit version for personal enrichment.

Related to the open-access movement is the *open-source* movement that has its roots in the history of software development (Perens 1999, Raymond 2001). The revolutionary idea of this movement was to give end-users free and open access to a software's source code by relaxing copyright restrictions, hence the term *open source*. Perens (1999: 171–2) likens open source to a 'bill of rights for the computer user' that establishes the following:

1. the right to make copies of the computer program and distribute those copies

2. the right to have access to the software's source code, a necessary preliminary before you can change it
3. the right to make improvements to the program

The principles behind the open-source movement soon spread to other areas of content development. Today, the term *open content* is commonly used to refer to any kind of published content that may be freely copied and modified. The best-known example of open content is Wikipedia, a free online encyclopedia project begun in 2001.[4] Written collaboratively by end-users, Wikipedia has rapidly expanded since its inception and now includes versions in several languages.

An excellent example of open-source educational content is Connexions, a non-profit publishing project that 'brings textbooks and other learning materials into the Internet Age' (http://cnx.org/). Founded in 1999 by Baraniuk, a professor of electrical engineering at Rice University, the goal of Connexions is to make high-quality educational content available via the internet to anyone, anywhere, at anytime. (Baraniuk 2007b) offers this description of the open-education movement:

> A grassroots movement is on the verge of sweeping through the academic world. The open education (OE) movement is based on a set of intuitions shared by a remarkably wide range of academics: that knowledge should be free and open to use and re-use; that collaboration should be easier, not harder; that people should receive credit and kudos for contributing to education and research; and that concepts and ideas are linked in unusual and surprising ways and not the simple linear forms that today's textbooks present. OE promises to fundamentally change the way authors, instructors, and students interact worldwide.

Baraniuk encourages authors, teachers and learners to 'create, rip, mix, and burn' learning materials made available at Connexions' open-access reposi-tory. Baraniuk purposefully borrows the phrase – 'create, rip, mix and burn'– from an Apple computer marketing campaign that attempts to capture the experience of personalizing and sharing music in the internet age. And yet, Baraniuk is quick to point out that many of the activities referred to by this catchphrase are illegal. He emphasizes that Connexions is not about pirating copyrighted materials but rather about entering into a legal and mutually beneficial relationship with other online producers and consumers:

> In Connexions, anyone can create 'modules' of information—smallish, Lego™ block documents that communicate a concept, a procedure, a set

of questions. Connect some modules together, and you have a web course or textbook, or build a curriculum entirely of your choosing. All content is open-licensed under the Creative Commons attribution license; all tools are free and open-source.[5] (Baraniuk 2007b)

Baraniuk claims that the transformational impact of Connexions on academic publishing is evident in three areas:

1. A redistribution of power and control from publishers to end users.
2. A faster publishing cycle, that is, the time needed to develop materials and get them into the hands of the student.
3. A drastic reduction of printing costs. By allowing students to download and print materials for themselves or use the materials online, Connexions helps students save time and money.

(New York Times, 1 May 2007)

While many consumers are convinced that open publishing will lead to lower costs and greater convenience, they are not sure about the quality of online materials. Is it possible to allow end-users to become producers and still maintain a quality product? This question raises two other questions: What is quality? And who decides? Traditionally, academic publishers have employed a careful pre-publication review process before allowing access to the finished product. Baraniuk argues that such a pre-publication review process makes sense when the publication medium is expensive and scarce (for instance, the paper and ink for book printing). However, he maintains that such a process is ill-suited to the world of open-educational resources because it is unable to keep up with the fast pace of editorial change of online materials and, more importantly, it violates the collaborative culture of the internet, which values social equality and sharing:

> [T]he traditional binary decision to accept/reject a work is inappropriate when an open educational resource can improve in an evolutionary fashion. Accept/reject decisions also create an exclusive rather than inclusive community culture. And finally, pre-review does not support evaluation of modules and courses based on actual student learning outcomes.

In place of a pre-publication review process controlled by the publisher, Baraniuk advocates quality control via *lenses*. The metaphorical term *lens* refers to a group of end-users who have a particular focus. The groups are typically quite heterogeneous: professional societies, informal groups of colleagues, school administrators, etc. An excellent example of a foreign-language lens is EDSITEment (http://edsitement.neh.gov/), a collaborative effort of the National Endownment for the Humanties, Verizon Foundation and the National Trust for the Humanities. EDSITEment reviews content, design and educational impact of digital materials in the humanities covering a wide range of subjects: art, history, language and literature. EDSITEment employs humanities specialists to review and select digital materials of high intellectual quality for inclusion in a searchable, online database. Another example of a lens is Multimedia Educational Resource of Learning and Online Teaching (MERLOT), an online community of faculty, students and instructional technologists (www.merlot.org). According to the website, 'MERLOT is a leading edge, user-centered, searchable collection of peer reviewed, higher education, online learning materials created by registered users and a set of faculty development support services.'[6]

The effectiveness and feasibility of quality control via lenses has been greatly aided by the recent emergence of Web 2.0 social software. Social software not only allows people to affiliate and form online communities, but it also enables community members to share digital content more easily. Baraniuk (2007b:) refers to the website *Del.icio.us* as 'the prototype lens incarnation based on social tagging' (http://del.icio.us/). A tag is a keyword descriptor created by an end-user and assigned to a given book-marked web page. For example, if a user comes across a French-language site, he or she may assign it a tag such as *French grammar* or *French exercises* or simply *French*. Tags automatically link all the content in a massive repository of related information based entirely on end-users' personal interests and organizational schemes. Thus, a learner searching for high-quality French grammar materials can go to *Del.icio.us* and conduct a keyword search that would not only yield thousands of relevant sites but also thousands of reviews posted by end-users.[7]

Improving digital materials
through formative evaluation

While *Tex's French Grammar* and *Français interactif*, the two websites that form the first-year French-language programme at the University of Texas at Austin, are not open-source materials in the same sense as a Wikipedia entry or a Connexions module, nevertheless they were heavily influenced by the values of inclusion and collaboration that lie at the core of the open education movement. The results of a decade-long process that included three separate yet related projects, the digital materials owe much of their effectiveness to the input of classroom teachers and students, who tested the materials during multiple phases of formative evaluation. (See Blyth and Davis 2007 for a complete description of the iterative process that included initial development followed by formative evaluation and final modification.) Put into Baraniuk's terms, the digital materials were based on actual student learning outcomes and attitudinal data that were taken into account in a systematic post-review process. Taken together, these three projects tell a story of how one language programme that adopted a more 'open' framework was able to move away from commercially produced print materials towards locally produced digital materials.

The first project (1994–7) is best characterized as an effort to improve and extend a commercially produced first-year French textbook by creating ancillary digital materials: online grammar drills, a CD-ROM and web-based writing activities. The second project (1998–2000) was motivated by a desire to improve and amplify the textbook's grammar explanations and resulted in a pedagogical grammar website. Even though their point of departure was the textbook, the project developers decided to design the grammar website as independent from the textbook. In other words, the second project decoupled an important part of the curriculum – explicit grammar instruction – from the textbook. Finally, the third project (2001–5) replaced the textbook entirely and resulted in an online first-year French course produced entirely in-house. The online course included multiple media components (for example, audio, video, downloadable textbook and self-correcting exercises).[8]

First project (1994–7): *Parallèles Interactive*

In 1994, the lower-division French programme at the University of Texas at Austin adopted a new textbook called *Parallèles: communication et culture* (Allen and Fouletier-Smith 1995). While the textbook's cultural content appealed to the instructors, the book was found to be less than user-friendly by the students. In particular, many students complained that the chapters' opening sections, a presentation of grammar and vocabulary in context via texts and realia, proved too difficult. For example, the opening texts contained many challenging vocabulary words but no glosses. Furthermore, these texts were recorded on an audio cassette that students rarely used. In addition to finding the opening sections too difficult, students complained that they were unfamiliar with the authors' metalanguage (in other words, the names and functions of parts of speech), and as a consequence, they found the text's grammatical explanations opaque. And, finally, both students and instructors agreed that the end-of-chapter synthetic activities were well beyond the proficiency level of beginners.[9]

In response to these apparent problems, several French faculty members teamed up with a computer-design specialist at the university in an effort to create digital materials that would make the textbook's grammar and vocabulary presentation more accessible. To that end, three different computer tools were developed: online grammar drills, a multimedia CD-ROM entitled *Parallèles Interactive* and web-based activities. Carefully following the textbook's grammatical syllabus, the online drills required students to fill in a blank and submit the set of answers for automatic correction. The goal of the CD-ROM was to make the textbook's contextualized vocabulary and grammar presentation more accessible by adding glosses and comprehension questions. In essence, the CD-ROM was an electronic version of much of the textbook's original content. The publishing company gave the faculty developers full copyright permission to repurpose the book's digital files of texts, realia and photos in the making of *Parallèles Interactive*.[10] And finally, the web-based activities synthesized the chapter's lexical, grammatical and thematic content in a process-writing task.

Assessment of the first project's digital materials yielded generally positive results (Blyth and Davis 2007). Students reported that the online grammar drills were both easy to use and valuable in helping them understand the grammar. While most students found the CD-ROM enjoyable and interesting, they reported that it was of less direct utility than the drills. And finally, reviews of the online writing activities were mixed. Some students criticized these activities as too difficult and time-consuming, while others found them appropriately challenging. The developers modified the materials in response to the student feedback.

Second project (1998–2000): *Tex's French Grammar*

Despite the favourable reaction to the initial attempts at improving the textbook, students continued to report low levels of satisfaction with the textbook's grammar explanations. The students' most common complaint was that the grammar explanations found in the textbook assumed too much prior knowledge. Furthermore, faculty teaching upper-level courses asserted that students coming from the lower-division courses required increasing grammatical remediation. Again, the decision was made that the textbook needed improvement and that the easiest fix would be the development of an in-house digital supplement.

Several factors had changed since the creation of the first project's materials however. By the time of the second project, the developers were strongly encouraged to seek a technological solution to curricular problems, as monies for instructional technology had become widely available on campus. In addition, the developers felt obliged to create materials that would benefit intermediate French students as well as beginning students, that is, all the students enrolled in the basic French language programme. Given that the second year of the French-language programme comprised many different courses, each using a different textbook, the website was conceived as a stand-alone product. The resulting website, called *Tex's French Grammar*, is an online pedagogical reference grammar that combines grammatical explanations with cartoon images and humorous dialogues woven together to tell a hyperlinked story.[11] Arranged like many traditional reference grammars with the parts of speech (e.g. nouns and verbs) used to categorize specific grammar items (e.g. gender of nouns and irregular verbs), the website features explanations in English, recorded French dialogues with translations and self-correcting fill-in-the-blank exercises. To facilitate reference and learning, all grammar items are thoroughly cross-linked. In direct response to complaints about class time being used for grammatical remediation, the developers decided to define all grammatical terminology more completely than is typical of commercial materials.

Course evaluation surveys indicated a high level of student satisfaction with *Tex's French Grammar*. The developers were gratified to discover that the students found the grammatical explanations more comprehensible and easier to follow than the textbook's explanations. Students also reported appreciating the humorous dialogues and cartoons. Negative feedback focused on the site's overall navigability and usability. As a result of this negative feedback, several modifications were made to improve the website's user interface.

Third project (2001–5): *Français interactif*

Student feedback, gleaned from attitude surveys and usability testing following the first two projects, uncovered many ideas that were not fully realized in commercially produced materials. In particular, users repeatedly said that they wanted a clearer and more deliberate pedagogical sequence from decontextualized vocabulary words to contextualized discourse. In other words, students kept asking for more practice aimed at the word level so that they would feel more comfortable tackling contextualized language samples. The developmental team set out to design a programme based on suggestions from students and guided by their understanding of the lexical approach (Lewis 1993). Lewis (1993) notes that language teaching has traditionally been organized around the supposedly central grammatical system. In the lexical approach, students first learn to collocate words and then to grammaticalize meaning progressively: from word to sentence to discourse. The developers began by identifying various communicative tasks that they wanted their students to be able to perform (e.g., describing a dormitory room, comparing the personalities of family members, narrating the events of the day). Then, they videotaped native speakers performing these tasks and inventoried the vocabulary and grammar spontaneously used to perform the task.

These inventories became the basis for the lexical and grammatical syllabus of an online course entitled *Français interactif.* The course content is organized into 13 chapters that deal with themes relevant to beginning French learners. For instance, Chapter 9 focuses on ways for communicating and learning about current events in the context of French media – newspapers, radio, internet, television, cinema, etc. (see Figure 12).

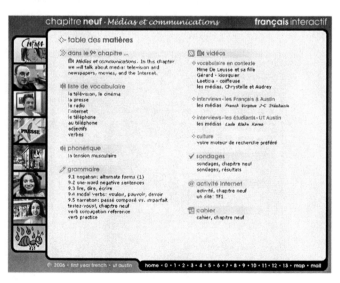

FIGURE 12 Table of contents

The website gives users access to various media components (video and audio files) as well as a downloadable chapter (*cahier*) that includes classroom activities based on the media components. Figure 12 displays the Table of Contents page for Chapter 9 and demonstrates the components that every chapter includes: *liste de vocabulaire* (text and audio of the chapter's vocabulary), *phonétique* (a brief phonetics lesson with accompanying audio), *grammaire* (grammar explanations and self-correcting exercises), *vidéos* (linguistic and cultural videos), *sondages* (polls that recycle the chapter's vocabulary) and *activité Internet* (a chapter-ending writing activity).

Français interactif contains three different types of videos: chapter-opening introductions, vocabulary-in-context presentations and open-ended interviews. The introductory video, as shown in Figure 13, features an American student living in France who presents the chapter's thematic and grammatical material in a way intended to pique the learner's interest. In Chapter 9, *Médias et communications*, the introductory video features a student buying a newspaper from a kiosk. This introductory video not only serves to preview the chapter's content, but also to personalize the content and to relate it explicitly to a student's lived experience. For example, the student making the purchase at the kiosk comments on the differences between American and French newspapers that she discovered while living in Lyon during the summer programme.

In response to students' repeated requests for more practice focused on vocabulary, vocabulary presentation videos were created to give listeners

FIGURE 13 Introduction

the opportunity to hear the vocabulary item used by a native French speaker in an authentic cultural context. To make these contexts more accessible for beginners, the videos maximize the redundancy between the visual image and the spoken language. In the video shown in Figure 14, a newspaper vendor explains the political differences between newspapers commonly sold in France. The primary pedagogical goal of these videos is to improve students' listening discrimination, that is, to help students identify relevant vocabulary in the natural, unrehearsed speech of native speakers. The listener does not need to understand every word of the native speaker's discourse in order to perform such a listening discrimination activity.

FIGURE 14 Gérard

The last type of video features an interview with a speaker responding to questions concerning the chapter's thematics as shown in Figure 15. Four native French speakers and three non-native French speakers (American students) were interviewed. In these unscripted interviews, speakers respond to questions that require them to employ the grammar and vocabulary featured in the chapter. Unlike the vocabulary videos, the interview videos have little visual support to aid listening comprehension. In fact, because the language is spontaneous and produced at a fairly rapid rate, optional transcripts and English translations are made available to learners. Moreover, many of the interview questions elicit paragraph-length responses. Thus, the language produced in these videos is considerably more challenging than in the vocabulary-in-context videos.

FIGURE 15 Karen

Blyth and Davis (2007) claim that the evolution of the digital materials from a textbook ancillary to a complete online course was due in large part to the inclusion of student feedback in the process. Moreover, an open process required the developers to strike a balance between what they believed students needed (more contextualized language input and practice) and what students said they wanted (more decontextualized language input and practice).

> This 8-year iterative process of development and evaluation demonstrated that students wanted two things: a greater emphasis on vocabulary as opposed to grammar and more decontextualized language used in presentation and practice. These student preferences ran counter to the developers' presuppositions about how language should be taught, that is, with a greater emphasis on contextualized grammar from the beginning. The developers believe that their materials have also improved and that the improvements are directly attributable to a clearer understanding of their students' preferences.

Blyth and Davis (2007) conclude that teachers and curriculum developers often think they know how their students learn best, when in fact, that is not necessarily true. This case study illustrates that the only way to be certain is to include students in the development process.

Focusing on the learner

While the methodological changes requested by the students were significant, the most profound impact of student involvement in the developmental process was a complete shift of focus – from the native speaker as a role model to the non-native speaker as a language learner. Blyth (1995) notes the irony of using monolingual speakers as role models for learners striving to overcome their own monolingualism. In addition to calling for multilingual speakers as role models, Blyth (1995: 170) argues for the inclusion of non-native speakers in pedagogical materials:

A Cambodian, a Senegalese, a Tunisian, or, for that matter, an American, who speaks French well enough to be interviewed on television by a French journalist sends a more encouraging message to students than do a thousand Parisians whose flawless, monolingual French is simply their birthright. In other words, adopting a different set of language norms can have a felicitous effect on our students' motivation: Bilingual norms encourage students to see their 'competence glass' as half-full whereas monolingual norms make them see their glass as half-empty.

Even though most commercial textbooks focus exclusively on the native monolingual speaker as the pedagogical norm (Train 2003, 2007), such a norm was explicitly rejected and, in its place, a multilingual norm adopted. In 2004, the lower-division French programme at the University of Texas at Austin sought to reframe the first-year French course in terms of bilingualism. The new online curriculum focused on the subjective language-learning experiences of a group of University of Texas students during their study-abroad programme in Lyon, France (see Figure 16). In essence, the study-abroad students act as virtual tour guides assisting students 'back home' in their own exploration of the French language and culture. The study-abroad students speak in a mixture of French and English and communicate with native speakers as best they can. Since the goal of the videos was to capture authentic samples of speech, both native and non-native, no attempt was made to remove the inevitable grammatical and lexical errors.

Français interactif accords a place of privilege to bilingual French-English speakers exhibiting a wide range of proficiencies: from balanced bilinguals to so-called 'incipient' bilinguals (i.e. American students learning French). All native French speakers had lived in the United States for many years, were married to an anglophone spouse and had achieved a superior level of proficiency in English. In contrast, the American students possessed variable levels of French proficiency – from novice to intermediate. Their frequent grammatical mistakes and communicative disfluencies were captured on the videos and became part of the input for learners.

By juxtaposing videos of incipient and fluent bilinguals, the developers hoped to raise learners' awareness about the nature of bilingualism and L2 learning. More specifically, the developers aimed for learners to

FIGURE 16 Français interactif

understand that bilinguals use both languages depending on situational circumstances and that use of the L1 did not always signal a deficiency. Furthermore, the developers wanted students to notice differences between incipient bilinguals and balanced bilinguals in order for them to construct a more realistic picture of the development of L2 skills.

The pedagogical agenda of *Français interactif* was inspired, in part, by recent work in the field of Critical Language Awareness (CLA). Train (2003) describes CLA as an attempt to problematize the notions of accuracy and appropriateness based on native-speaker norms that reflect the language practices of a dominant group in society. According to Fairclough (1992), language awareness in most classrooms is uncritical and prescriptive, leading students to become aware of their language production only in terms of how it deviates from the native standard. In other words, the goal of language awareness in most educational programmes is to facilitate self-correction and conformity to the native standard. Arguing that the ultimate goal of CLA is to create 'more inclusive conceptions and practices of language and culture', Train (2003: 16–17) cites five opportunities created by CLA projects:

1. The exploration (and ultimately the transformation) of speakers' individual and collective beliefs (ideologies, attitudes, biases, prejudices) surrounding language.

2. An appreciation of variation as inherent in language and learning.
3. The questioning of dominant linguistic and cultural knowledge (e.g. native-standard language) and how it is constructed and represented.
4. Critical reflection on the tension and interplay that exist in language education between creative individual uses of language and conformity to institutionalized norms.
5. Insight into the sociocultural construction of speakers' identities and 'realities' in a multilingual and multicultural world.

In a recent study of student awareness of native versus non-native discourse in *Français interactif*, Blyth (forthcoming) found that students attended more closely to the non-native speakers than the native speakers. Blyth reports that all participants in the study claimed that watching videos of non-native speakers proved highly beneficial. The two most commonly cited benefits were a greater awareness of communication strategies such as circumlocution and a greater awareness of errors and strategies for self-correction. Participants in the study also mentioned that watching videos of non-native speakers gave them a more realistic picture of L2 acquisition and helped them gauge their own language development. Based on these preliminary findings, Blyth claims that beginning foreign-language students are more likely to use *proficient non-native speakers* rather than native speakers as the basis for their own *projective linguistic identities* (Gee 2003).

Representing language as communicative practice

As a largely video-based programme, the linguistic content of *Français interactif* differs from many commercially produced textbooks. In particular, by taking videotaped interactions (interviews and conversations) as their point of departure, the developers of *Français interactif* emphasized oral French more than most textbook authors. The use of video for language teaching has become increasingly popular because it allows the elusive but all-important context to be turned into a text for subsequent manipulation and analysis:

> The problem with learning a language from live context is that context itself cannot be learned, it can only be experienced, or apprenticed in. Therefore in order for context to be made learnable, especially in an academic setting, it has to be transformed into analyzable text. As an educational tool, multimedia technology opens up immense possibilities of

contextualization by textualizing knowledge through its representational capabilities, that is, its endless reproducibility. (Kramsch and Andersen 1999: 33)

Even though Kramsch and Andersen argue for digital multimedia in instrumental terms, that is, in terms of its reproducibility and representational ability, they obviously value the tool for its association with a special kind of content – live interactional events. In other words, digital video furthers a pedagogical agenda that views language as situated communicative practice rather than as a system of abstract structures:

> From a discourse or anthropological perspective, linguistic structures, as they are used in communicative situations, are embedded in the whole social and historical context of culture (e.g., see, Gumperz, 1982; Malinowski, 1923; Sapir, 1949); they are but one system of signs among many that people use to give meaning to their environment. (Kramsch and Anderson 1999: 32)

In order to discern the effects of conversational videos on pedagogical materials, it is first important to understand conversation as a sociolinguistic phenomenon. In their book entitled *Conversation: From Description to Pedagogy*, Thornbury and Slade (2006: 25) define conversation as follows:

> Conversation is the informal, interactive talk between two or more people, which happens in real time, is spontaneous, has a largely interpersonal function, and in which participants share symmetrical rights.

This definition highlights three adjectives typically used to describe conversation – informal, spontaneous, and interpersonal – that correlate with the linguistic content found in *Français interactif*:

1. vocabulary and syntax normally associated with an informal, oral register
2. disfluencies and errors characteristic of spontaneous, unplanned discourse
3. language play to index friendship and intimacy

Informal oral grammar

Despite more than two decades of Communicative Language Teaching and the Oral Proficiency Movement, there remains a strong bias against oral norms of usage in many university foreign-language departments where literature is still the primary focus of study (Blyth 2000). Katz and Blyth (2007) note that printed textbooks invariably fall short when it comes to accurately reflecting how French speakers converse. In fact, textbooks are usually based on the written language and, as a consequence, fail to mention or exemplify grammatical constructions that are prevalent in the spoken language. Commenting on an outdated textbook dialogue replete with written language forms, Katz and Blyth contend that 'students in the 1970s did not realize that the conversations in their textbooks were stilted and unnatural. They learned French believing, for example, that *nous* was commonly used as a subject pronoun, that *ne* was needed for negation, and that inversion was standard in conversations.'

Katz and Blyth (2007: 150) note that textbooks generally employ so-called canonical sentences that follow an SVO order (for instance, *Marie déteste Jean*, Mary hates John) and that prefer full noun phrases in place of pronouns. These canonical sentences are invariably based on written norms; however, studies of spoken French reveal that such structures are actually quite rare in face-to-face interaction (Lambrecht 1987). Katz and Blyth (2007) outline four different oral variants of the canonical written sentence cited above:

1. *Marie, elle déteste Jean* (left dislocation)
2. *elle déteste Jean, Marie* (right dislocation)
3. *il y a Marie qui déteste Jean* (il y a cleft)
4. *c'est Marie qui déteste Jean* (c'est cleft)

The effect of orality is not limited to declarative sentences as exemplified above but is evident in interrogative syntax as well. For example, the formal inverted interrogative (*Comment s'appelle-t-il?* What's his name?) has two common oral counterparts (*Il s'appelle comment? Comment il s'appelle?*) (Katz and Blyth 2007: 190).

In the following example taken from an interview in Chapter 7 of *Français interactif*, the French speaker Franck lists various French holidays. Note that the syntax of both the interviewer and the interviewee reflects an informal register.

Interviewer:	Quelles sont les fêtes françaises?
Franck:	Ah, comme tout bon français, il y a beaucoup de fêtes en France. Donc, on prend beaucoup de vacances. Forcément, il y a le . . . le jour de l'an . . .
Interviewer:	Oui . . .

Franck:	Ensuite, on a Pâques, on a la fête du travail le premier mai. On a le quatorze juillet, la fête nationale . . .
Interviewer:	Oui . . .
Franck:	On a le onze novembre, on a . . .
Interviewer:	C'est quoi, le onze novembre?
Franck:	Ben, c'est la fin de la première guerre mondiale donc . . .
Interviewer:	L'armistice!
Franck:	L'armistice. Oui. Oh, c'est moi qui parle, c'est pas toi!

Translation:

Interviewer:	What are the French holidays?
Franck:	Ah, like all good Frenchmen, there are a lot of holidays in France. So, we take a lot of holidays. Certainly, New Year's Day . . .
Interviewer:	Yes . . .
Franck:	Then, we have Easter. We have Labour Day, the first of May. We have July 14th, the national holiday . . .
Interviewer:	Yes . . .
Franck:	We have November 11th. We have . . .
Interviewer:	What's that, November 11th?
Franck:	Well, it's the end of World War I so . . .
Interviewer:	Armistice!
Franck:	Armistice. Yes. Oh, I'm the one talking, not you!

The informal register is indexed by several syntactic items, such as Franck's use of the pronoun *on* (one, we). Note too that the constructions are essentially a repeated frame that is typical of listing (e.g. *on a le X, on a le Y, on a le Z*). The interviewer interrupts Franck to ask for clarification with an interrogative structure typical of French conversation (*C'est quoi, le onze novembre?* What's that, November 11th?). When Franck explains that it is to celebrate the end of World War I, the interviewer shouts out the name of the holiday (*L'armistice!*). Franck responds to this conversational move with a *c'est cleft* construction typically employed in conversation for contrastive purposes (*C'est moi qui parle, c'est pas toi! I'm* the one who's speaking, not *you!*). Note too that Franck omits the negative *ne* in the second *c'est cleft* (*c'est pas toi!* Not you!).

Spontaneous, unplanned discourse

Discourse analysts have noted that the unplanned nature of oral discourse is evident in the abundance of repetition, false starts and (self-)repairs (Ochs 1979). In addition, grammatical errors and violations of normative language rules are frequent in spontaneous conversation. Sometimes the speakers self-correct but other times they do not appear to realize that they have made an error. Given that *Français interactif* focuses primarily on bilingual speakers, it is not surprising that there are many examples of anglicisms and codeswitching. In the following interview, the native French speaker responds to a question about the French high-school exit exam, the baccalaureate. Instead of using the standard French word *examen* (exam), he hesitates and finally employs an incorrect English cognate (examination):

Interviewer:	Et le bac? Qu'est-ce que c'est?
Franck:	Le bac? C'est le baccalauréat. C'est une . . . un . . . une examination qui a lieu à la fin de l'année de terminale.[12]
Translation:	
Interviewer:	And the bac? What's that?
Franck:	The bac? It's the baccalaureate. It's a . . . a . . . an examination that takes place at the end of your last year.

Français interactif is unusual compared to many French materials in that it includes the voices of American students trying their best to communicate in their imperfect French. This leads to various forms of French–English mixing. For example, codeswitching, both intersentential and intrasentential, is frequent in the introductory videos where an American student presents the chapter's content:

C'est Karen encore et aujourd'hui nous sommes au centre ville Lyon. That is . . . right in the middle of downtown Lyon. And today we are going to learn about *la maison*. In this chapter you will learn how to talk about your *appartement* or *maison*.

Translation:

It's Karen again and today we are in downtown Lyon . . . That is . . . right in the middle of downtown Lyon. And today we are going to learn about *the house*. In this chapter you will learn how to talk about your *apartment* or *house*.

Codeswitches are not limited to introductory videos, but are also found throughout the interviews. In the following example, Karen inserts the word *check* in an otherwise French conversation to compensate for her lack of knowledge of the equivalent French word (*regarder* in this case):

Interviewer: Est-ce que tu aimes surfer l'internet? Est-ce que tu surfes souvent?

Karen: Je ne surfe pas souvent, mais je *check* mon email souvent.

Translation:

Interviewer: Do you like to surf the internet? Do you surf often?

Karen: I don't surf often, but I do check my email often.

Interpersonal function of language play

Guy Cook (2000) notes that current orthodoxies of language teaching emphasize the informational-cognitive functions of language, such as the exchange of referential information, rather than the psychosocial functions of language, such as the creation of solidarity or the display of aggression. He claims that current teaching methods downplay 'linguistic patterning, controversial and imaginary content, or emotionally charged interaction' (Cook 2000: 158). In fact, it is not unusual for commercial publishers who wish to avoid contentious content to draw up explicit guidelines for authors that forbid certain topics (e.g. alcohol, AIDS, religion, sex). The result is that many contemporary foreign-language materials exclude examples of spontaneous language play and focus instead on so-called ordinary, referential discourse (also variously called cognitive, informational and denotative) (Blyth 2003).

In contrast, the videotaped interviews of native and non-native speakers in *Français interactif* are full of overt examples of language play. Interviewees jokingly give intentionally wrong answers to interviewer's teacher-like display questions (What is the color of your hair?). On some occasions, interviewees play with the forms of the language. For example, when asked to describe himself physically, an interviewee responds by playing with the adjective *marron* (brown).

Interviewer: Alors, comment êtes-vous? Décrivez votre portrait physique et moral.

Franck:	Physique, je . . . j'ai les cheveux marron, les yeux marron, les oreilles marron [laughs]. Mmmm . . . portrait physique, j'ai les cheveux bruns, les yeux marron, taille moyenne.
Interviewer:	So, what do you look like? Describe your appearance and your personality.
Franck:	Appearance, I . . . I have chestnut hair, chestnut eyes, chestnut ears [laughs]. Mmmm . . . physical appearance, I have brown hair, chestnut eyes, medium build.

The humour of this video derives from the fact that the invariable French adjective *marron* is part of a fixed collocation (*les yeux marron*, 'brown eyes'). The native speaker purposely violates the grammar of French by using the adjective *marron* with other incongruous parts of the face. A similar effect can be achieved in English by using the adjective *auburn*, normally reserved to describe hair colour, with the noun *eyes* ('auburn eyes') or *ears* ('auburn ears'). After his silly linguistic joke, Franck quickly resumes the interview by answering the question with culturally and linguistically appropriate collocations.

This example points up a common fallacy in current teaching orthodoxy that equates real communication with referential language. Cook (2000) maintains that language play figures prominently in all real communication and is not a marginal feature of language. Moreover, language play of this kind naturally draws students' attention to formal properties of the language in a meaningful yet enjoyable way. Note that Franck's playful manipulation of linguistic form deftly highlights the relevant collocational rules and functions as a metalinguistic comment.

Language play frequently arises whenever a potentially embarrassing situation occurs during filming. In the following example, a French mother points out her daughter's collage hanging above the bed. When the interview remarks that the collage contains images of partially clad men, the mother immediately grabs two stuffed animals and proclaims that her daughter likes teddy bears as well as men. Next, holding the bears against the collage, she playfully exclaims that the teddy bears serve to hide the provocative images:

Mother:	Et ici c'est la chambre de ma fille qui a dix-huit ans et qui est très créative. Donc il y a des collages. Il y a de la peinture. Il y a des créations. Et euh . . . pratiquement, euh . . . elle a fait tout ce qui est au mur. [Points to sign] Danger de mort. [Laughs]

Interviewer:	Donc je vois . . . elle aime bien les hommes nus, là, hein?
Mother:	Elle aime les hommes nus mais elle aime aussi les peluches. Il y a des peluches encore dans son lit.
Interviewer:	Des peluches?
Mother:	Les peluches, OK? Je vous montre une peluche?
Interviewer:	Oui.
Mother:	Voilà, ça c'est toutes les peluches. [Holds the teddy bears against the collage] Voilà, on cache les hommes nus.
Translation:	
Mother:	And here is the bedroom of my daughter who is 18 years old and is very creative. So, there are collages. There is painting. There are creations. And uhm . . . practically, uhm . . . she did everything on the wall. [Points to sign] Danger of death. [Laughs].
Interviewer:	So, I see she likes naked men there, huh?
Mother:	She like naked men, but she also like teddy bears. There are still teddy bears on her bed.
Interviewer:	Teddy bears?
Mother:	Teddy bears, OK? Want me to show you a teddy bear?
Interviewer:	Yes.
Mother:	Here, these are all teddy bears. [Holds the teddy bears against the collage]. There you go, you hide the naked men.

Conclusion

In this chapter, the metaphor of ecology was employed to capture the size, the complexity and the interconnectedness of the changes that are affecting education in the digital age. The introduction of digital technology into the ecosystem of higher education has sent shock waves in all directions – from academic publishing to universities to individual classrooms. Baraniuk (2007b) envisions open education and open publishing as ultimately leading to *disintermediation*; that is, cutting out the middle man. Such an open model promises to revolutionize foundational concepts of higher education: authorship, teaching, learning, peer review, promotion and tenure.

The ecological metaphor was also employed to underscore the shift from textbook to digital materials as a longitudinal and contextualized process focusing primarily on the dynamic relations between agents and their artefacts. By allowing the end-users to play a more central role in the publishing process, the faculty developers created pedagogical materials that were more learner-centred and user-friendly. Nowhere is this more evident than in the focus on the language-learning experience itself that allowed the students to take centre stage in the materials. Repeated post-publication sessions of usability testing and formative evaluation were also crucial to achieving a more user-friendly online course. These sessions led to a greater emphasis on vocabulary learning and a slower progression from decontextualized to contextualized language samples in keeping with student feedback. Finally, the materials included many videos of interactions of native and non-native speakers, including the students themselves. The oral language captured by the digital videos differs notably from the French language as traditionally represented by commercial textbooks that continue to emphasize the prescriptive, written norm.

Notes

1 *Tex's French Grammar* (www.laits.utexas.edu/tex/index.html) and *Français inter-actif* (www.laits.utexas.edu/fi/index.html) are open to the internet public. Open-access websites do not require fees or passwords.
2 To view the homepage of MIT's *Open CourseWare Initiative*, go to www.ted.com/index.php/talks/view/id/25.
3 To view OLI's French online course, go to http://www.cmu.edu/oli/courses/enter_french.html.
4 Wikipedia may be accessed at www.wikipedia.org/.
5 Creative Commons (http://creativecommons.org/) is a non-profit organization whose mission is to provide 'free tools that let authors, scientists, artists, and educators to easily mark their creative work with the freedoms they want it to carry'.
6 For the MERLOT review of *Tex's French Grammar*, go to www.merlot.org/merlot/viewMaterial.htm?id=88018.
7 The most common tags for labelling *Tex's French Grammar* on the *Del.icio.us* website are *French, language, grammar, reference, learning*. The most common tags for *Français interactif* are *French, language, français, learning, tutorial*.
8 For a description of the impact of these materials on the ecology of the university's instructional technology services, go to http://tltc.la.utexas.edu/tltc/about/history.html.
9 Subsequent editions of the textbook addressed these issues by adding glosses and by lightening the lexical load.
10 For further information about the CD-ROM, go to www.laits.utexas.edu/fr/pi.f.
11 For further information, see www.laits.utexas.edu/tex/index/html.

12 Whenever a speaker commits a grammatical or lexical error, both the error
    and the correct form are highlighted in the transcription, e.g. *une examination*
    (correct form: *un examen*).

References

Allen, W. and Fouletier-Smith, N. (1995), *Parallèles: communication et culture*. Upper
    Saddle River, NJ: Prentice Hall.
Baraniuk, R. (2006), *Goodbye, Textbooks; Hello, Open Source Learning*. Online video
    available at www.ted.com/index.php/talks/view/id/25.
—(2007a), *New York Times*, 1 May 2007.
—(2007b), 'Challenges and opportunities for the open education movement:
    a Connexions case study', in T. Iiyoshi and M. S. V. Kumar (eds) *Opening Up
    Education: The Collective Advancement of Education Through Open Technology, Open
    Content, and Open Knowledge*. Boston: MIT Press.
Bax, S. (2003), 'CALL—past, present, and future'. *System*, 31, 13–28.
Blyth, C. (1995), 'Redefining the boundaries of language use: the foreign language
    classroom as a multilingual speech community', in C. Kramsch (ed.) *Redefining
    the Boundaries of Language Study*. Boston: Heinle, pp. 145–83.
—(2000), 'Toward a pedagogical discourse grammar: techniques for teaching
    word-order constructions', in J. Lee and A. Valdman (eds) *Form and Meaning:
    Multiple Perspectives*. Boston: Heinle, pp. 183–229.
—(2003), 'Playing games with literacy: the poetic function in the age of com-
    municative language teaching', in P. Patrikis (ed.) *Reading Between the Lines:
    Perspectives on Foreign Language Literacy*. New Haven, CT: Yale University Press,
    60–73.
—(forthcoming), 'The impact of pedagogical materials on critical language aware-
    ness: assessing student attention to patterns of language use', in M. Turnbull and
    J. Dailey-O'Cain (eds) *First Language Use in Second and Foreign Language Learning:
    Intersection of Theory, Practice, Curriculum and Policy*. London: Multilingual
    Matters.
Blyth, C., Kelton, K., Myers, L., Delyfer, C., Munn, Y., Lippman, J. and Eubank, E.
    (2000), *Tex's French Grammar: la grammaire de l'absurde*. Available at www.laits.
    utexas.edu/tex/.
Blyth, C. and Davis, J (2007), 'Using formative evaluation in the development of
    learner-centered materials'. *CALICO Journal*, 25, (1), 1–21.
Bronfenbrenner, U. (1979), *The Ecology of Human Development*. Cambridge, MA:
    Harvard University Press.
—(1993), 'The ecology of cognitive development: research models and fugitive
    findings', in R. Wozniak and K. W. Fischer (eds) *Development in Context: Acting
    and Thinking in Specific Environments*. Hillsdale, NJ: Erlbaum, pp. 3–44.
Cook, G. 2000, *Language Play, Language Learning*. Oxford: Oxford University Press.
Fairclough, N. (1992), 'The appropriacy of "appropriateness"', in N. Fairclough
    (ed.) *Critical Language Awareness*. London and New York: Longman, pp. 33–56.
'Frequently asked questions on connexions and open-access education', 1 November
    2007.

Gee, J. P. (2003), *What Video Games Have to Teach Us About Learning and Literacy*. New York: Palgrave.

Gumperz, J. (1982), *Discourse Strategies*. Cambridge: Cambridge University Press.

'Help, by the Book' (editorial). *New York Times*, 1 May 2007.

Iiyoshi, T. and Kumar, M. S. V. (eds) (2007), *Opening Up Education: The Collective Advancement of Education through Open Technology, Open Content, and Open Knowledge*. Boston, MA: MIT Press.

Katz, S. and Blyth, C. (2007), *Teaching French Grammar in Context*. New Haven, CT: Yale University Press.

Kelton, K., Blyth, C. and Guilloteau, N. (2004), *Français interactif: An Online Introductory French Course*. Available at www.laits.utexas.edu/fi.

Kern, R. (2006), 'Perspectives on technology in learning and teaching languages'. *TESOL Quarterly*, 40, 183–210.

Kramsch, C. (2003), 'Introduction: how can we tell the dancer from the dance?', in C. Kramsch (ed.) *Language Acquisition and Language Socialization: Ecological Perspectives*. London and New York: Continuum, pp. 1–30.

Kramsch, C. and Andersen, R. (1999), 'Teaching text and context through multimedia'. *Language Learning & Technology*, 2, (2), 31–42.

Kress, G. and Leeuwen, T. van (2001), *Multimodal Discourse: The Modes and Media of Contemporary Communication*. London: Arnold.

Lambrecht, K. (1987), 'On the topic of SVO sentences in French discourse', in R. Tomlin (ed.) *Coherence and Grounding in Discourse*. Amsterdam: John Benjamins, pp. 217–61.

Leather, J. and van Dam, J. (eds) (2003), *Ecology of Language Acquisition*. Dordrecht: Kluwer Academic Publishers.

Lewis, X. (1993), *The Lexical Approach*. Hove: Language Teaching Publication.

Lier, L. van (2004), *The Ecology and Semiotics of Language Learning: A Sociocultural Perspective*. Dordrecht: Kluwer Academic Publishers.

Malinowski, B. (1923), 'The problem of meaning in primitive languages', in C. K. Ogden and I. A. Richards (eds) *The Meaning of Meaning*. New York: Harcourt Brace.

Meskill, C. (2005), 'Metaphors that shape and guide CALL research', in J. Egbert and G. M. Petrie (eds) *CALL Research Perspectives*. Mahwah, NJ: Lawrence Erlbaum, pp. 25–40.

Ochs, E. (1979), 'Planned and unplanned discourse' in T. Givón (ed.) *Syntax and Semantics, 12, Discourse and Semantics*. New York: Academic Press.

Perens, B. (1999), *Open Sources: Voices from the Open Source Revolution*. Beijing: O'Reilly Media.

Raymond, E. (2001), *The Cathedral and the Bazaar: Musings on Linux and the Open Source by an Accidental Revolutionary*. Beijing: O'Reilly Media.

Sapir, E. (1949), 'The selected writings of Edward Sapir', in D. G. Mandelbaum (ed.) *Language, Culture, and Personality*. Berkeley, CA: University of California Press.

Thornbury, S. and Slade, D. (2006), *Conversation: From Description to Pedagogy*. Cambridge: Cambridge University Press.

Train, R. (2003), 'The (non)native standard language in foreign language education: a critical perspective', in C. Blyth (ed.) *The Sociolinguistics of Foreign-Language Classrooms*. Boston: Heinle, pp. 3–39.

Train, R. (2007), 'Language ideology and foreign language pedagogy', in D. Ayoun (ed.) *French Applied Linguistics*. Amsterdam and Philadelphia: John Benjamins Publishing, pp. 238–69.

Warschauer, M. (1999), 'CALL vs. electronic literacy: reconceiving technology in the language classroom'. Available at www.cilt.org.uk/research/resfor2/warsum1.htm (accessed 6 December 2007).

Conclusion: variations on a theme

Michael Evans

Do the different stories recounted in this book about the uses and potential of digital technologies in language learning allow us to draw out common salient themes and principles which might provide valuable guiding insights for policy-makers, researchers, teachers and learners of languages? Despite or perhaps because of the diversity of educational domains covered in the book, the reader might be encouraged to identify recurring insights reflected across the different language teaching and learning contexts represented in the chapters. What follows is not presented as a systematic or analytical synthesis of findings but as a listing of principles and ideas which have arisen from my reading of the evidence and arguments elaborated in this book.

One of the strongest leitmotifs, which is implicitly shared by all the contributors and which runs through all the chapters in this book, is that of integration; it is a perspective that seems to provide the key for looking at different levels, dimensions and objects of linkage between the use of technology and the context of language teaching and learning.

- Insights into the potential contribution of digital technology for instructed language learning are arrived at by combining research-based evidence from the broader social perspective of educational research, and the subject-specific perspective obtained through the lens of CALL and applied linguistics. As part of the former macro-framework we need to be aware of relevant priorities in national policy-making on foreign-language education. As Chapter 7 indicates, national policies and initiatives can define the parameters for change and can act as a spur to innovation in classroom practice. Knowledge about the role of digital technology in foreign-language teaching and learning, therefore, can be said to turn on the development of an open and flexible definition of the concept of 'integration' which requires greater empirically supported clarity about the different modalities, components and dimensions of integration in this context.

- Digital technology as represented by the internet provides access to an infinite variety of authentic material; but the transformative power of the resource resides essentially in how it is exploited rather than in the content alone. Use of the material needs to be mediated carefully by the teacher, with appropriately designed tasks for listening and reading based on principles that are grounded in second-language pedagogy objectives and rationale. The internet provides the authenticity and diversity of material and stimulus (which should, where possible, remain minimally edited); second-language pedagogy provides the tools for maximizing the communicative and acquisitional benefits for the learner.

- Adoption of technology by trainee teachers as an integral part of their approach to teaching develops under the influence of a process of acculturation to the use of computers for language teaching. This acculturation is affected by interaction with different professional cultures (such as school and peer cultures), which the trainees negotiate as they develop their skills and understanding relating to language teaching in general. Acculturation is also accelerated through discovery of the positive effects of classroom use of technology on learners through evidence elicited in the teachers' own classroom practice. Appropriate integration must be balanced against the risk of excessive visibility through overexposure to the digital medium. Computers best serve the purposes of language teaching and learning when they are least conspicuous. This does not mean infrequent use but that, on the contrary, when they are accepted as a normal resource ('normalized' through recurrent and integrated use) which provides a platform for interesting and purposeful language-learning activities, they draw less attention to themselves and target instead the teaching and learning aims in question.

- With more experienced teachers, adoption of a technology-mediated approach to language teaching is experienced either as a process of integration with or resistance to prior, firmly held pedagogical perspectives and commitments. Allegiance to a constructivist or didactic view of language pedagogy seems intially to correspond, at least in the TEFL case studies presented in Chapter 7, with approval or disapproval of the VLE as a platform for language learning. Even when the threshold of acceptance is crossed, different formats of digital interaction appeal to teachers of different pedagogical leanings. The constructivist welcomes the communicative immediacy of synchronous interaction between learners because it supports the development of communicative fluency; the didactic teacher prefers the asynchronous medium since it allows space for the teacher's interventions with corrective feedback and encourages greater explicit focus on form. What seems to be happening here is a dynamic of integration, or at least reconciliation, between use of technology and prior conceptions of what approaches are best for language pedagogy.

- With an experienced, technology-committed languages teacher working in the context of mainstream secondary schooling, integration between use of the medium and subject-related objectives takes on a different form. Here teacher use of the digital medium is interwoven into a wide range of different pedagogical functions and contexts for a given class of learners. Hawkes, in Chapter 4, shows how ICT becomes a transparent yet ubiquitous medium in her pedagogical approach, which is broadly encapsulated under the category of 'active learning'. In her classroom and that of others in her department, PowerPoint is used, for instance, as a 'planning tool', as a provider of visual backup for supporting the target language as medium of communication in the classroom, and as a vehicle for modelling Assessment for Learning by visual demonstration of the criteria and systems of language assessment in the classroom. Email is used to bolster learning beyond the classroom through corrective feedback on homework submitted via the medium, and through regular communications and updates with the pupils' parents. The social framework of teaching and learning is thus stretched beyond conventional boundaries. Technology in this example is consonant with an explorative and experimental pedagogy that seeks out different learning contexts within classroom practice, and in doing so allows the medium to create new pedagogical opportunities.

- For Blyth the notion of the 'ecology of the e-learning environment' allows for a reversal of the conventional pattern of incorporation of digital teaching and learning within the real classroom. Here, within the setting of the *Français interactif* online course, it is reality that is incorporated into the virtual environment. Reality is present at different levels in this setting: the 'real' as represented by interview videos with native and non-native speakers of French; the 'real' as represented in the incorporation of spontaneous and informal use of language, as opposed to exclusive presentation of clinically edited language; the 'real' in the form of the inclusion of imperfect French spoken by American students of the language, with a natural recourse to codeswitching between English and French. Such a perspective entails a challenge to the norm of the model of the ideal native speaker and instead creates an awareness of the distinction between incipient and balanced bilingualism.

- While *Français interactif* can be said to embed the real within the virtual, and thereby in a sense to transform the real into a virtual stimulus at the service of the educational goals of the online course, the distance-learning programme provided by the SIDE project described by Durrant provides an example of a different form of integration between the real and the virtual. Driven by the need to overcome 'the tyranny of educational space' within the great expanse of WA, the teachers and coordinators of the project strive to connect the programme with the real world in two main ways: through visits to partner schools and institutions and through the use of a conferencing facility, Centra, which enables face-to-face tuition with individual learners. In this way, the pedagogical activities provided by the virtual environment are reinforced through direct connections with learners and their institutional bases.

- From the language learner's perspective, the digital environment is often seen as an attractive and favourable platform for autonomous communication and language learning. The voices of students from the diverse projects described in this book express an awareness of different ways in which the technology facilitates the various dimensions of integration that support their language learning. The TEFL students interviewed by Hamilton see the VLE as 'a way of maintaining contact with their teacher'. In this way, continued contact beyond the classroom would seem a natural extension of the immersion setting of their study-abroad experience. The pupils participating in Tic-Talk, on the other hand, preferred their teachers to adopt a more back-seat role in the CMC interactions. This is because, for these pupils, the overriding impulse was that of bonding with their partners based in different countries yet sharing the same virtual space. Social integration here took the form of interpersonal, intercultural and metalinguistic collaboration between peers. As well as learning from each other, language learners used the medium to perform to each other and thus mutually reinforce their motivation and learning. This phenomenon appears repeatedly in the accounts given in many of the chapters in this book. Digital technology thus serves to support and develop in foreign-language learners of all ages and stages of proficiency a core feature intrinsic to all language use (Duranti 1997: 16):

Performance in this sense is an ever-present dimension of language use because it is an ever-present dimension of language evaluation and there is no use without evaluation. We are constantly being evaluated by our listeners and by ourselves as our own listeners.

Reference

Duranti, A. (1997), *Linguistic Anthropology*. Cambridge: Cambridge University Press.

Glossary

AATE	Australian Association for the Teaching of English
ABC	Australian Broadcasting Commission
ACTFL	American Council of Teachers of Foreign Languages
ALL	Association for Language Learning
ASL	Average Sentence Length
CALL	Computer-Assisted Language Learning
CILT	Centre for Information on Language Teaching
CLA	Critical Language Awareness
CMC	Computer-Mediated Communication
DCSF	Department for Children, Schools and Families
DEST	Department of Education, Science and Training
DfEE	Department for Education and Employment
DfES	Department for Education and Skills
ESRC	Economic and Social Research Council
FLOTE	Facilitating the Learning of Languages Other Than English
IWB	Interactive WhiteBoard
L1	Mother Tongue or First Language
L2	Second Language
MCEETYA	Ministerial Council on Education, Employment, Training and Youth Affairs
MERLOT	Multimedia Educational Resource of Learning and Online Teaching
MIT	Massachusetts Institute of Technology
NALSAS	National Asian Languages and Studies in Australian Schools
NC	National Curriculum
NSLI	National Security Language Initiative
NSW	New South Wales
OLI	Open Learning Initiative
PACCIT	People at the Centre of Communications and Information Technologies

QTS	Qualified Teacher Status
RFDS	Royal Flying Doctor Service
SIDE	School of Isolated and Distance Education
SOTA	School of the Air
SSAT	Specialist Schools and Academies Trust
TBL	Task-Based Learning
TDA	Training and Development Agency
TEE	Tertiary Entrance Examinations
TELL	Technology-Enhanced Language Learning
TL	Target Language
VAK	Visual, Auditory and Kinaesthetic
VLE	Virtual Learning Environment
WA	Western Australia
WP	Word Processing

Index